'C

'O

Ac
con
the
exc
tioı
rac
rieı
cla:

'Ot
'bl
cor
bet
nist
traı

'Ot
ical
the
a w
studies, 'race' and ethnic studies, women's studies and all those with
an interest in race relations and political activism.

Julia Sudbury is an assistant professor in Ethnic Studies at Mills
College, Oakland, California, and the former director of Sia: The
National Development Agency for the Black Voluntary Sector,
based in London.

Gender, Racism, Ethnicity
Series editors:
Kum-Kum Bhavnani, *University of California at Santa Barbara*
Avtar Brah, *University of London*
Gail Lewis, *The Open University*
Ann Phoenix, *University of London*

Gender, Racism, Ethnicity is a series whose main concern is to promote rigorous feminist analysis of the intersections between gender, racism, ethnicity, class and sexuality within the contexts of imperialism, colonialism and neo-colonialism. Intended to contribute new perspectives to current debates and to introduce fresh analysis, it will provide valuable teaching texts for undergraduates, lecturers and researchers in anthropology, women's studies, cultural studies and sociology.

Other titles in the series:

White Women, Race Matters
Ruth Frankenberg

Fear of the Dark
Lola Young

Gendering Orientalism
Reina Lewis

Cartographies of Diaspora
Avtar Brah

'Other Kinds of Dreams'

Black women's organisations and the politics of transformation

Julia Sudbury

London and New York

First published 1998 by Routledge
11 New Fetter Lane, London EC4P 4EE

Simultaneously published in the USA and Canada
by Routledge
29 West 35th Street, New York, NY 10001

© 1998 Julia Sudbury

Typeset in Times by Routledge
Printed and bound in Great Britain by Creative Print and Design
(Wales), Ebbw Vale

British Library Cataloguing in Publication Data
A catalogue record for this book is available from the British Library

Library of Congress Cataloging-in-Publication Data
A catalog record for this book is available on request

ISBN 0–415–16731–0 (hbk)
ISBN 0–415–16732–9 (pbk)

For the women of Osaba Women's Centre who dared to dream

Contents

Foreword

Julia Sudbury has produced a remarkable study of black women's organisations in Britain. Her work poses a formidable challenge to those accustomed to framing their ideas in terms that place black women at the proverbial intersection of multiple forms of domination, while denying their roles as conscious actors. Black women, Sudbury powerfully argues, are not simply victims, but rather can claim a rich and complex recent history of political activism. In supporting this claim, she illuminates previously unexplored dimensions of the organisational histories of women of African and Asian descent in Britain while also raising central questions that bear upon the potential of women of colour organising projects in the United States. *'Other Kinds of Dreams'* moves to a new level of ongoing theoretical efforts to rethink and transform narrow definitions of feminism. As such, Sudbury's work should be as exciting for scholars and activists in the United States as in Britain. British readers familiar with the histories of such groups as Organisation of Women of African and Asian Descent (OWAAD) and Brixton Black Women's Group will appreciate her nuanced analysis of these pioneering organisations. Many who have decided, for a range of reasons, that the particular construction of blackness that characterised the work of OWAAD and similar organisations has become obsolete, will be encouraged to reflect on the contemporary potential of this political/racial identity to facilitate the building of cross-racial and transnational coalitions in the age of global capital.

In developing a sociological history of black women's autonomous organisations from the 1970s to the 1990s, Sudbury weaves an engrossing context for the interviews she conducted, using her extensive and impressive knowledge of British and North American literature on race, gender, sexuality, and class. Moreover, her own history of involvement in black women's organisations provides her work with an urgency that is frequently absent in sociological analyses. Her findings therefore not only allow her to make important interventions into contemporary debates regarding such issues as the usefulness of organising around racial identities; in an important critical move, she also foregrounds the ways in which her interviewees contest prevailing notions of what counts as 'political activism'.

Among the reasons Sudbury proposes for the scholarly neglect of British black women's organising practices are precisely the rigid definitions of political activism which fail to take into account the creative strategies black women have deployed. The way in which the activists she interviews describe and theorise their work demands a reconceptualisation of political activism that moves beyond electoral and parliamentary constructions of politics. She interprets her interviewees' contributions as contesting the exclusion of their work from new social movement history. For example, the specific way in which the private sphere was theorised in organising efforts by Black Women for Wages for Housework caused important connections to be drawn between the unpaid labour of women in industrialised countries and the unpaid labour of women in the Third World, thus pointing toward the need for transnational visions and movements.

Drawing upon the growing North American literature in the areas of black and women of colour feminism, Sudbury places these writings in productive conversations with the British literature by such scholars and cultural producers as Avtar Brah, Gail Lewis, Hazel Carby, Kum-Kum Bhavnani and Pratibha Parmar. In constructing these conversations, she identifies the creative contributions of black British writers, who, with a few exceptions, are not as widely known in the United States as they should be. Precisely through her abundant and illuminating use of both literatures, she effectively contests the hegemonic tendencies of the North American literature.

A recurring theme of Sudbury's research is the importance of probing the particular way the category 'black' took shape in the organising practices of British black women during the late 1970s and early 1980s. The seemingly interminable work of disarticulating blackness from its biologistic resonances can be facilitated, she argues persuasively, by seriously scrutinising the ways women of Asian and African descent consciously took on a 'black' political identity. Blackness, within this organising context, was hardly a simplistic notion of nonwhiteness summoned forth as opposition to the prevailing racism. For African, Caribbean, Asian and Middle Eastern women who were concerned with police brutality, reproductive politics, the welfare system, education, immigration and other issues, black political identity accomplished a number of strategic goals. It allowed women to link histories of colonialism and repression that were both similar and different, as well as histories of resistance to both racism and sexism. And precisely because they were compelled to build this identity consciously, they were able to develop a consciousness of their own political agency.

These lessons Sudbury gleans from her interviews and archival research do not comprise a nostalgic project of recovery which portrays black women's organising history as a consummate model for the present. On the contrary, she always unflinchingly confronts problematic and contradictory moments in this history. In this spirit she asserts that the exclusion of lesbians and the failure to address the influence of homophobia on black women's organisations was an enormous obstacle. Her analysis of the reception among black women in Britain of North American black nationalist discourse points out that its appeal not only to people of African descent, but also to people of Asian descent, helped to encourage African–Asian unity, but that at the same time, the masculinist thrust of this discourse served to discourage deeper engagements with black patriarchy. She acknowledges the greater authority and access middle-class black women's organisations have acquired recently, and the potential for developing mutually beneficial cross-class relationships with poor and working-class women. At the same time, she points out that there is a great likelihood that these developments may lead to a blunting of the radical potential of black women's organising.

Sudbury's intellectual courage bears the mark of the activist who knows she will have to accept the consequences of her political choices, both individually and collectively. Thus her choice to embrace a 'womanist' as opposed to 'feminist' methodology links her with those in Britain who express solidarity with North American women of colour, who – using the term Alice Walker coined – describe their research and/or organising as 'womanist'. At the same time, by not calling their work 'black feminist', they reject the hegemonic tendencies of North American black feminist theory and practice. In so far as it constructs a history of British black women's organisations that simultaneously embraces and distances itself from 'black feminism', Sudbury's work, while not directed primarily to women-of-colour feminists and womanists in the United States, nevertheless is an extraordinary gift to us. Both research and organising strategies that attempt to recognise the cross-cutting linkages among race, nationality, gender, class, sexuality and their increasingly transnational character are becoming more and more complex. Sudbury has developed a method that will help us to understand and appreciate that complexity and to recognise it as part of a new landscape for radical political struggle.

Out of the organisational experiences of women of African and Asian descent in Britain, as documented and analysed here by Julia Sudbury, emerges a radical transformative vision and a determination to preserve difference, diversity and even conflict in the very process of building unity. As we trek into the next millennium, asserting, maintaining and defending our humanity in the face of global capital, we very much need '*Other Kinds of Dreams*'

Angela Y. Davis

Acknowledgements

I would like to thank my parents, Mary and George Sudbury, for their constant faith in my ability to choose the right path; my partner, Stephen Small for bringing love, encouragement and laughter, through the good and bad times; my father, Sonny Oparah, for giving me the inner peace out of which creativity grows; my sister, Andrea Cork for her spiritual guidance and wisdom.

I could not have written this book without the emotional, intellectual and spiritual nurturance of many women – Carmen Allen, Yaa Asantewaa Adade, Hasnah Sheriff, Sobia Shaw, Juliet Coke, Maud Blair, Valentina Alexander, Ekanem Hines, Linda Bellos, Yvonne Joseph, Molara Solanke, Pat Hilden, Maria Cecilia Santos and the women I interviewed. Much love goes out to all the women who have been involved in Osaba Women's Centre over the years, and particularly those who helped make my time there a space for dreaming other kinds of dreams.

A special thanks to Annie Phizacklea whose supervision gave me the freedom to develop my own ideas and to Deborah Steinberg and Philomena Essed for their detailed comments on an earlier version. To the series editors, Avtar Brah, Kum-Kum Bhavnani, Gail Lewis and Ann Phoenix, many thanks for your support, analysis and debate at every stage of this project. Thank you also to the Institute for the Study of Social Change, the Department of Ethnic Studies at the University of California, Berkeley and Mills College for providing me with a community away from home during the writing process. Acknowledgement is also due to the University of Warwick and the European Social Research Council.

Abbreviations

AMwA	Akina Mama wa Afrika
BBWG	Brixton Black Women's Group
BNP	British National Party
BPA	Black People's Alliance
BUFP	Black Unity and Freedom Party
BWA	Black Women Achievers
BWfWfH	Black Women for Wages for Housework
CAACO	Confederation of Afro-Asian-Caribbean Organisations
CALPS	Campaign Against Labour Party Suspensions
CAPA	Campaign for Police Accountability
CBWSG	Cambridge Black Women's Support Group
CCCS	Centre for Contemporary Cultural Studies
CIO	Confederation of Indian Organisations
CR	Consciousness Raising
DAWN	Disabled Asian Women's Network
EOC	Equal Opportunities Commission
EOP	Equal Opportunities Policy
GLC	Greater London Council
HIV	Human Immunodeficiency Virus

INWOC	International Network of Women of Colour
LWLN	London Women's Liberation Newsletter
MP	Member of Parliament
NAWAD	National Association of Women of Afrikan Descent
NLCB	National Lottery Charities Board
NNBWO	National Network of Black Women's Organisations
OWAAD	Organisation of Women of African and Asian Descent
PAAWA	Professional Afro-Asian Women's Association
Ph.D	Doctorate of Philosophy
RAAS	Racial Adjustment Action Society
SBS	Southall Black Sisters
SUS	Search under Suspicion
SWAPO	South West African People's Organisation
SWP	Socialist Workers Party
SYM	Southall Youth Movement
UCPA	United Coloured People's Association
WACAWN	Warwickshire African Caribbean and Asian Women's Network
WAF	Women Against Fundamentalism
WHC	Wages for Housework Campaign
WLM	Women's Liberation Movement
ZANU	Zimbabwe African National Union

Chapter 1

Introduction

Community activists love to hark back to a golden age, that mythical era when 'the movement' was united in purpose and determined in action; when divisions and resentments did not distract one from the struggle; when it was clear who was oppressed and who the oppressor; when leaders had integrity and passion, and when confidence and optimism were boundless. The black[1] women's movement in Britain is no exception: we are haunted by the spectre of the 'OWAAD days'[2] (Brah 1992b; R. Bhavnani 1994). According to this popular mythology, the collective empowerment experienced by black women in the late 1970s and early 1980s has since been dissipated and black women have become introspective, fragmented and competitive (Grewal *et al.* 1988; Parmar 1990). A certain magic and innocence has been forever lost.

Black women's activism has come under criticism from all sides. Socialist feminists have accused black feminists of fostering divisions at a time when unity and collective determination are required to ensure that the few gains won by women are not undermined, and of ignoring critical differences between black women such as class, nationality and citizenship (Tang Nain 1991; Anthias *et al.* 1992). Increasingly Asian scholars and activists have refuted the project of building unity under the banner of blackness, claiming that 'black' only ever meant compromise under an African leadership (Modood 1988, 1990; Cole 1993). Some African Caribbean activists have joined the critique of blackness, preferring to identify their struggles within the rubric of Pan-African or Afrocentric ideology (Ackah 1993). 'Black and Asian', a phrase coined by the Commission for Racial Equality has become the basis for governmental classification and a symbol for the disintegration of black unity (Mason 1990; Owen 1993). Black women themselves have begun to question whether that unity was ever more than a facade for rigid authenticity codes and exclusionary practices (Grewal *et al.* 1988; Mama 1995).

Yet black women's organisations have demonstrated remarkable staying power. As established groups celebrate their second and third decades and new groups spring up in places as far afield as Aberdeen and Cardiff, we must question the suggestion that they have been unable to deal with the complex realities of black women's lives in the 1990s. It is time to revisit these organisations and ask what lessons they hold for us. How have black women's organisations adapted to the 1990s? How have they dealt with the challenge of difference and the stripping bare of the myths of a unitary black womanhood? Can we continue to make 'truth claims' about black women organising or does the recognition of multiple and shifting identities challenge such a project? Have black women retained their commitment to action, or has political activism given way to internal divisions? How have the inclusion and exclusion of lesbian women at different moments influenced the development of organisations? What does the rise of a (so-called) black middle class of professional women mea\n for the politics of black women organising? These are some of the questions that this book will address.

The title of the book owes a debt to June Jordan, an African American activist intellectual who, in conversation with Pratibha Parmar, states that black women's visions are not limited to a narrow and essentialist identity politics (Parmar 1990: 108). Black women have 'other kinds of dreams' which are broader and far more revolutionary (ibid.: 109). This dialogue, which takes place across borders created by ethnicity, nationality and space, offers a starting-point for this study. It speaks to my own commitment to bridging racialised and national identities in search of alliances. It also creates a new framework for the examination of the political, cultural and increasingly contested space which many of us still call 'black'[3] (R. Bhavnani 1994; The 1990 Trust 1993). This framework enables us to examine the complexities and practicalities of black women's organising while keeping one eye on the dreams and aspirations of social transformation which underpin these organisations. It allows us realism without despair, honesty without cynicism and perhaps charts a path for a more reflexive and self aware form of black women's activism.

The goals of this book are twofold. First, I aim to redress the erasure of black women's collective agency in current thinking about social change. My second aim is to explore black women's organisational responses to diversity and differentiation within black communities along lines of gender, ethnicity, sexuality, class and political ideology. The book interrogates contemporary theories of racism and racialisation, gender and political mobilisation through an empirical study of black women's organisations in Britain from the 1970s to the present day. Implicit in my approach to this study is my belief, from personal involvement in autonomous organisations, that first, the black women's movement is far from dead and second, black women are engaged in everyday acts of theorising about their lives, experiences and struggles (Sia 1996a, 1996b). My interest lies in drawing together the strands of the theorising taking place in autonomous spaces created by black women.

RETHINKING HISTORIES OF MIGRATION AND RESISTANCE

The landing of the *Empire Windrush* in 1948 with its human cargo of 492 Jamaicans is for many scholars the symbolic dawn of modern British 'race relations'. While few would claim that these were the first black people in Britain, writers point to the increased visibility that the arrival of ships full of black migrant workers created (Ramdin 1987: 189; Jarrett-Macauley 1996: xii). If the Windrush is the symbolic moment, it is also important to note the make up of its passengers: ex-servicemen seeking refuge from unemployment and low wages in the Caribbean. These 'men from Jamaica' left an imprint on the British consciousness[4] (Fryer 1984: 372). It is hardly surprising then, that subsequent studies of black people in Britain have focused on male migrant workers, with only passing reference to their 'wives and children' (ibid.: 372). Women were seen not as workers, but as wives and mothers, their experiences of productive work obscured by their unwaged domestic role (R. Bhavnani 1994: 14; Parmar 1982: 250)[5]. These black women never quite came to the forefront of the academic imagination.

Revisionist researchers of British history have established beyond doubt the presence of people of African descent in Britain from the third century AD and a continuous and significant African, Indian and Chinese presence from the sixteenth century onwards (Fryer 1984; Shyllon 1977). Scanning these histories for the role of black women, we will find black ladies inspiring Scottish poet Dunbar in the sixteenth century, captive African women and girls brought to England as sex workers, maids and entertainers from the 1570s to the end of the nineteenth century, Asian women and girls brought to Britain as maidservants and 'ayahs' by English women returning from travels to India in the eighteenth century, wealthy Indian women students and impoverished British born daughters of Indian, Chinese and African sailors found in British ports in the nineteenth century (Walvin 1971; Visram 1986; Myers 1996).

Yet while we can find evidence of their presence filtered through the perceptions of white chroniclers, we find little reference to black women as agents in shaping the destiny of black communities in Britain. Nor is this omission remedied by the common approach of describing black resistance to racism and colonialism, whereby the lives of 'great' black leaders and thinkers are revisited. Ramdin (1987), for example, struggling to include a black women's presence in his history of the black working class in Britain, describes the life stories of Mary Seacole and Mary Prince. Yet the inclusion of these histories of women engaged in caring – the former as a nurse, the latter an enslaved servant – appears peripheral to Ramdin's thesis of black working class resistance. Within this resistance black engagement in political struggles and organisations which change the face of British politics, is led by black men, from Robert Wedderburn and William Cuffay in the eighteenth century, to Pan-Africanists George Padmore, W.B. DuBois, Marcus Garvey and Indian Nationalists Shapurji Saklatvali and Joseph Baptiste in the twentieth century (Ramdin 1987).

In order to correct this omission, the woman-centred researcher could focus on those black women who have been remembered in political journals and the minutes of conferences and rallies – Cornelia Sorabji[6], Amy Garvey[7], Claudia Jones[8] to mention three – and draw out how these women's contributions have shaped the movements in which they were involved. However, this 'history of the greats' will by necessity ignore the masses of women who have been the backbone of the black struggle, those women who ran the hostel services and food kitchens in the League of Coloured Peoples in the 1930–50s; women who made sure that the minutes of meetings and conferences were kept which have made an analysis of the Pan-African and Home Rule movements in British history possible. Those women who cooked, nurtured and supported, but also whose radical vision of black community liberation was central to the continuation of black activism. To capture the role of black women in community resistance, we must by necessity look beyond individual contributions, to the organisations which have formed and continue to form the basis of black community struggles.

While the seeds of black women's political activism in Britain can be identified as far back as the black women who attended the Somerset case of 1772[9] and the societies of escaped enslaved and indentured servants[10] which enraged white Londoners in the late eighteenth century, it was not until the early 1970s that black women began to organise autonomously (Fryer 1984: 69; Walvin 1971). What were the motors for this new movement? First, the social, economic and political environment of Britain in the early 1970s was particularly harsh for black people. The cycle of racism and exclusion began with education where African Caribbean pupils were labelled educationally sub-normal and all black pupils suffered from 'bussing' (dispersal) policies (Coard 1971; Troyna and Williams 1986). Poor education combined with endemic institutional racism in the workplace and unions led to high levels of unemployment, low pay and unsafe conditions (Phizacklea and Miles 1980; Hiro 1971). In the field of health, racist practices led to disproportionate numbers of black people being diagnosed as mentally unstable (Bryan *et al.* 1985). Black women in particular suffered from unsafe and irreparable birth control methods (Bryan *et al.* 1985; Amos and Parmar 1984). The criminal justice system was also embedded with racist practices, police brutality and harassment that went unchecked and biased media coverage contributed to the criminalisation of young black people (S. Small 1983; Gilroy 1987). In addition, the 1960s and early 1970s witnessed the institutionalisation of the equation of black presence with social disorder through the introduction of racist criteria into immigration laws[11] (Solomos 1992; Miles 1993).

Second, the late 1960s offered a new ideological weapon which could be brought to bear in the struggle against racism. Inspired by massive political and social mobilization in the United States and in the recently independent African and Caribbean nations and by visits by Malcolm X in 1965 and Stokely Carmichael in 1967, black people in Britain embraced the assertiveness and symbolic energy of Black Power (Heineman 1972; Hiro 1971). Black Power in Britain was never entirely a North American borrowing but drew heavily from ideas and strategies generated in the Caribbean and influenced by the interaction of activists and thinkers from Britain, Africa, the Caribbean, North America and Asia[12]. In Britain, Black Power captured the militant mood of many young black people infuriated by attitudes encapsulated in Enoch Powell's infamous 'River of Blood' speech[13]. Moreover, Black Power offered a renewed emphasis on Pan-African unity which appeared to offer a solution to the divisions between and within African and Caribbean communities. While it is often assumed that Black Power appealed most to 'alienated Caribbean youth', two of the first Black Power organisations, the Radical Adjustment Action Society (RAAS) (1965) and the Black Peoples' Alliance (1968) were initiated by coalitions of West African, Caribbean, Indian and Pakistani activists (Hiro 1971: 145). By the late 1960s, branches of the Black Panther Party, Black Unity and Freedom Party (BUFP) and Black Liberation Front were established in London, Liverpool, Manchester, Birmingham and Nottingham.

Unlike the American experience, where Black Power was limited to those of African descent, Britain's black communities forged a rallying cry which would unite men and women of African and Asian origin in challenging racism and state brutality. African, Caribbean and Asian communities in Britain had faced common obstacles and had developed a history of joint struggles. In 1963, for example, a march in solidarity with Martin Luther King's March on Washington had been convened in London by the Confederation of Afro–Asian–Caribbean Organisations, the Campaign Against Racial Discrimination (CARD) established in 1964 was also a pan-ethnic group (Anwar 1991: 42; Heineman 1972). 'Black' was therefore expanded in the British context (Hensman 1995; R. Bhavnani 1994). Many Black Power organisations had African, Caribbean and Asian members and were instrumental in supporting Asian community struggles, such as the strikes at Red Scar mills in Preston in 1965 and Crepe Sizes in Nottingham in 1972 (Ramdin 1987: 450; Sivanandan 1974: 20). Both the Indian Workers Association GB, which had long been central to political organising in Punjabi communities, and the National Federation of Pakistani Associations which formed in 1963, embraced the notion of solidarity under the political umbrella of blackness (Hiro 1971). Radical Asian youth organisations had also begun to emerge in communities such as Southall, Newham and Brick Lane in London, Bradford, Birmingham, Leicester and Manchester (Bains 1988; Mukherjee 1988). At times, these groups formed campaigns in conjunction with African Caribbean young people. Bradford United Black Youth League and Hackney Black

People's Defence Organisation were two such pan-ethnic groups (Ramdin 1987; Mason-John and Khambatta 1993).

Michelle Wallace (1978) in her much maligned exposé of black gender relations has captured the exclusion from decision making, the sexual objectification and the pressure to conform to the role of 'African queen' imposed on African American women in the Black Power movement (see also Brixton Black Women's Group 1984b). African Caribbean women in Britain had similar experiences:

> We could not realise our full organisational potential in a situation where we were constantly regarded as sexual prey. Although we worked tirelessly, the significance of our contribution to the mass mobilisation of the Black Power era was undermined and overshadowed by the men. They both set the agenda and stole the show.
>
> (Bryan *et al.* 1985: 144)

The Black Power movement was not unique in its attempted restriction of women's participation. Women of African descent who turned to Rastafari in search of an alternative to 'babylon culture', were also forced to struggle with patriarchal ideologies. These were given justification by Bible readings, but were firmly rooted in the nationalist vision of black male liberation:

> Rasta 'queens' could not cook if menstruating, women could not 'reason' with the 'kingmen' nor partake of the chalice (smoke marijuana). Biblical support was found for limiting Rasta women's access to knowledge except through the guidance of their 'kingmen'.
>
> (Turner 1994: 30)

Asian women had a similar battle for recognition in community struggles against racist attacks, deportations and miscarriages of justice. The young Asian men who transformed themselves into urban warriors defending their communities from racist attacks were quick to chastise young women who wished to stray from traditional gender roles and participate in political activism:

> Any girl who tries to take an active part in the running of SYM [Southall Youth Movement] is popularly regarded as 'loose', with the consequences that those who do try to get involved very quickly leave.
>
> (Bains 1988: 237; see also A. Wilson 1984: 174)

These barriers did not prevent black women from throwing them-selves into community activism. Black women refused to take a backseat role, they were active in sit-ins, boycotts, Saturday schools, defence committees, conferences and study circles. Above all, this activity was critical in politicising young black women, many of whom had been educated in Britain and had little knowledge of anti-colonial struggles. Young black women championing the black berets, socks and shoes of militant resistance were inspired by women activists from the United States, in particular Angela Davis: 'Angela Davis was such an inspiration to black women at the time. She seemed to have liberated herself mentally and fought in her own right, showing us all a lead' (Bryan *et al.* 1985: 145).

In response to women's demands to be allowed to play a full role in community struggles, and in an attempt to increase numbers of women members, some of the black organisations at the time estab-lished women's sections. These groups, such as the Black Women's Liberation Movement and the Black Women's Action Committee were not autonomous and were viewed by the 'parent' organisation as a means to induct black women into the movement. Moreover, as these organisations began to shift towards a Marxist line, black women found themselves alienated from the ideological position exemplified by Sivanandan:

> For the black man (*sic*), however, the consciousness of class is instinctive to his consciousness of colour. Even as he begins to throw away the shackles of his particular slavery, he sees that there are others besides him who are enslaved too. . . . He acknowledges at last that inside every black man there is a working class man waiting to get out.
>
> (Sivanandan 1974: 96)

For many black women, the promise of solidarity between black and white male workers was a poor substitute for an oppositional black unity based on egalitarian relations between men and women (Bryan *et al.* 1985: 145–6). Alienation from mixed gender black organisations created the need for another channel for black women's activism. The Women's Liberation Movement (WLM), also blossoming in this period, ostensibly offered a platform for addressing women's concerns (Whelehan 1995; Feminist Anthology Collective 1981). The problems facing black women who sought alliances with white women are explored in Chapter 6. Here it is adequate to note the reluctance of the WLM to face racism either as an internal problem or as part of an agenda for political action (Amos and Parmar 1984; Mama 1995: 3). The leadership and achievements demonstrated by women involved in national liberation organisations such as ZANU Women's League and SWAPO women's campaign offered an alternative model. Inspired with a new sense of their own efficacy, black women established the first black women's autonomous organisations[14].

BLACK WOMEN'S AUTONOMOUS ORGANISATIONS

> Grassroots women (and men) don't know ourselves the history we are making, and this is the greatest deterrent to our recording it. Such lack of self consciousness is one of the most debilitating effects of the power of education and the media against us.
>
> (James 1985)

The failure to maintain archives has meant that the records of many black women's organisations which folded during the 1970s or early 1980s were lost, scattered among former members' personal belongings and often eventually discarded. Those organisations which did manage to combine community activism with keeping written records or contributing to newsletters or journals have therefore taken the fore in documented black women's histories. We must therefore treat with caution the many accounts which imply that black women's activism occurred only in London-based groups such as Brixton Black Women's Group, Awaz and the Organisation of Women of African and Asian Descent (OWAAD) (Hart 1984; Parmar 1990; R. Bhavnani 1994). What is certain is that the black women's groups which formed in the 1970s did not have the benefit of communicating with other organisations in a cohesive 'black women's movement'. Instead they were creating their own models of organisation:

> As the first autonomous black women's group of its kind, certainly in London, there were no models for us to follow, no paths laid out. We just had to work it out as we went along.
>
> (Bryan et al. 1985: 150)

Amrit Wilson describes a similar sense of breaking new ground in Awaz, one of the first Asian women's organisations:

> I think the group meant a lot to all of us because it was for

us and about us – which was something we never had before. It meant that you put yourself first – your dreams and hopes and collective experiences – and that political action came out of that.

(A. Wilson 1984: 175)

Outside London and therefore less likely to be incorporated into black histories which have tended to focus on the capital (Carter 1986; Bryan *et al.* 1985), the 1970s saw women of African and Asian descent establishing autonomous organisations in Birmingham, Coventry, Nottingham, Liverpool and Manchester (see Appendix II).

It would be misleading to imply that the majority of black women were involved in these early black women's organisations. Even an organisation such as Southall Black Sisters in a densely populated black community would be unlikely to have more than fifty active members at any one time. Black women in smaller black communities and isolated in largely white communities would be unlikely to have access to such an organisation (Goldsmith and Makris 1993). Most would still rely on the traditional venues, hairdressing salons and places of worship, as well as mixed gender black organisations for their community involvement (Bryan *et al.* 1985; V. Small 1994). It was not until the early 1980s that black women's organisations were established on a large scale and became prevalent in most major cities as well as some smaller towns. The catalyst for this came from the first black women's organisation to organise at a national level, the Organisation of Women of African and Asian Descent (OWAAD).

Although OWAAD is commonly known as the Organisation of Women of African and Asian Descent, it came into being as a rather different organisation: the Organisation of Women of Africa and African Descent (Mason-John and Khambatta 1993: 12). OWAAD was founded in 1978 with the aim of linking struggles of women in Africa with those in the African diaspora and in particular Britain. This Pan-Africanist vision, promoted largely by women from the African students' union many of whom were active in anti-imperialist movements in Africa, was countered by those that felt the organisation should unite all black women around common issues such as immigration controls and racist attacks. This second view took precedence in 1979 when the organisation was renamed (Brixton Black Women's Group 1984a). Contrary to the experience of earlier black women's groups, women in OWAAD consciously documented their achievements and struggles via the organisation's newsletter *FOWAAD!*. We therefore have detailed records of the campaigns which they created around immigration legislation, 'virginity tests' and deportation cases; rape and domestic violence; school exclusions and 'sin bins'; 'SUS' laws and police brutality; Depo Provera and reproductive rights and in support of industrial action by black women (OWAAD 1979, 1980). OWAAD also stood out as the first organisation to bring black women together from across Britain and came to form a loose umbrella group for black women's organisations nationwide. National conferences brought together hundreds of women and created a renewed vigour and excitement among those women that attended (Brixton Black Women's Group 1984a; Bryan *et al.* 1985; Hart 1984).

While OWAAD was the catalyst for the creation of many new black women's groups and community struggles throughout Britain, it was unable to incorporate the experiences of all black women within its ranks. The experiences of black lesbian women were particularly painful and the public denouncement of lesbian women at the 1981 conference led to the establishment of the first documented black lesbian group (Mason-John and Khambatta 1993: 13). While black lesbian women had been active in many of the Black Power and black women's groups in the 1970s and early 1980s, the empowering experience of black women gathering *en masse* at the OWAAD conferences, combined with the anger and pain of exclusion created a new assertiveness among them. No longer willing to pass as heterosexuals or face rejection, black lesbian women decided to claim an autonomous voice within the newly emerging black women's movement.

This new assertiveness led to the creation of the first black lesbian conference in Britain. The conference, Zami I took place in London in October 1985 and attracted over 200 women from as far afield as Scotland (Mason-John 1995b). While Zami conferences were open to all women who self defined as 'black', the term 'Zami' draws on a Caribbean tradition, popularised by Caribbean American poet and activist Audre Lorde[15]. Shakti groups were later established in order to attract more lesbians and bisexual women of Asian descent (Mason-John 1995b: 13). From the mid 1980s onwards black lesbian groups were established in most cities with significant black populations. The implementation of Section 28 of the Local Government Act 1988, banning local authority support of the 'promotion' of gay and lesbian lifestyles heralded a rolling back of some of the gains that black lesbians had made. Some of the few groups that had been funded saw their funding cut: those that used local authority venues as a meeting place were often ejected and some had their promotional literature removed from public places such as libraries (Hayfield 1995: 189). This, combined with the ever increasing difficulties of daily survival in a hostile right-wing environment, has led some black lesbian groups to disband or cease active existence. Nevertheless, black lesbian groups continue to meet in London, Birmingham, Bradford, Nottingham, Manchester and Bristol well into the 1990s (Mason-John and Khambatta 1993; *Caribbean Times* 23 January 1997).

THE CREATION OF A FUNDED BLACK WOMEN'S INFRASTRUCTURE

The local black women's groups which formed out of the catalysing experience of national conferences such as OWAAD (1979–82), We Are Here (1984) and Zami (1985), as well as out of the daily experiences of black women, were born into an environment in which black organisations had gained some acceptance within the mainstream. In the aftermath of the uprisings which swept Britain in the early 1980s, self help groups were seen by central government as a way of offering 'alienated black youth' a stake in society (Scarman 1982; Gilroy 1987). Funding for black community organisations under existing programmes such as Urban Aid and Section 11 of the Local Government Act 1966 was significantly increased (Anthias *et al.* 1992). Furthermore, the 1980s saw significant grant aid programmes being offered by the Greater London Council, which funded many black women's organisations for the first time (Greater London Council 1986). Numerous scholars have identified this as the turning-point where black struggle was transformed into a 'professional ethnic community' run by a state-created petit bourgeoisie of 'career militants' (Bains 1988: 240; A. Wilson 1984: 177; Gilroy 1987). This argument will be examined in some depth in Chapters 3 and 4. However, this kind of analysis creates a false dichotomy between oppositional black struggle and coopted ethnic organisations. These critics ignore the complexity of community organisations which engage in both campaigning and service delivery and embrace both black politics and ethnic identities (Qaiyoom 1993b; Brixton Black Women's Group 1984a: 89). Black women's groups which obtained funding under these programmes gained stability and were able to reach more women. Government grants provided the necessary funds for organisations to obtain premises and provide a range of services including hostel provision for women escaping violence, nurseries, Saturday Schools and training programmes (Sia 1996a, 1996b). Funding also created an organisational longevity which many unfunded groups such as Awaz and OWAAD could not sustain.

By the early 1990s, then, a phenomenal increase in the numbers of black women's organisations, both funded and unfunded, had ensured that black women's organisations existed in all cities with significant black populations, as well as in many smaller towns and rural areas in Britain. A national directory produced by Sia: the National Development Agency for the Black Voluntary Sector in 1996 included over 110 organisations and approximately four hundred groups could be identified via sources such as the *Ethnic Minority Directory*, *Confederation of Indian Organisations' Directory of Asian Organisations* (CIO), as well as listings held by Racial Equality councils and local authorities (Sia 1996b; *Hansib Directory* 1994; CIO 1995). Autonomous organisations had become part of the collective consciousness of a large proportion of black women in Britain, both migrants and British born.

DOCUMENTING BLACK WOMEN'S AGENCY

As my research will show, black women's organisations are not fixed in time, but change and are constantly reborn over time. In the 1990s these organisations are extremely heterogenous; some are funded; others remain unfunded; some have entered into contracts in order to deliver services; others retain a greater degree of independence and are campaign orientated; some have developed a cultural and ethnic homogeneity; others embrace a political definition of blackness. In their diversity, they represent a unique synthesis of struggles and histories in Britain, the Indian subcontinent, Africa, the Caribbean and the Americas and of gender, racialised and class relations. Black women's autonomous spaces offer fertile ground for the examination of the intersection of economic, ideological and political structures, forces and counterforces in Britain. Yet these organisations have been largely ignored by sociologists and historians alike.

How can we explain this absence? For white feminist scholars, black women have seldom been more than a mirror, held up to enable white women to know themselves better (Carby 1982). Black women's autonomous political praxis has therefore been recreated as a problem for feminism. This tendency is reflected in the numerous texts which locate the catalyst for the break up of the Women's Liberation Movement in the rejection by black women of a homogenous sisterhood and the establishment of autonomous ('separatist') spaces. The Feminist Review Collective (1986) and Griffin (1995a: 4) criticise this tendency. Research by white feminists has therefore focused on how to solve the 'problem' of black women's alienation from [white] feminist organisations, while marginalising black women's actual participation in autonomous organisations (Ferree and Martin 1995; Albrecht and Brewer 1990). By focusing on black women as an absence, this approach perpetuates the stereotypical notion of black women's victim status, ignoring their participation in communities of resistance and foregrounding their subjection to 'backwards' cultural practices or to 'double discrimination'.

The last decade has seen a shift from universalist 'imperial' feminisms which viewed black women through the prism of white womanhood, to the development of white feminisms which recognise and indeed embrace women's diversity (Spelman 1988; Griffin 1995a). In groundbreaking work which owes much to black feminist critiques of white womanhood, white feminists have acknowledged white women's participation in racialised structures and ideologies and have recognised that they too have ethnicity (Ware 1992; Frankenberg 1993a, 1993b). This new-found self awareness has not, however, led to a dramatic change in the way in which black women's activism is perceived. Instead, the focus on 'whiteness' can be utilised as a new language and legitimacy for marginalising black women's agency while drawing on their theoretical contributions to illuminate white women's subjectivities.

While white feminist scholars have been slow to recognise black women's agency, sociological studies of black participation aim to move away from definitions of black people as passive victims towards a view of black political agency (Goulbourne 1990; Anwar 1991). Nevertheless, these studies too have been severely restricted by the systematic fashion in which they have ignored black women's agency. Since these works measure black political participation by the extent to which it is visible to and impacts on the liberal democratic political machinery, they are slow to acknowledge any activity which is targeted at black audiences. They are therefore limited to the study of elections, political parties, unions and similar processes such as black sections and formally structured organisations such as the Campaign Against Racial Discrimination (CARD) and the Indian Workers Association (Anwar 1991; Saggar 1992; Jeffers 1991). Informal and organic community groups are considered peripheral in achieving gains for black communities.

Studies of black political participation are also limited by their failure to utilise a gender transparent approach. Where these scholars do acknowledge gender differentials, they are faced with a remarkable absence of women (Layton-Henry 1992). This has been 'explained' by untheorised references to the cultural barriers experienced by Asian women and to a 'hierarchy of oppression' experienced by African, Asian and Caribbean women (Geddes 1993: 55). These generalisations stand in sharp constrast to the otherwise painstaking analysis of the data and are informative in revealing the extent to which stereotypical images of black women as passive victims have yet to be exorcised from the sociological imagination (Brah 1993: 142). They relieve the scholar of the task of questioning in which other ways black women may be expressing their political vision and reinforce sociological explanations which have little do to with black women's subjective realities.

Since scholars of [white] women's and black [male] political activism have erased black women's organisations, we might expect the black women intellectuals who have emerged since the early 1980s to document their presence. Hazel Carby's strident call to arms 'White woman listen!: black feminism and the boundaries of sisterhood' (1982) marked a turning-point in the publication of critical thinking by black British women (1982: 214). Carby reflected the frustration and anger of black women faced by a Women's Liberation Movement which consistently refused to acknowledge the existence or experiences of black women. Carby's critique was shaped by her interaction with black women activists such as Pratibha Parmar, Kum-Kum Bhavnani and Valerie Amos, and was very much an expression of intellectual currents developed within the context of a burgeoning black women's movement (Parmar 1990: 105). Members of Organisation of Women of African and Asian Descent (OWAAD), the Black Lesbian Group and Brixton Black Women's Group had made similar comments at feminist conferences, in newsletters and journals (OWAAD 1979; Brixton Black Women's Group 1980).

Carby's article is mostly borrowed for the theoretical framework she offers for the critique of white feminism(s), based on her analysis of key areas of feminist theorising including family, patriarchy and reproduction (Amos and Parmar 1984: 4; S. Small 1994: 201). Equally important was her analysis of the importance of networks and organisational infrastructure among black women in Africa, the Indian sub-continent and Britain (ibid.: 231). Rejecting inaccurate portrayals of black women's oppression by white feminists, Carby claims black women's right to create autonomous spaces from which to define their own realities. Black women have made the same demand throughout the 1980s and 1990s in conferences and publications with titles such as *Black Women Speak Out* (Osaba Women's Centre 1993), *Making Voices Heard* (Equal Opportunities Commission 1993) and *Black Women Talk* (Chapeltown Black Women Writers' Group 1992). Black women have expressed their determination to come to voice, to be listened to rather than examined or spoken for. Yet this demand has not been matched by a blossoming in literature written by black women about black women organising in Britain. Since the edition of *Feminist Review* edited by members of OWAAD in 1984, in which Brixton Black Women's Group, Brent Asian women's refuge and OWAAD were examined, there has been startling paucity of writing on black women's organisations.

This paucity needs to be set within the context of black women's intellectual production in Britain. Despite increasing numbers of black women accessing higher education in the late 1980s and 1990s, black women in Britain are dramatically under-represented in academia and very little of their theoretical and intellectual work is published (Mirza 1992; Sulter 1988). Black women in Black Women in Research group meetings which I attended in London in 1994 shared experiences of alienation and intimidation by white male colleagues who assumed their work would be marginal and irrelevant to the major issues within the disciplines of sociology, education and history (see Marshall 1994). This exclusion of black women from institutionalised notions of what constitutes legitimate knowledge production has been explored in the American context, but has not been extensively documented in Britain (Collins 1990; James and Farmar 1993; Omolade 1995). However, it is clear that the promise of Carby's call to arms was in part curtailed by the exclusion of black women from positions where their intellectual work would be recognised and paid for. Where black women's groups have addressed this problem by publishing their own work documenting the achievements of such organisations, the resulting publications rarely achieve the wide readership and distribution they deserve (Southall Black Sisters 1989; Chapeltown Black Women Writers' Group 1992; Chatterjee 1995).

Where articles and books by black women are published by mainstream presses, they tend to focus on individual women's lives rather than exploring black women's collective activism (Grewal *et al.* 1988, A. Wilson 1984). Such publications often respond to gendered racism through poetry and creative writing (Cobham and Collins 1987; Ngcobo 1988). An exception is Bryan *et al.*'s seminal book *The Heart of the Race* (1985). However this important portrayal of black women organising is as partial as it is powerful, since the contributions of Asian and lesbian women are largely absent (Sisters in Study 1988). By the mid 1990s, a number of black women had produced theoretical works on black women (Afshar and Maynard 1994; Bhavnani and Phoenix 1994; Mama 1995; Jarrett-Macauley 1996). However, once more black women's organisations were at most a backdrop rather than a subject deemed worthy of in depth analysis.

Pratibha Parmar's (1990) analysis of the movement of the 1980s perhaps explains this lost opportunity. In describing her sense of alienation from the 'optimism and stridency' of the late 1970s and early 1980s, Parmar writes:

> To assert an individual and collective identity as black women has been a necessary historical process which was both empowering and strengthening. . . . It is also based on an assumption of shared subjectivities, of the ways in which our experience of the world 'out there' are shaped by common objective factors such as racism and sexual exploitation. However, these assumptions have led to a political practice which employs a language of 'authentic subjective experience'. . . . Identity politics or a political practice which takes as its starting-point only the personal and experiential modes of being has led to a closure which is both retrogressive and sometimes spine-chilling.
>
> (Parmar 1990: 107)

By the 1990s black women intellectuals who were at the forefront of national black women's organising in the 1980s were beginning to feel a sense of disillusionment with the methods of that very movement. Experience of the more excessive and essentialising forms of identity politics, 'guilt tripping' of white women, aggressive comparisons of oppression in a hierarchy of 'isms' all led to a questioning of the assumptions underlying black women's organisations (V. Alexander 1995; Grewal *et al.* 1988).

In questioning the grand narrative of the 'black woman's experience', these intellectuals began to explore ways of expressing the diversity and complexity which made up the heterogenous notion of black women (Brah 1992a; Mama 1995). The shift from totalising notions of race and gender to explorations of the shifting nature of culture, identity and subjectivity will be explored in depth in Chapter 4. For now I will simply note that the intellectuals formed out of the black women's movement of the 1980s, had lost interest in the necessarily simplified dichotomies of black/white, man/woman, state/community which formed the backbone of many grassroots black women's struggles in the early 1980s. The disintegration of the Organisation of Women of African and Asian Descent (OWAAD) in 1982 among antagonistic and painful recriminations, due in part to the failure of many members to conceive of a black womanhood that could incorporate lesbian sexuality, served to undermine further the continuing relevance of black women's organisations in the 1990s (Mason-John 1995b; Brixton Black Women's Group 1984a).

MAKING VOICES HEARD[16]

The previous section examined the ways in which the black women's organisations which developed from the early 1970s, have been an important blind-spot for many researchers of black [male] and [white] women's agency. The aim of this chapter has not been to capture the nuances of different strands of the genres discussed, but to present a broad brush picture of the ways in which the scholars in question have been blinkered by ways of thinking and knowing which preclude recognition of black women's collective agency. Subsequent chapters will revisit much of the literature discussed here and begin to develop a more textured analysis of their usefulness in the study of black women's organisations.

I have examined how black women's activism has been overlooked and neglected by the existing methodologies of most social scientific research. In the light of this problem, the second chapter of this book carries out the necessary task of constructing an alternative research methodology, drawing heavily on the work of black feminist theorists such as Patricia Hill Collins, Gail Lewis and Chandra Mohanty, but also acknowledging the innovative thinking of male African-centred and white feminist scholars. With this grounding in place, the third chapter revisits the question of black women's political participation and via an examination of the views of black women involved in twelve case study organisations comes to a new definition of politics. This chapter then evaluates the political content and impact of these organisations and examines whether previous assertions that funded organisations have been coopted by the state are a valid assessment.

An evaluation of the political content of black women's organisations leads us to the theme of the fourth chapter which analyses the importance of constructions of identity. This chapter questions whether black women's organisations can be described as posited on a narrow identity politics and examines the relevance of the (anti)essentialism debate to the women interviewed. It also asks whether black women have developed ways of organising and forms of leadership unique to black women and what this means for new theories of subjectivity. The fifth chapter undertakes an in depth analysis of the relevance of class analyses to black women's organisations and asks whether black women involved have a class consciousness and whether this impacts on their organising effectiveness.

Chapter 6 looks beyond the internal organisation of black women's groups and asks in what ways black women have built coalitions. This chapter looks in depth at coalition building between black men and women, and between white and black women. It asks whether, as has been suggested, mobilising around racialised identities hinders an appreciation of struggles which have broader constituencies and attempts to identify what factors have prevented or encouraged effective coalition building. The final chapter returns to my initial questions in order to illustrate how these have been addressed. First, I outline a new framework for analysing black women's agency by reiterating the key conceptual shifts which have formed the basis for this research. Second, I draw together the strands in this research by highlighting their implications for black women organising into the next millennium. The futuristic conclusion continues the visionary theme of this book, enabling me both to reiterate my central arguments and to set out some key ideas for debate and discussion among black women's activists and their allies. I conclude with a call for black women's organisations to build on their most outward looking tendencies, to create coalitions and to develop an analysis of gendered racialised inequalities which utilises local struggles as a basis for fundamental changes in the global socio-economic order.

NOTES

1 Throughout the book, I use 'black' to refer to people of African, Asian and Middle Eastern descent in the British context. I recognise that the usage of this term is currently under much contestation, not least within black women's organisations themselves, and this debate is addressed at length in Chapter 4. I argue that the term reflects a political and cultural space which arose out of and is sustained by specific forms of organising in Britain. I have avoided the conflation of 'black' with African heritage by using the term African Caribbean where appropriate.

2 The Organisation of Women of African and Asian Descent. For a brief description of the history of OWAAD, see under heading, 'Black women organising autonomously', Hart 1984 and Brixton Black Women's Group 1984a.

3 In a survey of 2,500 black voluntary organisations carried out by Sia: the National Development Agency for the Black Voluntary Sector, the majority voted for the term 'black and minority ethnic' being dropped from its title in favour of 'black' (1995: 3).

4 In fact, one of the occupants of the *Windrush* was a woman stowaway, Averill Wauchope, a dressmaker from Kingston (R. Bhavnani 1994: 17).

5 By 1953 women seeking work were arriving from the Caribbean in equal numbers to men (R. Bhavnani 1994: 17). Parmar points out that while women from India, Pakistan and Bangladesh were brought as dependents of male migrant workers from the mid 1960s, most of these women came from a background of back-breaking work as subsistence farmers (Parmar 1982: 254). Many East African Asian women, forced out of Kenya and Uganda in the late 1960s and early 1970s, had also worked in family businesses. On arrival, many Asian women obtained unskilled wage labour, much of it undocumented, in the clothing and service industries (Wilson 1978). Many African women arriving as students from Nigeria and Ghana and refugees from Somalia and Ethiopia did not have work visas and therefore tended to be engaged in undocumented cleaning and manual jobs (R. Bhavnani 1994: 18).

6 Cornelia Sorabji, the first woman law student at a British university, returned to India in 1894 and dedicated her life to fighting legal battles on behalf of women in purdah (Visram 1986: 187–8).

7 Amy Garvey, a leading member of the Pan-African Congress, headed the Association for the Advancement of Coloured People which also ran a hostel and club in north Kensington (Ramdin 1987: 224).

8 Claudia Jones, a Trinidadian, was deported from the United States for

her role in communist and anti-racist activities. In 1956 she came to Britain where she founded the *West Indian Gazette* and the Confederation of Afro–Asian–Caribbean Organisations. In 1963 she led a British freedom march in solidarity with Martin Luther King's March on Washington (Bryan *et al.* 1985:136–9).

9 A celebration of Chief Justice Mansfield's ruling that James Somerset, an enslaved African who escaped while in England could not be forcibly shipped to Jamaica by his former owner was attended by 200 black men and women. The ruling was taken by many to imply that slavery was unenforceable within England and led to widespread acts of resistance by enslaved Africans and Asians in Britain (Ramdin 1987).

10 These societies caused considerable concerns to the authorities at the time, who noted that rebellious blacks would 'enter into Societies and make it their business to corrupt and dissatisfy the Mind of every fresh servant that comes to England' (Fryer 1984: 71). This hidden history has its counterparts in the 'quilombos' of Brazil, the maroon societies in Jamaica and the 'seminole' communities of what is now North America and Mexico, some of which were led by women such as Nanny of the Maroons and Cubah 'Queen of Kingston' (Bryan *et al.* 1985: 128).

11 The laws referred to are the 1962 Commonwealth Immigrants Act, the 1968 Commonwealth Immigrants Act, the 1969 Immigration Appeals Act and the 1971 Immigration Act.

12 Black Power's ideological debt to the Caribbean becomes evident when we recognise that Earl Little, father of Malcolm X was a staunch follower of Garvey, who first called for the black man to see 'beauty in himself' and that Stokely Carmichael, one of the most influential Black Power activists and thinkers was born in Trinidad (Ramdin 1987: 105; Gilroy 1987). Less often acknowledged is the extent to which central tenets of Black Power ideology – cultural pride, integrity and self determination – were core elements of Indian and Pakistani organisations in Britain (Hiro 1971: 148).

13 In 1968 Conservative MP Enoch Powell made this grim prediction about black immigration to Britain: 'As I look ahead, I am filled with foreboding. Like the Roman, I seem to see the River Tiber foaming with much blood' (Hensman 1995: 30).

14 Organisations established in this period include Brixton Black Women's Group (London 1973), Liverpool Black Sisters (early 1970s), Manchester Black Women's Co-operative (1973), Muslim Ladies Circle (Nottingham 1972) and Awaz (London mid 1970s).

15 'Zami. A Carriacou name for women who work together as friends and lovers' (Lorde 1982: 255).

16 Taken from the title of the All Wales Black and Ethnic Minority Women's Conference, Cardiff, 5 June 1993.

Chapter 2

Writing against the grain: towards a womanist methodology

Having illustrated some absences in the current literature, it is necessary to create a methodological framework for this study of black women's organisations. The past three decades have witnessed the problematising of the validity or even possibility of value-neutral and objective social scientific research (Ladner 1973; Collins 1990). The deconstruction of white masculinist social science occurred as the new social movements for racialised equality, women's liberation and gay and lesbian rights broke into the academy (Omolade 1995; Harding 1991: 115). Black men and women and white women activists in grassroots organisations initiated these critiques. The creation of black and ethnic studies, cultural studies and women's studies programmes provided oppositional spaces where theory could be honed and disseminated (Ladner 1973: xxv). Black scholars in Britain and the United States pointed out the ways in which social science had pathologised black people, portraying black family structures as deviations to a white (heterosexual) norm and black cultures as inevitably leading to deprivation and social exclusion (Lawrence 1982; Brah and Shaw 1992). At the same time, feminist scholars pointed out the masculinist bias in the social sciences which had led to distorted analyses of issues such as domestic violence, mothering and women's work (Oakley 1981; Stanley and Wise 1993). Meanwhile, poststructuralist theorists were questioning the very epistemological assumptions upon which claims to know social 'facts' were based (Spivak 1990b). These accounts reveal that social science is far from the detached pursuit of objective 'best truths' utilising 'scientific canons of proof and evidence' (Mason 1990: 131). Rather, sociological accounts are embedded with stereotypical assumptions about black communities and white women and frequently serve to perpetuate social inequalities by justifying oppressive policy interventions (Ani 1994; Cheney 1996).

While critiques of social science orthodoxy have emerged from diverse social and political locations, three broad groups of scholars have offered arguments which are particularly pertinent to this study. Writing in the 1970s, African American social scientists highlighted white sociology's[1] failure to further humanist goals, its indifference to social inequity and its collusion with white supremacy (Staples 1973: 162; Alkalimat 1973). These scholars established 'black liberation sociology' as 'the science of liberation' (Staples 1973: 168; Walter 1973: 201). Black liberation sociologists rejected the misleading claims to value-neutrality which masked white sociology's covert support of the status quo and declared themselves to be overtly politically committed. This commitment was expressed programatically in several ways. First, the liberation sociologist would advocate for and valorise African American family structures and institutions. Second, his or her ideological viewpoint would differ from that of the white sociologist. She/he would reject consensus models of society in favour of a rigorous analysis of racism and oppression and shake off the obsession with integrating into the host community in favour of analysing solidarity among African peoples. Third, she/he would focus on the end result of the research rather than simply on the findings and analysis. The black liberation sociologist was therefore not only a scholar, but also an activist and was accountable for her/his research findings to 'the black community'.

While black liberation sociology's claim to provide a blueprint for liberatory research may appear to the contemporary eye to rest on an imaginary notion of a unitary black community, it nevertheless provided an essential counter to the pathologisation of African Americans. Building on these early insights, Afrocentric scholars have developed a research agenda which seeks to relocate African subjects from the margins to the centre of analysis (Asante 1990; Ani 1994). In contrast to the former, African-centred scholars seek to change not only the content and ideological assumptions of their research, but to question the very epistemological beliefs upon which knowledge claims within the social sciences are based. They therefore place a critique upon two tenets of social scientific rationalism. First, white social scientists' claims to objectivity are problematised on the grounds that the separation of subject from object, knower from known, on which objectivity is predicated, is both a damaging enterprise which has 'allowed European social scientists to immobilize us and to exploit us' (Ani 1994: 516), and that it is 'invalid operationally', that is, the subjective decisions, emotions and opinions of the researcher will always be a part of any research (Asante 1990: 24). Second, the search for universal truths is rejected as a form of European expansionism:

> Europeans use universalistic terms to describe themselves; they are 'modern man', 'civilised man', and 'universal man'. It is above all the nature of their *utamaroho* [cultural energy] that they project themselves onto the world. They are world saviours and world conquerors; they are world peace-makers. . . . It is ultimately the European obsession with unlimited 'power over other' that brings universalism into their conceptions.
>
> (Ani 1994: 514)

The Afrocentric method is proposed as a means of countering the distortion of social reality which occurs when traditional methods are utilised. While specific practitioners may vary, Molefi Asante offers an overview of this method. First, he counters the separation of the subject from the object of research with the notion of the 'wholistic impulse' (ibid.: 27). This impulse locates the African subject within a collectivity which thus prevents the separation of the individual. Second, Asante proposes that the researcher deploys introspection and retrospection to ensure that no obstacles exist to a fair interpretation of data (ibid.: 27). Third, he advocates social and cultural immersion in the social environment of the research project to ensure that the researcher retains a committed and ethical attitude towards his research subject. Where the researcher is not of the culture or society under examination, Asante suggests that two people should undertake data collection and evaluation, of which one should be a local person. Finally, the Afrocentric researcher will locate her/his research subjects in the context of their history. For African subjects in the diaspora, that implies starting analysis from the African origins of civilization (ibid.: 14).

The Afrocentric method is designed to eliminate bias in the research process. In so doing, however, it adheres to some of the very concepts which it criticises in Eurocentric social science. Afrocentric scholars berate white social scientists for presenting self interest as objectivity, and expansionism as a humanistic urge to the universal good. However, while such false claims to objectivity are questioned, the Afrocentric method itself uses methods such as triangulation and the use of dual collectors and evaluators in order to increase the accuracy (objectivity) of its data collection (Asante 1990: 25). Similarly, while white appropriation of humanistic rhetoric is a problem for Afrocentricity, the search for an authentic humanistic voice by African scholars is not:

> The aim of the Africalogist is to make the world more meaningful to those who live in it and to create spaces for human understanding. Our task is not like that of the Western social scientist who seeks to predict human behaviour in order to advance more direct control over nature but rather to explain human nature.
>
> (Asante 1990: 28)

Afrocentric research is therefore represented as a more authentic version of social science, a method which resolves the biases of traditional research. In so doing, it becomes a humanising mission, in the tradition of the Enlightenment project, offering greater self knowledge to the world's population. Thus while Afrocentricity starts with the specificity of the African population in the diaspora, it ends up with far more expansive claims. As Asante reminds us, the Afrocentric approach: 'sees research as assisting in the humanizing of the world' (ibid.: 27). In their desire to humanise the world from an African-diasporic perspective, Afrocentric scholars fail to acknowledge the specificity of their project, located in the privileged halls of Western academia. In so doing, they replace one universal set of claims with another and thus leave little space for dissenting voices from formerly colonised countries, from other communities of colour or from marginal sections within African diasporic communities.

STANDPOINT THEORIES: TUNING INTO THE 'OUTSIDER WITHIN'

In a parallel development, but often in isolation from black scholars, white feminists in Britain and the United States have also criticised the objectivism and universalism of social science orthodoxy. While the former defined these characteristics as 'Eurocentric', feminists found the same characteristics to betray the self interest of male social scientists (Oakley 1981; Harding 1991; Stanley and Wise 1993). Thus, Ann Oakley describes the 'proper' interview, where the interviewer retains an emotional distance from *his* subject, as a 'masculine fiction' which obscures the actual relations of power and negotiation involved (ibid.: 55). In its place, she advocates the acknowledgement of personal involvement and commitment as a necessary part of researching women's lives. Taking Oakley's analysis further, Dorothy Smith argues that sympathetic interview techniques are not enough. If women are to speak in ways which differ from the 'fathertongue', they must begin sociology from 'women's standpoint':

> To begin from the standpoint of women is to insist on the validity of an inquiry that is interested and that begins from a particular site in the world. It is to be committed to an inquiry that violates the conditions of sociological objectivity and yet insists that there is something to be discovered, to be known, a product of inquiry that can be relied on.
>
> (Smith 1990: 33)

Feminist standpoint theory therefore rejects the myth of the impartial observer who has no interest in or impact on *his* research, the 'god-trick of seeing everything from nowhere' in favour of situated knowledge(s) (Haraway 1991a: 189). This rejection of traditional notions of impartiality does not however imply the rejection of objectivity as a goal of social science research. Standpoint theorists, in a move comparable to the Afrocentric method, rebuff objectivism – the insistence on value-neutrality – while retaining a revised concept of objectivity. By introducing the notion of different degrees of objectivity, strong versus weak, theorists such as Sandra Harding are able to claim superiority for feminist standpoint theory rooted in its ability to get closer to the 'best claims' of social science. In so doing, Harding replaces the traditional [male] impartial observer who is distanced from his research object through the processes of objectification, with the committed woman researcher who is distanced not from her research objects, but from the culture-wide assumptions framing the research: 'The stranger brings to her research just the combination of nearness and remoteness, concern and indifference, that are central to maximising objectivity' (Harding 1991: 124). Thus, women, as outsiders to the social order, are more likely to produce research findings which challenge the status quo.

When black liberation sociologists focus on white supremacy and when white feminists focus on patriarchy as the primary locus of oppression, they produce one-dimensional remedies to the bias inherent in social scientific theory and praxis. It has been the goal of the third broad grouping of critics to produce a 'way of seeing' which makes transparent the simultaneity of gendered racialised inequalities, to develop a black feminist epistemology (Collins 1990; Bannerji 1995). Black feminists have long claimed the right to speak for themselves, rather than having others speak for them. In this sense, they have challenged the false claims of traditional social scientists, black [male] liberation scholars and [white] feminists that they represent the concerns of all (hu)mankind, black communities and women respectively and asserted the validity of their unique standpoint as black women. Speaking 'as a black woman' has been a powerful basis both for political action and for social scientific critique (Lewis 1996: 25). In Britain, black women demanded the space to 'bear witness to our own herstories' (Carby 1982: 212) using the integrative analytical framework which they had developed:

> As Black women. . . . We have to look at the crucial question of how we organise in order that we address ourselves to the totality of our oppression. For us there is no choice. We cannot simply prioritise one aspect of our oppression to the exclusion of others, as the realities of our day to day lives make it imperative for us to consider the simultaneous nature of our oppression and exploitation. Only a synthesis of class, race, gender and sexuality can lead us forward, as these form the matrix of Black women's lives.
>
> (Amos and Parmar 1984: 18)

In the United States, African American feminists have developed a similar conceptualisation of their location at the intersection of 'race', gender, class and sexuality. In so doing, they have claimed a unique perspective of the interlocking nature of systems of oppression (hooks 1981; Combahee River Collective 1983). Where white women are blinded by 'race' and perhaps class privilege and black men are limited by the mask of their masculinity, black working class women alone may be free of ideological blinkers.

bell hooks sees black women's position as one of radical marginality (hooks 1984: vii). Using the spatial exclusion from the white 'center' enforced by North American segregation as a symbolic statement, hooks reclaims that location both as a space of resistance and of understanding. Experiences of oppression are therefore recast as creating the opportunity for epistemic privilege.

Patricia Hill Collins (1986) develops this notion of marginality as a resource into a comprehensive and coherent theory of African-centred feminist epistemology. For Collins, 'being in touch' with her marginality in the academic sphere is a necessary precursor to writing from an authentic black women's standpoint. It is this positioning which enables black feminist critics to reject the white male sociological worldview and to become 'outsiders within':

> As outsiders within, Black feminist scholars may be one of the many distinct groups of marginal intellectuals whose standpoints promise to enrich contemporary sociological discourse. Bringing this group – as well as others who share an outsider within status *vis-à-vis* sociology – into the center of analysis may reveal aspects of reality obscured by more orthodox approaches.
>
> (Collins 1986: 5)

Collins makes it clear that her analysis would also apply to other oppressed groups. She thus alludes to a wider category of 'subjugated knowledge' which may be tapped by other men and women of colour, white women, gays and lesbians (Collins 1990: 202).

African American feminists' standpoint theories have been highly influential in Britain as well as the United States (Marshall 1996; Young 1996). For some black British feminists, though, there is a wariness about using such a positionality as a basis for claims of a superior viewpoint. In a review article on several works by women of colour in America, Lewis and Parmar warned of the limitations of such an assumption:

> A common experience of discrimination is not of itself a sufficient basis from which to bring about the structural and institutional change essential to our liberation. . . . What Afro-Caribbeans and Asians in Britain have been concerned to unite around is an experience which is both historical and contemporary, both collective and individual.
>
> (Lewis and Parmar 1983: 89)

The need to create a politics of African–Asian unity prohibited an identity politics based only on narrowly defined sameness of experience. Rather, black feminists in Britain focused on common histories of resistance to colonialism and racism and a shared analysis of 'race', class and gender. Nevertheless, black feminist standpoint theory contained within it the seeds of a divisive essentialism. By asserting that experiences of oppression created a unique accuracy of vision, standpoint theorists created the basis for claims of superior knowledge based purely on degrees of oppression. Thus 'darkskinned' black women could claim to be better judges of racism than 'lightskinned' black women: heterosexual women could be silenced in the light of lesbian women's assumed insight (Brah 1992a; Grewal *et al.* 1988). What had begun as an empowering way to enable previously silenced women to gain a voice, became at times a means to silence those who were not quite oppressed enough. Collins had in fact attempted to resolve this problem in her characterisation of black women's standpoint as 'a partial perspective on domination' which could only be made more complete by adding partial perspectives from other subjugated groups:

> Each group speaks from its own standpoint and shares its own partial, situated knowledge. But because each group perceives its knowledge as partial, its knowledge is unfinished. Each group becomes better able to consider other groups' standpoints without relinquishing the uniqueness of its own standpoint or suppressing other groups' partial perspectives.
>
> (Collins 1990: 236)

However, Collins' theorisation does not address the internal contestation which can occur within the category of 'black women'. It is highly likely, for example, that black British women might dispute the characterisation of black women's perspective offered by Collins and hooks, which are based entirely on African American women's experiences. Similarly, a young African American woman living in social isolation on a segregated housing estate, is unlikely to have the 'outsider within' perspective on white families which Collins attributes to black women domestic workers (Collins 1986: 4).

The weakness of standpoint theories, as they have been elaborated by black feminists, is their tendency to essentialise, to assume that black women's characteristics can be described with little more than lip service to their specific historical or spatial location. Ironically, this is the very criticism which has been made of white feminist standpoint theories, as Denise Riley points out, it is not enough to move from 'Woman' to 'women': ' "being a woman" is also inconsistent, and can't provide an ontological foundation' (Riley 1988: 2; D. Smith 1990). While the shift from 'women' to 'black women' has been an empowering moment, the latter category is equally unable to provide a consistent foundation for knowledge claims. That is, the fact of being a black woman researcher does not guarantee a more accurate understanding or representation of racism and oppression. Bat-Ami Bar On argues that accounts which afford epistemic privilege to marginalised groups tend to rely on idealising certain assumed characteristics as the basis for that privilege (Bar On 1993: 91). Thus, caring and nurturing roles, domestic work and resistance are identified as authentic practices for black women (hooks 1990; Collins 1990). Implicitly, then, those who do not juggle caring for children while carrying out research, or do not identify with an African American tradition of resistance to slavery, become unauthentic and are thus silenced. The 'black woman researcher' becomes a very narrow space which perhaps marginalises as many as it empowers:

> Traditionally excluded from the creation of sociological and feminist thought, the position of the Black female researcher is unique. She is aware that Black women have been pathologised by sociological and feminist literature . . . for example, notions of Black matriarchs and Sapphires. . . . This awareness is extremely alienating as the (so-called) 'angry Black woman' struggles to tackle the negation of her experiences.
>
> (Marshall 1996)

Marshall's description is an interesting example of the construction of the black woman as authentic agent of knowledge. Written in the British context, her definition of the black female researcher clearly excludes Asian women, many of whom identify as black (Brah 1992a). Marshall's use of stereotypes draws heavily on American imagery, the 'Sapphire' in particular was developed as a stereotype to describe African American women (Jewell 1993). Marshall's 'Black woman' is not after all as universal as she seemed at first glance. Instead, she is rooted in an African American tradition of black women theorists. In constructing this voice, other black women are silenced. Bar On's (1993) analysis points to a flaw in the ideal of coming to voice without silencing those other subjugated groups which are also attempting to find their voices. The concept of authority inherent in standpoint theories undermines this democratic goal. Standpoint theories implicitly valorise the authentic marginalised voice. But as the marginal is moved to the centre, new margins are created.

RELOCATING 'EXPERIENCE'

Few critiques of standpoint theory have been concerned with the new margins, the voices which have never made their way to the centre. Instead, theorists who have found themselves deposed have begun to envision ways to centre their voices once more. Thus there has been a blossoming of literature on how white feminists may speak now that their relation to the centre has been revealed as rather less disinterested than was previously claimed (Ware 1992; Frankenberg 1993a). It has been asserted that men can 'do' feminism and white women can 'think from' the lives of people of colour (Harding 1991, 1993; Whelehan 1995: 184–9). In this amended version of standpoint theory, Harding asserts that people can in fact speak from standpoints of others: 'It is only necessary to learn how to overcome – to get a critical, objective perspective on – the "spontaneous consciousness" created by thought that begins in one's dominant social location' (Harding 1991: 287).

In shifting standpoint theory away from the somewhat discredited category of 'experience', Harding's new notion of standpoint loses its political power – the ability to claim a platform for subjugated groups. While learning to 'think against the grain' of dominant discourse by engaging in texts written by a range of oppressed groups is important, it has little to do with standpoint (Harding 1991: 289). Or put another way, the fact that such texts can be labelled as 'African American theorists', 'gay and lesbian writers' means that the category of experience has not yet gone away. 'Others' are defined by their social location, but the 'critical, objective' thinker can escape hers. The return to critical thinking therefore becomes an opportunity for white feminists and other (in some contexts) dominant groupings to silence the margins and to reclaim their voice, as Haraway states: 'There is no immediate vision from the standpoints of the subjugated. Identity, including self identity, does not produce science; critical positioning does, that is objectivity'[2] (Haraway 1991b: 193).

Haraway makes an important point, that 'experience' is not simply 'out there', waiting to be conveyed faithfully by the subject, but that it is constructed and mobilised through discourse. But Haraway and Bar On are perhaps wishful when they call for subjugated groups to reject authority claims based on experience as an example of using 'the master's tools' (Bar On 1993). This call fails to acknowledge the complex processes of validation which enable those operating within social scientific orthodoxy to speak (Collins 1990). It is hardly surprising that oppressed groups look for similar validation. The important question is how we can retain both a grounded understanding of the political necessity for the knowledge of subjugated groups to be validated and an appreciation that experience is not in fact 'the final empirical authority' (Asante 1990: 25). Drawing on poststructuralist theory, a number of feminists in Britain and the United States have begun to suggest new ways in which experience may be theorised (Glucksmann 1994; Mohanty 1992). Rather than starting from experience as evidence of social phenomena and a foundation for analysis, its foundational status is problematised. As a result: 'The very category of "experience" is established as in need of examination, so that the web of historical relations in which all "experience" is inscribed is brought to the fore' (Lewis 1996: 26). Lewis utilises this insight to question when and where 'experience' is mobilised and to what ends. It is no longer possible to speak 'innocently' of black women's experience(s), she suggests, we must instead look at how the location of specific women within multiple systems of subordination shapes the ways in which black women represent themselves as individuals and as a group. This 'politics of location', differs from a politics of identity in that it insists on the specific 'historical, geographical, cultural, psychic and imaginative boundaries' which shape our definitions of self and other (Mohanty 1992: 74). Thus, it is not enough to speak of black women: we need to know whether we are speaking of Britain, the United States or Nigeria, whether we mean women of African or Asian descent, whether we refer to contemporary or historical women, whether we are discussing heterosexual women, lesbians and so on. Within those broader categories, we need to look at narrower groupings, as Lewis illustrates in her analysis of black women social workers who are located both in a subordinate location in relation to white staff and one of authority over their clients, both black and white (ibid.). This focus on location insists on the standpoint of its speakers, yet it does not essentialise. It enables examination of the specificities of the 'partial story' without losing sight of the macro structures which locate and illuminate those details. Finally, it creates the space for the critical analysis of subordinated voices without re-centring those voices which have been deposed.

If the politics of identity means that I write 'as a black woman', then the politics of location demands that I write as a specific black woman located within a particular time-frame, ideological perspective and geographical framework. This perspective allows little complacency with regard to the subject of research. Rather than assuming that my research subject, being intimately related to my own position as a black British woman, will be easily accessible, I have to question the apparent ease of my access to the topic. That is, to draw on Lewis again, I need to read my own experience as a black woman researcher 'against the grain of common sense' (Lewis 1996: 49).

FROM THEORY TO METHOD: CONSTRUCTING A RESEARCH MODEL

Utilising the politics of location required that I develop a research methodology which integrates the insights of black feminist standpoint theorists with the reflexivity of thinking against the grain. I was committed to what I felt to be the tenets of black woman-centred research. First, drawing on Collins' notion of the interdependence of thought and action, I wished to produce a study which would be of use to black women (Collins 1990: 28). I would not seek primarily to explain black women's lived experiences to an audience of white male social scientists, but would produce knowledge which could lead to greater insight and improved effectiveness by black women activists. Writing for an audience of black women had serious practical implications. It implies that my work would have an audience beyond the academe and therefore would have a broader accountability. It made me question the type of language I would be using, how I could utilise sociological concepts without reverting to obscure jargon which excludes rather than includes the non-academic. Nevertheless, since the research was originally carried out for a Ph.D dissertation, my task was clearly that of writing for two audiences, one with the power to grant or withhold the Ph.D, the other with the power to grant 'community legitimacy', and my creativity would be stretched to the utmost as I attempted to remain faithful to the vitality, emotion and audacity of black women's activism while justifying my claim to write sociologically.

My second concern lay with the ethical treatment of the women I was researching. This went much further than the practice of informed consent advocated by many methodological texts, but involved treating them as knowing subjects of their own realities (H. Smith 1975: 12; Bulmer 1982: 221). Barbara Omolade has noted how African American women in North America have historically been constructed as sub-human manual workers and therefore as incapable of abstract reason and independent thought (1995: 119). bell hooks notes further that black women often internalise this distinction between theory and practice and develop a hostility to theory and to those who embrace theory: 'The stereotype would have us believe that the "real" black woman is always the one who speaks from the gut, who righteously praises the concrete over the abstract, the material over the theoretical' (hooks 1994a: 68).

In Britain, Pragna Patel (1991) of Southall Black Sisters points out how black women who explicitly theorise about social inequality are often depicted as elite intellectuals imposing their ideas on grassroots communities. In addition, the distant and 'objective' approach of much academic research into black communities has stoked a growing hostility to academia in general and sociological theory in particular, which is felt to have little to offer black women seeking to understand the oppression they face (Mason 1990: 131). My work seeks to challenge this false dichotomisation of theory and practice by recognising that black women activists engaged in black women's organisations are also engaged in everyday acts of theorising. Black women's activism does not just happen spontaneously, but is the result of painstaking analysis about the nature of socio-economic inequalities, the intersection of racism, gender and class and the means of social change. In utilising in depth interviews with black women activists, I sought to elicit their analyses of the historical development and present day struggles of black women's organisations. I aimed to relocate black women as thinkers and knowers.

My third methodological insight related to the critique of objectivism. What would I use as evidence to substantiate my claims about the scope and content of black women's organising? While I wished to focus on women's accounts of their experiences of organising, I was also aware of the possible accusations that my claims were not applicable outside the twelve organisations I had chosen to examine. My initial research proposal had included a questionnaire which I intended to send to approximately one hundred black women's organisations. At a superficial level, this would legitimate the information gained in the interviews. As the research developed, however, it became evident that such a questionnaire could not hope to enter beneath the surface of the public face of these organisations, which could just as easily be gleaned from leaflets, annual reports and voluntary sector directories. The information which I was interested in, women's subjective views about self and identity, political activism and organisational debates could only be elicited through face to face contact. The questionnaire had become a legitimating exercise which I was using to 'hedge my bets' on the question of objectivity and was in this sense symbolic of the power of social science hegemony to impose inappropriate methods on the researcher. I therefore decided to omit the questionnaire and to rely instead on collections of written materials, interviews and participant observation.

While I wished to avoid engaging in a formulistic objectivism, I also needed to select a broadly representative sample of case study organisations if I was to ensure that my interviews did not simply reflect a small part of the diverse range of organisations in existence. I therefore spent some time investigating the axes of difference which distinguished black women's organisations and then chose organisations which reflected this diversity. In order to facilitate selection of organisations I developed a grid which incorporated the key variables which I wished to study (see Table I).

I drew on personal knowledge, written sources, the *Confederation of Indian Organisations Directory*, *Grapevine Directory of African Caribbean Organisations* and *Third Sector*, a directory of business and community organisations compiled by the publisher of *Asian Times* and *Caribbean Times* newspapers to compile a list of over sixty organisations which were well established and unlikely to fold before the completion of the study and which had an organisational base and an easily accessible contact person. I then used the sampling grid to eliminate those which created duplication of variables, that is, I deleted many London-based groups to ensure regional variation. Finally, I ensured that I included groups from major urban conurbations of considerable black population: London, Manchester, Liverpool, West Midlands, as well as a town with a smaller black population: Cambridge. I did not wish to perpetuate English hegemony and therefore included an important Scottish group. As the research progressed, I became aware that the schema represented in Table I could not adequately reflect the full complexity of each organisation. In particular, the section on activity masked organisations which, for example, were primarily funded to deliver training but also offered support to women who were escaping from domestic violence. However, this schema offered a way into the organisations which acknowledged that diversity would be an integral aspect of the study.

Table I: Sampling grid for organisational variables

Geographical location and remit	Cambridge	(1)
	Coventry	(2)
	Edinburgh	(1)
	Liverpool	(1)
	London	(5)
	Manchester	(1)
	Sheffield	(1)
	National	*(5)*
	Local	*(7)*
Group membership	Asian women	(1)
	Muslim women	(1)
	Chinese women	(1)
	Caribbean women	(3)
	African women	(1)
	Inclusive definition – all 'black' women	(5)
Key activity	domestic violence	(2)
	education/ training/childcare	(4)
	arts/culture	(1)
	counselling	(1)
	campaigns	(2)
	consciousness raising	(1)
	overseas development	(1)
Sexual orientation	Mixed	(11)
	Lesbian	(1)
Funding	Grant-aided	(8)
	Unfunded	(3)
	Donations	(1)
Date established	1970s	(2)
	1980s	(6)
	1990s	(4)

Organisations also have internal divisions and fractures and one of my concerns was how I could avoid receiving a one-sided portrayal of organisational struggles and concerns. I therefore interviewed more than one member of each organisation where possible, ultimately interviewing twenty-five women from twelve organisations. In fact, this was impossible in two cases where I felt unable to demand more time from the organisation than had been granted. In one instance, it was clear to me that the staff member viewed me very much as an outsider and was giving me the 'official' version. However, due to the confidential nature of the organisation's service, I was unable to speak to any of the volunteers or users. In most cases, however, I was able to interview both staff and volunteers or users, and in many cases, I spoke to founders as well as current members.

The main body of interviews took place between October 1995 and June 1996. I was very flexible about where they took place although I did try to ensure that I was able to tape record the conversation. All but two interviews were taped and all taped interviews were transcribed in full. The varied locations included my home, the interviewee's home, black women's centres and other community venues and involved travel to Manchester, Liverpool, Sheffield, Edinburgh, Cambridge and Coventry. Many interviewees outside London were evidently impressed that I had travelled to see them and in several cases, provided transport from the station, hospitality and even accommodation. In one instance, the members of a group expressed their discomfort with a formal interview. I therefore asked questions in a far more discursive way and wrote up notes within twenty-four hours. While most interviews were one to one, where women felt uncomfortable with this format, more than one woman would attend. Four interviews took place in this way. Several interviews took place in the presence of children or spouses. In one instance, an interviewee's partner who had been very involved in accessing funds for the group, joined in the discussion. After a short time, I emphasised that the tape recorder would not pick up what he was saying and in this way politely encouraged the interviewee to pick up the story. His involvement and the support of other men is discussed in Chapter 6. In several instances, children or television created background noise which hindered transcription. However, they also contributed to the creation of a more relaxed atmosphere.

While interviews provided rich qualitative data, I was keen to create a layered, multiple-sourced study. I therefore contextualised the interviews with the following data: Unpublished materials – annual reports, leaflets, pamphlets – from over thirty organisations produced between 1979 and 1996; newsletters from a range of women's organisations, including *FOWAAD!* (OWAAD), *Speak Out* (Brixton Black Women's Group), *London Women's Liberation Newsletter*, *Women Against Fundamentalism Journal*, *We Are Here*, *Transitions*; articles in black newspapers and magazines including the *Voice*, *Caribbean Times*, *Asian Times*, *Black Perspective*, *The Alarm*, *CARF*; published literature by and about black women in Britain and black women's autonomous organisations. Materials by and about black women and especially black women organising are not easily accessible. While there are a number of feminist and women's libraries in Britain, their collections on black women are limited. In particular, the journals and newsletters produced by black women's organisations such as OWAAD, We Are Here Collective and Awaz are often buried in obscure locations. In addition to asking the women I interviewed and other women engaged in black women's struggles and writing to thirty organisations for any materials they could provide, I utilised the following resources: the Institute of Race Relations, Akina Mama wa Afrika Resource Centre, Fawcett Library, Feminist Library and the Centre for Research in Ethnic Relations Library. For additional theoretical material by American feminists of colour, I utilised the DOE library at the University of California, Berkeley.

In addition to what might be perceived by traditional social scientists as 'data', I had a wealth of observations gained during two years volunteering with Cambridge Black Women's Support Group, three years as the coordinator of an African Caribbean women's centre and two years as the director of a national development agency for black voluntary organisations. I had gained invaluable insights from attending and presenting papers at conferences organised or attended by black women's groups and from my involvement during 1995 in establishing a National Network of Black Women's Organisations. These non-traditional activities were nevertheless legitimate sources of information. In other words, only by acknowledging my dual roles as a researcher and activist could I accurately portray the multi-sourced nature of my written work.

Black feminist researchers have been concerned to place their understandings of the intersection of 'race', gender and class at the centre of the research analysis. This was my fifth concern. Many scholars problematise the conceptualisation of 'race' and gender as separate and discrete entities, but then carry on using the phrase 'racism and sexism' to describe black women's experiences (Anthias et al. 1992: 103). This phrase suggests that black women experience the same racism as black men plus the same sexism as white women. They therefore experience a double burden. Scholars of the intersection of 'race', class and gender have convincingly demonstrated that black women's experiences of racism are not the same as those experienced by black men, for they are uniquely gendered (Collins 1990; Bannerji 1995). Thus the subjection of Asian women to 'virginity tests' by immigration officials in London was an integral part of their racialised objectification and abuse (Brah 1992b). Similarly, rape, sexual abuse and commodification of their reproductive functions were integral to African women's oppression under slavery and continue to shape modern day representations (Davis 1981; Omolade 1995).

Rather than describing these incidents as examples of racism and/or sexism, as if we can analyse separately which aspects are racist and which sexist, it is more accurate to describe the above acts as gendered racism. In other instances, where, for example, stereotypes about Asian women's cultural confinement to the home are used by black or white men to justify their exploitation in poorly paid piecework in the garment industry, we might talk about racialised sexism. Without entirely resolving the difficulties associated with a language system based on either/or dichotomies (at what point on the spectrum does racialised sexism 'fade' into gendered racism?), the complementary concepts of racialised sexism and gendered racism enable us to move towards a more integrated understanding of oppressive acts or situations. In so doing, we make the necessary break from analyses which imply that one form of oppression can exist in isolation from the other.[3]

Utilising a conceptual framework which emphasises the intersection of 'race', class and gender is insufficient if these categories are inadequately theorised. Scholarly work on the social construction of 'race' and gender has illustrated that 'race' and gender are not biologically given and static but vary according to specific ideological, socio-economic and demographic contexts (Omi and Winant 1994; S. Small 1994; Fuss 1989). Thus, it is possible for a woman who is Tamil in Bangladesh to migrate to England and become 'Asian' or 'black' and then by moving to the United States to become 'East Indian'. Or, for a woman with one grandparent of African origin and one of European origin to be 'black' in the context of one society (USA where the 'one drop rule' applies) and 'white' in another (Ghana where both whites and lightskinned Western blacks are labelled 'bruni'). Or for the same woman in another time-frame in the United States to 'pass', and thus for her children to 'become' white. In other words: ' "Race" is not something that just exists. It is a continuing act of imagination. It is a very demanding verb' (Scales-Trent 1995: 3).

And while the biological evidence of sex difference is inescapable, what it is to be a 'woman' also varies immensely according to 'race' and class locations (Davis 1981). These insights should not lead us simply to replace the commonsense of *race and sex* with the more questioning 'race' and gender. As Miles (1993) has pointed out, many social scientists acknowledge that 'race' is a social fact, rather than a biological one and then proceed to act as if it exists as a static and known phenomenon (1993: 2). Instead, this theoretical position must inform the research questions we ask. Rather than assuming the 'race' and gender attributes of my respondents, I was forced to problematise my own assumptions about their identities, which are shaped by the context of 1990s British society. I therefore asked women explicit questions about whether they viewed themselves as 'black', what this meant to them and how they had come to define themselves as black, Asian or Muslim women. These questions forced into sharp relief the processes of racialisation and gender formation which underpin black women's activism. While 'race' can be shown not to exist, at least in any of the commonsense ways in which we utilise it in everyday speech, racism is very much alive. Thus acknowledging the artificial nature of 'race' should not lead us somehow to forget its power as a social fact which structures black people's opportunities and life expectancy in a society in which racism is systematic and endemic. In asking questions about black women's ability to 'imagine' their identities, I was also aware of the constraints on black women's subjectivity and the need to portray as accurately as possible the barrage of stereotypical representations, political exclusion and socio-economic exploitation which are the context for racialisation and gender formation in Britain.

If constructions of 'race' and gender vary according to historical as well as geographical location, it is essential to position discussions of black women's activism in the context of a specific time-frame and a particular history. I was unconvinced by black British scholarship which adopts an analytical framework from African American women writers without also acknowledging the very different history of oppression and resistance which took place in the United States. Black British women's activism is shaped not only by the African American Civil Rights and Black Power movements but also by African and Asian struggles for national self determination. The inclusive definition of 'black' is one phenomenon which makes little sense outside of that specific history. Yet British history is often represented as the history of its white residents and 'black history' in the West is often seen as coterminous with the African American experience. To present a historicised account of black women's organisations in Britain, I needed to give an account of their activism. This would offer a backdrop against which we could interpret the debates and struggles in which black women participated from the 1970s onwards. This account is found in the introductory chapter.

My sixth methodological question was inspired by my engagement in black women's political movements. A key theme of this activism has been to establish the basis and limits of African-Asian unity and to ensure that the voices of Asian women are neither obscured nor dominated by those of African and Caribbean women (Sisters in Study 1988; Amos and Parmar 1984). My own experience as the coordinator of an African Caribbean women's centre meant that much of my experience and knowledge about black women organising came from within the context of an African-centred perspective. I was therefore concerned to ensure that I did not universalise the experiences of women of African descent as representative of all black women. My groundwork therefore included reading poetry and prose by Asian women, especially activists, writing to twenty Asian women's organisations for additional materials, and informal discussions about the research with Asian women activists. Claire Alexander (1996), an anthropologist who undertook a study into the lives of African Caribbean young men in Britain found that her position as an Asian woman gave her a useful outsider within perspective. She was not perceived to be as threatening as (she assumes) a woman of African descent would have been, but did not inspire the hostility and lack of trust that a white woman might have experienced:

> Had I been black, I may have been spared some of the overtly sexist assumptions I was confronted with, but I think that the group would have been threatened by my presence. Most of the boys were intimidated by black women – and they were especially fearful of intelligent black women, who, they felt, undermined their control over situations. I was, however, 'black enough'.
>
> (1996: 22)

While the gender dimensions make Alexander's a quite different study, I am not entirely convinced that her argument in favour of an outsider perspective outweighs the insider's additional insight and knowledge of the community being studied. My own participation in an African Caribbean women's organisation provided a wealth of cultural capital. I was able to share a common language, often refer to the same literature and to appreciate indirect or unexplained references to key events in the life of the African Caribbean community. I was also aware of the immediate sense of ease which many women of African descent felt when talking to me. I was a 'sister in struggle' and as such could be trusted with intimate details of personal development or difficult divisions and conflicts within organisations.

However, focusing only on differences in racialisation between myself and my interviewees affords racialised subjectivities a disproportionate primacy. There were other critical axes of difference and of power which could place me on the same 'side' as some Asian women interviewees and on the opposite side as some women of African descent. There are differences of power, access to resources and perspective between women from Africa and women of the African diaspora, between migrants, refugees and British citizens, between professional and non-professional black women, between women who work primarily around male violence, and thus perhaps have a heightened awareness of sexism, and those that focus on racism in education and employment. In each of these instances, I find myself relocated from centre to margin and back again in relation to my interviewees. This has very practical impact on the interviews. In two of the interviews, I sensed that lesbian women were trying to locate my sexuality and it was essential that I made my own commitment to representing the contributions of lesbian women clear. It was also notable that straight women who had assumed my 'straightness' were visibly taken aback when I began to ask about the contributions or exclusion of lesbian women. At that point, our assumed commonality as black women became secondary to my possible location as an outsider by virtue of sexuality.

There have also been ideological divisions between organisations which seek state funding and those that suspect that such funding leads to compliance with a state agenda (Sivanandan 1990; Anthias et al. 1992). As the director of an agency which was known by some of the interviewees to receive funding from central government, my own position therefore became automatically suspect to one group of interviewees with an overtly anti-statist stance. I was therefore questioned for over an hour by this group, both about the aim and audience of my research, and about my own background in black women's activism. In this instance, the fact that I had been involved in 'grassroots' activism was far more important than my ethnicity and our shared African origin was of little use as a means of facilitating access. While this was the most overt instance of having to 'win over' a group with my own credentials, in all cases my role as a committed activist played an important part in first the ease with which I made contact and arranged interviews and second the depth of the information with which I was trusted. It was not enough simply to be a black woman. As politically sophisticated activists, the interviewees were aware of the diverse ideological locations which black women can occupy. The quality of my research data was therefore largely dependent on the accountability which my position as a known activist implied.

WHOSE RESEARCH IS THIS ANYWAY? FROM ACCOUNTABILITY TO RECIPROCITY

Little of my extensive reading of sociological texts prepared me for the real problems and soul-searching which fieldwork in black women's organisations would present. In developing my own research method, I had dealt with the key dilemmas encountered by anti-racist and woman-centred researchers. How can research be anti-oppressive, that is not merely avoiding the reproduction of power inequalities existent in society, but challenging those inequalities and attempting to empower the 'researched'? How can the researcher, as part of the 'oppressed' group being researched, retain her integrity while wooing the acknowledgement of 'a scholarly community controlled by white men' (Collins 1990: 203). How can a rigorous critique and analysis occur, while acknowledging the non-objective subject position of the researcher?

These were familiar questions which I felt I had worked through in relation to my own research. My subject position as a community activist was clearly one of commitment to my subject matter far beyond the scope of the research. I was motivated by a desire to overcome the invisibility of black women's organisations and to identify ways of overcoming barriers to effective organising. I felt comfortable with this role. While other researchers were deliberating over the ethics of using disadvantaged groups as research materials, I was actively involved in improving the lives of the very women I was researching. And as a part-time student, moving between the parallel worlds of the leafy campus of Warwick University and the inner city community of Hillfields, I was a confident traveller. The rigorous grilling of an elite university education had more than equipped me to deal with the doubts which assail any black woman student within the halls of the academe. I had the confidence to make radical arguments because I knew I had the skills to argue my case and to critique 'their' scholars.

Yet one year into my fieldwork, I had barely progressed beyond the theory. What went wrong? Shortly after starting my research, I was offered a position as the director of a black development agency with a national profile. Rather optimistically, I was not too concerned about the impact on my research. In an agency with a database of over two thousand black voluntary organisations, I would have even more access to my subject matter. Two months into the new job, I realised that reaching my goal would not be so simple. Despite the support of some committee members, I felt that to announce my own interest and actively pursue the research would raise concerns about my commitment to the organisation. What would not have been a problem in my previous position at a black women's centre, where I had built a track record over three years and where there was a more flexible working arrangement which could incorporate individual interests, would have proven highly fraught at my new workplace. The split which I had thought I could retain between my role as researcher and as community activist was not sustainable in a context in which my name was becoming commonly known in the black voluntary sector. In practical terms, this meant that I could not expect to send out letters signed by myself, without some follow-up at the workplace by women who would recognise my name and assume it was a project developed by the agency. This could then lead to allegations that I was using the position of director to further my own personal goals.

The balance between carrying out research and contributing to social change is a difficult one to maintain. I needed to be accountable to the women whose activism I was studying and to my organisational responsibilities while retaining a sense of my own goals as a researcher. Rather than seeking to maintain dual identities, the solution lay in integrating my scholarly and activist endeavours. This solution was offered implicitly in my first few interviews when the interviewees began to use the interview session for their own goals. The session became an opportunity to draw on my expertise in organisational development, fund raising and voluntary sector management. A typical interview therefore started with an informal discussion about an organisational issue or problem. These included a crisis situation where a funder had withdrawn support due to allegations of mismanagement; an organisation which had lost its coordinator and was seeking to recruit a consultant in an interim position; and an organisation which had received a hostile review by a funder and wanted help in preparing a response. In addition, a number of issues on which I was able to offer advice arose during the interview. These included a project looking for sources of capital funding; an organisation which was concerned that acquiring charitable status might undermine its ability to campaign; and an interviewee who wished to pursue a Ph.D. In some cases, this advice involved follow-up work, for example, one organisation which I had advised to document their aims and achievements subsequently sent me an action plan for my comments.

The interviews were therefore a very practical example of a mutually beneficial exchange whereby I gained the information necessary for my research, and the organisation received useful advice and information which I was able to provide as an 'expert' in the field. From a difficult beginning, the interviews eventually developed through a process of negotiation with the interviewees in a way which reinforced my goal of carrying out research of practical benefit to the 'researched', both as individuals and as organisations.

OPPOSITIONAL NARRATIVES: DEVELOPING A WOMANIST VOICE

Writing as an *as a* declares the willingness to be held accountable to a given community. Writing *as a* feminist declares the writer's accountability to a community of women, ostensibly, although at times slippage occurs to limit that accountability to women of a similar class and racialised group. Writing *as an* Afrocentric, declares the writer's accountability to an African community in Africa and the diaspora. While these 'communities' may in fact be largely imagined, constructions of the writer's particular 'take' on what it means to be a woman, or an African, they nevertheless remind the scholar of the importance of the ethics and the outcome of her scholarship. To ask 'why write as an "as a"' ignores the fact that social scientists who do not declare their interest or allegiance, are in fact writing primarily for an audience of white men (Collins 1990: 203). Writing is never just 'writing', even writing as a disembodied observer infers a silent 'as a'. Nevertheless, writing as a black British woman is clearly different from writing as an African American feminist, which in turn differs from writing as an African diasporic womanist. Locating my writing requires that I declare from which ideological positionality I write, not simply from which 'identity'.

Popularised by Alice Walker, 'womanism' is a term which locates black women's struggles against gendered racism and exploitation within a tradition of black women who resisted (Walker 1985). Rather than speaking to a history of [white] women's struggles against patriarchy to which the fight against racism and imperialism was later included, womanism reminds us that black women and women of colour did not wait for feminist consciousness raising to initiate struggles for social justice in Africa, Asia, the Caribbean and in the West. While womanism has been characterised as arising from an African American tradition, Chikwenye Ogunyemi, a Nigerian literary critic, uses the phrase to define the simultaneous struggle against sexism, racism, poverty and international capitalism by writers in Africa and the diaspora:

> Black womanism is a philosophy that celebrates black roots, the ideals of black life while giving a balanced presentation of black womandom. It concerns itself as much with the black sexual power tussle as with the world power structure that subjugates blacks.
>
> (Ogunyemi 1985: 72)

In this sense, 'womanism' can be utilised wherever black women/women of colour integrate internationalist, anti-racist and anti-sexist politics. Rather than starting with 'feminism', broadly defined as opposition to the oppression of women *qua* women, and adding 'black' or 'anti-racist' (Tang Nain 1991), womanism cannot be defined without reference to opposition to racism: 'the politics of the womanist is unique in its racial–sexual ramifications' (Ogunyemi 1985: 68). Or to return to Alice Walker, a womanist is 'committed to survival and wholeness of entire people, male and female' (Walker 1985: xi).

Writing as a womanist declares that I refuse to subsume 'race' to class or gender, but that I equally refuse to wait until racism is defeated before raising issues of gender. Writing as a womanist with roots in Britain declares my solidarity with a small cohort of young black men and women who have scaled the walls of British academia and are currently completing Ph.Ds. It means that I view their struggles with hostile supervisors, indifferent institutions and internalised doubts and fears, as important to my own struggles (see Marshall

1996). It means that I view their successes as equally bolstering my confidence. This sense of collectivity is not abstract: it is rooted in the specificities of British academia in the 1990s. My writing as a womanist arises out of a second generation of black women warriors in post-war Britain, women who learnt our gender analysis nor from white feminist icons, but from Alice Walker, Audre Lorde, Pratibha Parmar, Pragna Patel and Hazel Carby. Nurtured by black women theorists, we did not rely on white feminism for our analyses, nor did we fight for our place within it. Instead, we came into an arena already mapped out by black women thinkers and activists. For this second generation of intellectual activists, for whom 'feminism' never quite shook off its association with white middle class women's concerns, womanism seems a much more inspirational space (see V. Alexander 1996: 104).

Womanism is also symbolic of my accountability to a community of black women activists for whom the term 'feminism' is associated with daily struggles against racist exclusion by white women's organisations. The interviewee whose funding application for a black women's refuge had been undercut by the local [white] women's refuge claiming to serve 'all' women. The organisation which had been allocated a white feminist project officer by the local authority only to discover that the latter was opposed to 'black separatism' and consistently sought to undermine their work. The black women who have had to oppose white feminist calls for increased policing in primarily black neighbourhoods, in the name of 'women's safety'. These are some of the many accounts of interactions between black women's organisations and white feminists which I was told during the course of this study. For many black women in 1990s Britain, 'sisterhood' with white feminists is a luxury which may be afforded at an abstract level, but when issues of funding and power are at stake, it would be naive to assume that sisterly solidarity will determine white women's actions. The turn to 'womanism' is therefore a response to a particular moment in the history of black women's activism in Britain, where sisterhood across racialised lines has yet to materialise.

The danger of writing as a member of an oppositional community, is the temptation to 'tell heroic stories' in order to counter negative stereotypes. In the context of the erasure and pathologisation of black women in Britain, constructing a counter-narrative which highlights our strength and resilience is a necessary task. However, the desire to portray black women in a positive light leads potentially to silencing those aspects of black women's organising which have been less than positive, or outright destructive. This idealisation ultimately is of little benefit to black women because it dulls our ability to think critically about our actions. Ultimately, the liberatory narrative becomes a tool to silence doubt and dissent, and thus prevents us from learning lessons from mistakes or turning weaknesses into strengths. Ogunyemi's (1985) conceptualisation of womanism is weakened by this celebratory approach to black communities. For Ogunyemi, the authentic womanist novel has a 'positive, integrative ending' (1985: 66). She therefore denounces Buchi Emecheta (1986) for being overly influenced by Western feminism because of the tragic fate of her heroines. The implicit censorship in such a stance is one outcome of the insistence on 'positive' images of black women (Haraway 1991c).

The Heart of the Race (1985) is an example of an important liberatory narrative in the history of black women in Britain. Since this was the first sustained account of black women's experiences of establishing lives in Britain, the collective authors focused on black women's strength, commitment and heroic struggles against racism and (to a lesser extent) sexism (Bryan *et al.* 1985; Ngcobo 1988). Yet in writing an account of black women's history which focused on the consensual and collective, the authors inevitably ignored voices of dissent. Thus, the text obscures the role of Asian women and the struggles to create Afro-Asian unity under the umbrella of blackness. Despite the extensive arguments which took place around sexuality, particularly within OWAAD, it erases the presence of lesbian women entirely (Sisters in Study 1988). While undertaking the interviews, I encountered some resistance to questions relating to conflict or dissent which had arisen within organisations. These questions were sometimes brushed off with a brief answer while questions about achievements of the group received a more detailed response. It was notable that women who knew me through my work as a black woman activist, were far more willing to share the conflict which had arisen. They trusted me to use the information ethically, that is, to present the difficulties within the context of black women's problem solving skills with the aim of shedding light on why conflicts may have arisen and how they could be avoided in future. For many of the interviewees, developing a critical approach was a key to building more realistic expectations:

I still feel there is something in this 'myth' if you like that when black women decide to get together and support each other there's no stronger bond in the world. It's just, I'm not sure what it is that you need to have, but maybe just a healthy scepticism to recognise that we are just as fallible as anyone else and shouldn't nail all of our high expectations and hopes and whatever onto this sense of solidarity.

(Lynette, Caribbean, African Caribbean organisation)[4]

Writing within a womanist tradition, part of my accountability to the multiple voices of black women is to retain a healthy scepticism towards the centred and celebratory voices which appear to speak 'for black women'. Utilising Lewis (1996) and Mohanty's (1992) insights into the politics of location, I remind myself to ask 'which black women', 'when' and to interrogate whether, in legitimating the voice of the speaker, these narratives also serve to erase the voices of black women at the margins.

NOTES

1   That is, those forms of sociological endeavour which adhere to the tenets of the discipline as established by white male academics.
2   Haraway is here using a feminist notion of 'objectivity'. She rejects the disembodied, value-neutral scientist's eye in favour of the notion of objectivity as 'partial vision' (Haraway 1991b:190).
3   Anthias *et al.* (1992) argue against this approach which they claim conflates racism and sexism. Their assertion that the dowry: 'is not part of the discourse and practice of racism but that of sexist social relations' (1992: 203) and thus should be examined separately from racism is highly inaccurate. In fact, Asian marital practices have not only been condemned by white feminists (ibid.:128), but have been utilised by the British state as a symbol of cultural backwardness and have been deployed as an integral part of racist immigration controls in preventing Asian family reunification (Rattansi 1994; Cheney 1996).
4   Brackets following interview citation should be interpreted as follows: (pseudonym, ethnic origin of interviewee, membership of organisation). Interviewees were asked to identify their ethnic origin and to describe the membership of the organisation. While many interviewees identified personally as 'black', providing their ethnic origin becomes important in later chapters to provide evidence of the diverse usage of the term. Where the organisational membership is given as 'black', this implies that the organisation utilises a political definition of blackness. Where 'black' was used by the interviewee interchangeably with African descent, I have specified 'African Caribbean'. After the first citation in a given section, the pseudonym is given with no further information.

Chapter 3

'We don't just make tea': redefining political activism

In Chapter 1, I suggested that many scholars have taken a gender blind approach, concentrating solely on black/white divisions and ignoring gender inequalities (Goulbourne 1990; Anwar 1986). A handful of researchers have made concessions towards gender transparency, acknowledging the small numbers of black women who have an active role in the processes they describe (Carter 1986; Geddes 1993). However, they have relied uncritically on conventional wisdom that black women, doubly burdened by the practices and ideologies of racism and sexism, have simply failed to access the political arena. This chapter will illustrate the shortcomings of both approaches and will utilise black women's own definitions in order to arrive at an alternative framework for the analysis of black political participation. I shall then examine political activism which has been developed by black women's organisations. Finally, I shall look at the role of key groups of black women as catalysts for political change.

Contemporary studies of black political participation can be broadly categorised around four themes. First, there are quantitative studies of electoral behaviour (Saggar 1992; Anwar 1986, 1991; Layton-Henry 1992). An early example of this approach is offered by the Community Relations Commission, whose 1974 study first posited the significance of the 'black vote' and thus put black voters on the mainstream political agenda (Fitzgerald 1984: 7). This analysis contains two elements: comparisons between rates of registration for white, African Caribbean and Asian potential voters and actual or estimated voting patterns. Analysts utilising such data tend to look at the real or imagined 'black vote' and at which party stands to gain from it. They aim to discover to what extent commonsense ideas about black political loyalty to the Labour

Party are valid. Recent studies have challenged the notion of a homogenous black vote and suggested that the diversity of black communities prohibits such a phenomenon from developing in Britain (Miles 1988; Solomos and Back 1995).

Second, scholars have analysed the numbers, locations and impact of black parliamentary candidates, MPs, Lords and councillors (Geddes 1993; Wadsworth 1992), and more recently, the racialised politics of selection and deselection processes (Solomos and Back 1995). This work aims to illustrate the contributions of black people to British politics and to facilitate a greater understanding of the barriers to their participation. The third theme is the examination of black caucuses within white political structures. Notable among these studies are Shukra (1990) and Jeffers' (1991) studies of black sections within the Labour Party.

Finally, there has been an increasing awareness by researchers of the existence and importance of autonomous black political organisations and institutions. A number of studies have analysed the political impact and agendas of local community organisations (Werbner 1991; Anthias *et al.* 1992; Carter 1986). Anwar (1991: 56) states that there are over two thousand 'ethnic minority' organisations in Britain. However, listings in *Hansib Directory* 1994 indicate that there are more than 9,000. Of these, the Notting Hill Carnival and associated local campaigns have been a particularly rich source of data (Carter 1986; Gilroy 1987). In addition, there has been some discussion of black organisations with a national brief (Josephides 1991; Heineman 1972).

These recent contributions have challenged the notion that black people are passive victims of exclusionary political practices. In examining black people's actions and decisions as voters, as politicians and as participants of grassroots organisations, they have shown that black people are active agents for change. Goulbourne (1990) has characterised this new approach as encompassing a 'view from below' which includes black people's own interpretations of their actions, focusing not just on institutional change, but also on the individuals who bring it about (1990: 3). Historically informed accounts are particularly important in that they illustrate that black people have been active in British politics for as long as they have been in this country, although most studies only record the actions of visible public figures from William Cuffay, son of Kittian slaves and a leader of the Chartists, to Shapurji Saklatvala, MP for Battersea in the 1920s (Wadsworth 1992; Anwar 1991).

THE TEXTUAL REPLICATION OF GENDER INEQUALITY

How do these studies attempt to engage with gender differentiation within the political sphere? The answer is that with few exceptions, gender inequities are unquestioningly replicated in the texts themselves. In many of the texts, 'black' could simply be substituted with 'black male' without changing any of the data. In most cases there is simply no reference to the gender of the black participants. When names are mentioned, however, it becomes clear that the politicians are men (Rex 1991). Activist intellectuals are no less phallocentric. For example, Wadsworth's (1992) illuminating description of black politicians in pre-Second World War Britain makes no reference to any black woman in her own right, but also fails to acknowledge this omission. Carter (1986) is an exception in that he acknowledges that his narrative is primarily male (and London-based), and attempts to redress the balance by including eulogies to Claudia Jones and Pansy Jeffries (1986: 17). However, this last minute inclusion merely serves to underline the stark absence of women in the remainder of the text.

A revealing twist on gender blindness is Solomos and Back's analysis of the Labour Party in Birmingham (Solomos and Back 1995). This work is notable for its erasure of black women while simultaneously foregrounding white women. This occurs, for example, when the authors describe the divergent political priorities of white and black [male] councillors. A male Asian politician discusses the imposition of women shortlists in the following terms:

> Why should we say that we have to support women, we have to support lesbians, we have to support homosexuals. . . . If you're a black woman fair enough. But they know we haven't got many black women who are politically active, they're trying to exclude us.

> (Solomos and Back 1995: 152)

This conflict between black and women's politics necessarily involves a reconfiguration of the term 'woman' to include a silent 'white'. Women, it is proposed, can only advance in opposition to black politicians and asking black politicians to support women is equivalent to asking them to support gays and lesbians, who are also conceptualised as white.

What is disappointing about this quotation is not the councillor's position – in a local political context in which powerful women's or gay and lesbian groups tend to be white, this construction is in part a response to a material reality – but the authors' failure to criticise the implicit racialisation of the term 'woman' and its implications for black women's participation. This failure in turn reinforces commonsense notions about black women's exclusion from political processes, to the extent that the authors do not find it necessary to explore the statement 'we haven't got many black women who are politically active'. Black women's passivity is simply a given and does not warrant further investigation. Solomos and Back's analysis of 'the uneasy relationship between black politics and sexual politics' is actually an exploration of the uneasy relationship between black men and white women politicians. Despite being a recent work, it ignores the simultaneity of black and 'sexual' politics, and thus erases the presence of black women (Solomos and Back 1995: 101).

Black women are visible in the few accounts which make use of gender transparent statistics. Layton-Henry (1992) acknowledges that black women in the 1987 general election were slightly less likely to vote Conservative than were black men and also 'less certain about going to vote' (1992: 57). However, this difference is not analysed and we are left unsure of its implications. Geddes (1993) undertakes a more in depth exploration of gender differences in his analysis of black representation at local level. Yet the major disparity he finds in participation by men and women is hardly reflected in the amount of time he puts into analysing his data:

> Of the 342 Asian and Afro-Caribbean councillors picked up by the survey around 6 per cent are women. This may be indicative of cultural constraints within, for example, the Asian community on female political activity. It may also suggest a 'hierarchy of oppression'.
>
> (Geddes 1993: 55)

This minimal analysis deploys stereotypes of women of Asian and African descent and certainly does nothing to unravel the complexities of racialised sexism. In describing the barriers facing Asian women as cultural, the author ignores the role of sexism in structuring dynamics within black communities. The implication is that such inequalities are inevitable and therefore not worthy of discussion.

Where black women do play a key role in accounts of black political mobilisation, that role is not of activists, but of symbols of black oppression. The deaths of Cynthia Jarret in Tottenham and of Cherry Groce in Brixton led to the uprisings in those areas in 1985. The parallels with the alleged murder by immigration officers of Joy Gardner in August 1993 are obvious. Joy Gardner's death sharpened black community awareness of the new immigration controls suggested in the Asylum Bill. Descriptions of her death, in front of her five-year-old son Graeme in Haringey, caused outrage in the black community. While recognising the very real pain that the loss of these women caused to family and friends, it is also possible to identify how these deaths are utilised to foreground a suffering and martyred black womanhood (Werbner 1991: 20). Images of black women as victims become alternatives to the possibility of black women's political agency. Black women are at once invisible, and highly visible in the public political sphere.

EN-GENDERING A NEW RACIALISED POLITICS

An alternative paradigm is needed. This paradigm should embrace what black communities and individuals are doing, rather than comparing them to white communities and finding them lacking. It should account for black agency, while retaining gender transparency and incorporating the active roles of women. It should seek to examine all aspects of black political participation, that which explicitly engages with mainstream [white] political processes and that which speaks primarily or entirely to a black audience.

We need to re-examine our conceptualisation of political activism. The aforementioned texts use a narrow definition of legitimate political expression. Political activism is expected to be collective, expressed via recognised bodies such as parties or unions, and addressed to the power-brokers or the white public. Many of the black women's organisations which I studied during the course of this research questioned such hegemonic notions of political participation. A common theme of the interviews was the failure of the parliamentary process to address the concerns of black women in any meaningful way. Many interviewees felt that their aspirations were not represented by any party. The traditional view that black voters' concerns are represented by the Labour Party is challenged by one respondent:

> I think black women wouldn't find an automatic easy alliance with political groups, the Labour Party, although a lot of black

women might have socialist perspectives in an informal sense. I think there are some issues which they might be seen as right-wing on, in terms of education and a clear traditional view of education, not what has been called '80s liberal education. But on other things they are very clearly, very strongly anti-Tory.

(Brenda, Caribbean woman, African Caribbean organisation)

Interviewees also felt that traditional forms of political participation were alienating and exclusionary. The black women interviewed tended to view the mechanisms of formal participation, both political parties and trade unions, as 'white politics'. This view may be shared by the high numbers of young black people in particular who are not on the electoral register (*Voice* 12 December 1995[1]; Fitzgerald 1984). One interviewee who had been actively involved in the Labour movement at local and national levels explained that black women were regularly 'ignored and marginalised' (Faith, African, black organisation). This situation was exacerbated by a lack of support for women activists juggling housekeeping, childcare and paid employment. The concentration of black women in low paid employment and the tendency for many women to work long hours to support their families also contributed to their exclusion:

A lot of us African women have been involved in bringing up our children, running homes, doing two or three jobs because our men are unemployed, dealing with day to day reality. And in those circumstances, it's not always possible for women to join political parties and go to ward meetings and go to constituency meetings.

(Faith)

Only one of the interviewees had expressed her political convictions through a mainstream political party. Most of the interviewees contrasted their perception of traditional political participation with their own, much more encompassing view:

I think that politics for black women is an everyday event, because we're always out there struggling and to actually struggle with your children and to get through the system is a political kind of thing.

(Alekiri, African, African Caribbean organisation)

Black women consistently asserted the immediacy of their politics compared to what they viewed as a much more theoretical and abstract approach by political parties. For them, political interventions are shaped by their personal experiences, which in turn provide a sense of urgency and importance in their campaigns:

> If you've been affected by domestic violence and you have experienced problems with services, because you've had first hand experiences, then you're going to be more involved in the political arena and saying what the issues are. I think you have a lot more to give.
>
> (Anita, Asian, Asian organisation)

Feminist scholars and activists, in their rejection of the division between public and private spheres, have also asserted the importance of personal experience in their assertion 'the personal is political'. By bringing aspects of what had previously been considered private life into the public arena – housework, abortion, sexual violence, domestic violence, incest and sexuality – they created a much broader notion of what is political. This is explained by Lorde:

> If what we are talking about is feminism, then the personal is political and we can subject everything in our lives to scrutiny. . . . The subject of revolution is ourselves, is our lives.
>
> (Lorde 1988: 14)

and elaborated by Essed:

> For women, everyday life can be a site of political struggle. The kitchen, living room, or doorway of a school becomes a political space where women cooking, drinking coffee, or waiting for children to get out of school exchange family stories, as well as consult with each other about the future of the children in school.
>
> (1996: 97)

This conceptualisation of the political sphere enables us to challenge the stereotypical notion of black women's non-engagement, by asserting that they are involved in a range of political struggles in their everyday lives:

> A lot of the time women are making sure their kids are not being expelled from school, making sure that they're doing their homework, very practical things which is political, which is involved in

the community, involved in churches. So I don't put a superior value to the way in which we manifest our political activity.

(Faith, African, black organisation)

In an educational system in which African Caribbean children are disproportionately excluded and in which Asian children are seen as linguistically deficient, the task of ensuring that black children receive an adequate education becomes a profoundly political act which challenges their social classification as uneducable or educationally sub-normal (*Voice* 9 April 1996: 19; OWAAD 1979). For black women, the family becomes a site of political resistance, not just to patriarchy[2] but to institutionalised racism.

The centrality of children to black women's politics was a feature of many of the interviews. In addition to expressing the need to fight for their children's right to receive an adequate academic education, many of the women felt that one of the most important gains from their involvement in a black women's organisation had been their children's politicisation. This had contributed towards the children's identity formation as well as helping them to challenge manifestations of racism. An African mother of three children of mixed heritage described the process thus:

Whereas before I became a member of the black women's group, my concern about my children's identity was very much more towards where my children don't look as black as me and therefore they're not going to experience prejudice. Which left them in a kind of limbo about 'who am I?'. But I think that giving them a black identity despite their light skin has actually given them a sense of who they are.

(Hilda, African, African Caribbean organisation)

Interviewees stated that their involvement in building alliances with black women of different ethnicities had influenced their children's perception of other black communities. In one instance, a Caribbean interviewee noted that her child had stopped using derogatory but commonplace language such as 'the Paki shop'. Another interviewee saw her children learning to have greater tolerance and understanding for the emotional and behavioural difficulties experienced by some Somali refugee schoolmates. One woman commented on her children's political education:

At school one of the things that's always said about my children is that they have a really strong sense of justice, and also the fact that our children have been equipped to challenge the racism that they experience at school constructively and they can tell the difference. They know about racism, they know about sexism.

(Sonia, Caribbean, African Caribbean organisation)

For many of the interviewees, children represented the intersection of the individual and the community. As one respondent emphasised: 'Many black women see children as communal' (Brenda, Caribbean, African Caribbean organisation). This view of children as a shared responsibility gives rise to a desire to create collective solutions to problems experienced initially at an individual and family level. Establishing daycare where children could be left in a safe, anti-racist environment was one common response. Children's programmes, such as that developed by one refuge worker, were often designed to counter the negative effects of racism and abuse on children's self esteem:

I believe in having a mirror and I think that's important therapeutically. So they can see that they are beautiful. To make comparisons that there are different shades in all of us. That can strengthen them to go into that world out there.

(Sophia, Asian, black organisation)

Another interviewee described how their group had undertaken trail-blazing work around the needs of black children with a violent parent: 'We were the first refuge in the city to have a children's worker and out of her action research type of work [what's happened] is that other hostels and refuges have followed suit' (Balwant, Asian, Asian organisation). Yet another group had been involved in raising awareness about the impact of the Child Support Act. The group had organised workshops on women's right to non-cooperation in naming violent fathers and had appeared on regional television to highlight the act's role in exacerbating the impoverishment of children with one resident parent. Black women's political activism around their children therefore encompasses education for political consciousness of their own children, dealing with a lack of adequate childcare, challenging racist abuse of children in institutional settings, recognising and challenging the impact of violence within the family on children and opposing changes in welfare benefits which disadvantage black single mothers. These struggles take place at the level of the family, within the community and with the local and national state.

INVISIBLE ACTIVISM: EMPOWERING SELF, FAMILY AND COMMUNITY

The above analysis illuminates the specific interpretation of the personal as political utilised by black women's organisations. This interpretation does not diminish the importance of collective action. It takes as the starting-point of that action the personal experiences of women and recognises the importance of political education as a basis of collective resistance. Sivanandan (1990) alerts us to the dangers inherent in embracing the personal as political without a commitment to collective action. We run the risk, he claims, of losing sight of the communal and organisational element crucial to the creation of social change:

> The 'personal is the political' has also had the effect of shifting the gravitational pull of black struggle from the community to the individual at a time when black was already breaking into ethnics. It gave the individual an out not to take part in issues that affected the community: immigration raids, deportations, deaths in custody, racial violence, the rise of fascism. . . . There was now another venue for politics: oneself, and another politics: of one's sexuality, ethnicity, gender. . . . I am, therefore I resist.
>
> (1990: 39)

Sivanandan's critique is pertinent to the feminist conceptualisation of political action. He warns us against seeing sustained political group action as inherently 'masculinist', and the only authentic women's politics as individual acts of self affirmation. These acts, while individually empowering, may do little to challenge oppressive structures and institutions. However, Sivanandan does nothing to resolve the apparent dichotomy of self actualisation versus collective action. He simply rejects the former in favour of the latter without acknowledging the necessary role of personal empowerment in the creation of alternative political discourses. Sivanandan's political actor is ready made and requires no personal growth in order to engage in black working class struggle. In reality, this black political actor does not simply exist, but is created and recreates herself constantly through resistance and struggle.

Writing in the North American context, Patricia Hill Collins (1990), rejects this either/or dichotomy of the individual versus the collective. In its place, she suggests a holistic approach which incorporates both the struggle to change structures of oppression and the creation of individual and familial sites of resistance:

> The Black women's activist tradition of individual and group actions designed to bring about social change has occurred along two primary dimensions. The struggle for group survival is the first dimension. Consisting in actions taken to create Black female spheres of influence. . . . The second dimension of Black women's activism consists of the struggle for institutional transformation.
>
> (1990: 141)

The experience of black women's organisations and the politics of childrearing is an empirical example of the strengths of Collins' theoretical approach. In examining African, Caribbean and Asian organisations it becomes clear that Collins' analysis is not unique to African diasporic women. Her theoretical approach speaks not only to the experiences of women of African descent in Britain, but also to the struggles of Asian women.

Crucial to this approach is an understanding that black political activism speaks to different audiences at different times. Therefore, both political discourses which engage with mainstream political processes and ideologies, and those which address dynamics internal to black communities are worthy of examination. Hence, the struggles of black women for recognition and respect from black men, and their opposition to black male violence, while often hidden from view to white communities and academics, are recognised as authentic expressions of political mobilisation. Similarly, the activism of black lesbians and gays, within organisations such as the Black Gay and Lesbian Centre, Zami and the Anti-Racist Alliance, can accurately be described as articulating not only a politics of difference, but also a politics of change.

An expanded conceptualisation of political action of the kind that is being proposed here enables us to acknowledge a wide range of political activity within black women's organisations. Drawing on Collins' analysis of black women's activism, we can identify six arenas of political activism (1990: 141–2). These arenas can be divided into those that are internal to the black communities: the individual, the family, the community and those which engage with mainstream power structures: the local, the national and the international. In the following pages I expand and develop this categorisation.

The concept of individual empowerment is an important one within social movements which aim to counter the internalisation of the dominant mode of social interaction (Lorde 1984; Freire 1972). For the organisations studied, the idea of the personal empowerment of black women featured as a common theme. Empowerment was seen as encompassing a broad range of practical and emotional issues which I have grouped around three themes: self confidence, education and economic development. The first area was the most commonly mentioned. One interviewee described women escaping violent partners in the following terms:

> They were at the lowest of the low and now they've rebuilt their lives and they've achieved so much. Those women have been so empowered, given so much confidence to go on and live their independent life.
>
> (Anita, Asian, Asian organisation)

There is an implicit danger, however, in focusing attention on black women's lack of confidence, rather than on discriminatory structures and practices. This approach can lead to black women being designated a 'problem' requiring remedial action. The latter conceptualisation is an all too familiar tenet of governmental programmes established to tackle 'disadvantaged' black communities such as Section 11 of the Local Government Act 1966 (Anthias et al. 1992: 164–6). An alternative understanding of the need for personal growth and confidence building is that many black women need a space in which they can distance themselves from the daily onslaught of derogatory and hostile representations and experiences which are a commonplace within British society:

> In terms of my political development, it's around having somewhere to take all that crap you experience in the outside world. . . . All black women in this country need a really good sisterhood network to survive. Because otherwise it's so easy to start internalising the crap and to start to think that you've got a problem which clearly isn't the case.
>
> (Sonia, Caribbean, African Caribbean organisation)

The second aspect of empowerment emphasises the need for an alternative to the mainstream education system. Most of the interviewees questioned felt that they had been bombarded with inaccurate representations of black womanhood which erased black women's historical contributions and current achievements. They therefore felt that they needed a re-education process in order to identify the gendered racialised barriers facing them, learn about the role of black women achievers both historically and in the present day and create alternative visions of social relations. An interviewee described her group's focus on personal empowerment as follows:

> I think to be able to take a political stance on something you have to know who you are, what you value and how you'd like to see that reflected in the way the society works. And we were many of us just getting to the stage where we were trying to work out our own norms, our own mores, so we weren't just accepting the stuff that we'd been fed.

(Abiola, African, black organisation)

This re-education process takes place through informal 'reasoning' sessions, in assertiveness classes and in black history courses.[3] It is the 'education for critical consciousness' described by bell hooks (1994a) in her development of a progressive politics of pedagogy and is resonant of Paolo Freire's (1972) notion of 'conscientazion', a concept which has had a significant influence on black feminism in Britain and the United States.

Many black women educated in the British school system have also been denied opportunities to gain mainstream academic qualifications and therefore need education, normally in the form of access courses which provide the opportunity to gain basic skills as the basis for further education. While education for political consciousness and access to basic education appear quite distinct, both suggest that the road to empowerment is via the acquisition of knowledge:

> Those women at our organisation who over a period of two years, sitting talking, reasoning, going out, getting on courses. Some of them are at university, others have got qualifications. All of that happened [in assertiveness courses] in three days where black women came to a consciousness of themselves as black women where they gained support and they share that indefinable something that just happens when black women get together.

(Brenda, Caribbean, African Caribbean organisation)

This educational process was also seen as equipping black women to deal with the personal impact of racialised discrimination and hostility. In this sense it was seen as creating an essential pragmatic underpinning to the hard-won self confidence: 'You've got be confident, yes you've got all of these rights, but you've also got to have strategies for dealing with failure which is not personal failure, but is societal and institutional' (Jennifer, Caribbean, black organisation).

The third realm of empowerment was that of economic development. Poverty is a critical issue facing many black women. Escaping poverty through employment or entrepreneurship was therefore an important goal. In addition, many women viewed dependence either on a male partner or on state benefits as preventing women from becoming fully self actualised and from pursuing their individual goals. Economic independence is also a key to creating options for women escaping violence. Women at the two women's refuges in this study actively assisted women to access employment in order to facilitate the choice to leave an abusive partner.

Empowerment has been conceptualised as a process whereby the boundary between the personal and the communal is transcended, enabling the individual to connect fundamentally with collective movements for social change (Collins 1990; Yuval-Davis 1994). Subjective feelings of empowerment should not be accepted at face value without interrogating the material basis for any claim that an individual or group's situation has improved. It is essential therefore that personal voyages of self discovery and assertion are accompanied by organised collective efforts for social change. As Collins accurately asserts: 'while individual empowerment is the key, only collective action can effectively generate lasting social transformation of political and economic institutions' (Collins 1990: 237). Most organisations studied emphasised that empowerment connected the individual to the collective sphere. One interviewee described the relation between confidence building and the willingness to challenge discriminatory institutional practices:

> How do you separate out empowerment of the self to empowerment and impact on your environment? I think that our organisation changed many women's lives and I think that one change would have had a knock on effect on other changes. . . . Inevitably I think, one of the outcomes was that some of those women were feeling confident to challenge the housing people, to say, 'look, I'm a confident person, you can't write me off'. So for me the notion of empowerment is taking or recognising what's ours by right.
>
> (Brenda, Caribbean, African Caribbean organisation)

However, the idea that personal empowerment has political ramifications was not uncontested. One interviewee insisted that empowerment and political activism were quite separate activities. Her organisation provides counselling for Muslim women and the coordinator was quite adamant in her claim that the group was apolitical:

> During the Gulf crisis, we used to get a lot of calls from Muslims trying to really get us to do something, to get involved. We could not. . . . Because our aim is really to concentrate on giving counselling to Muslim women and helping them.
>
> (Zaheda, Middle Eastern, Muslim organisation)

The interviewee suggested that if I wanted to know about Muslim women involved in politics, I should attempt to meet with the Muslim Parliament.[4] Nevertheless, enabling women to claim their rights was central to the organisation's counselling. Users were informed about their rights under Islamic law to education, divorce, a spouse of their choice and to property and money. The organisation's work was seen as equipping women with the emotional strength and self confidence to lead their lives more fully: 'How can you get involved in society fully if you have a lot of problems? . . . you have to be happier, you have to be inwardly and outwardly feeling very beautiful and once you have reached that stage, then you are able to contribute more' (Zaheda).

However, it also had a subtext of challenging cultural norms which are oppressive to women. The presentation of the organisation as simply 'helping women' was therefore a powerful tool in winning the support of Muslim communities and in particular religious leaders while actively challenging some of the very practices institutionalised by the more traditional mosques.

Recent feminist analysis has suggested that empowerment is a more problematic goal than has previously been envisaged. While proponents assert that the power gained in the process of empowerment is a benign power over one's own destiny, rather than an oppressive power over others, Yuval-Davis (1994) suggests that such an assertion is naive. It is unlikely that the empowerment of one oppressed group will in every instant be compatible with that of another. Indeed, empowering some members of a given group may involve the silencing of others within the group. The ostracism of black lesbians from some black women's organisations is a pertinent example of this problem. In practice grassroots activism has always engaged in a process of shifting the boundaries of who is included and who is excluded. The politics of empowerment is not inevitably exclusionary or oppressive to subordinate and marginal groupings, nor is it always progressive. Rather, it contains the possibility of building a diverse social movement which emerges vibrantly from the personal struggles of its members.

A second arena in which black women's activism is often invisible to 'outsiders' is the family. Since mordant critiques by Carby (1982) and Amos and Parmar (1984) revealed that white feminists had imposed their experience of the family as universal, it has become commonplace in the work of more progressive critical thinkers to indicate that for black women, the family is less a site of oppression than one of affirmation and resistance to racism (see also Whelehan 1995). A striking feature of many of the interviews was the support offered by many black male partners to women wishing to become involved in black women's organisations:

> So the people that had men in their lives at the time, [the men] were cooking the rice and peas, were coming to pick up the kids, maybe were looking after the children. And I would say that my husband played a role in that he would be supervising the children whilst I was going out on a Sunday afternoon to work with a group of women. And then they would come along at the end and maybe sit down for half an hour and get involved in the debates that women had.
>
> (Alekiri, African, African Caribbean organisation)

As a result of this support, many black women's organisations welcomed men onto their premises, with the obvious exception of those that were involved in refuge provision. The exclusion of men was seen as an aspect of white women's organisations from which black women wished to distance themselves:

> There was a white women's organisation in the High Street and the comments I had from black women I started talking to about setting up an organisation were 'we don't want to be like that'. . . . And one of the things we discussed was that a black women's centre can be whatever we want it to be. If we think that men should be a part of the centre, that doesn't mean that it's not a women's centre.
>
> (Pat, Caribbean, African Caribbean organisation)

In many cases, women were influenced by common experiences

of racism to turn a blind eye to oppressive gender roles. This apparent willingness to 'forgive' sexism from black men, and in particular family members, was rarely a result of a lack of awareness about the existence of sexism, rather it was a choice expressed by women facing multiple sites of oppression:

> I think we're quite forgiving really in terms of our menfolk. We forgive them loads in terms of sexism, because we have a much more pressing issue, the issue of racism and discrimination . . . we tend to be having more solidarity for our brother or our father or our husband, because he's suffering the same experiences as we do. Therefore we are more forgiving I think. That doesn't make the black man or the Arab man or the Asian man less sexist, but us much more tolerant.
>
> (Mona, Middle Eastern, black organisation)

Several of the interviewees associated sexism with white men and institutions such as the police, and employers generally. There was less willingness to address issues of black male sexism. Rather than consciously challenging the sexism of their partners, many women found their relationships gradually drifting apart. These changes were linked to men's failure to deal with their partners' newly found confidence and were often regretted:

> It was almost like I had been looking out of one window and all of a sudden there was another window there that I didn't know existed. And when that other window opened I couldn't get enough of it. And I just soaked myself in it twenty-four [hours] seven [days a week] and for me I suppose there were no boundaries around that and the impact and the toll it had was on my relationship with my ex-husband who unfortunately wasn't in there and moving at the same pace with me.
>
> (Alekiri, African, African Caribbean organisation)

The prioritisation of racism over sexism as separate systems of oppression was not uncontested. Women working within refuges on the issue of male violence against women were more likely to take a strong position against all forms of misogyny and to maintain an integrative analysis of racism–sexism. This was frequently in the face of accusations from male partners of women as users and of being 'marriage breakers' or of 'splitting families' (Southall Black Sisters 1989; Roy 1995). While many workers in such environments espoused a rigorous black feminist analysis of male violence, they were equally aware that not all women using the organisation shared such a perspective, but did not view this as problematic. Indeed, they felt that the feminist principles underpinning their work were often unstated. The practical implementation of these principles did not necessarily involve encouraging women to see themselves as black feminists, nor did it involve attempting to evangelise:

> We've got women coming to us who are in crisis. The last thing you do is shove in their face, 'look we're feminists and you've got to do this'. . . . But what you do see is that over the years, women empower themselves, knowingly, unknowingly they do it and it's really good to see that. They may not call it feminism, they may call it feminism, they may call it self esteem.
>
> (Misa, Asian, black organisation)

While police and housing officials appeared to expect white women's refuge workers to work to feminist principles, Asian women were pressured to handle cases of domestic violence in a more reconciliatory way. The idea that women's independence was alien to Asian communities in particular was reinforced by male 'community leaders' who were most often involved in consultative mechanisms on work with Asian communities:

> There is that pressure and that stereotype that Asian women's organisations have got to offer reconciliation work from the community. In those days, it was very difficult because one, where do you go, and two, it was unheard of that a woman would live on her own with her children, it just didn't happen.
>
> (Manjit, Asian, Asian organisation)

The interviewees' feminism was therefore as much an expression of their opposition to the racialised gender stereotypes fostered by these agencies as a response to black male violence (Mama 1989b). Where feminism was embraced as a method of understanding and challenging gender relations, it was explicitly defined as 'black feminism'. In this way, black refuge workers distanced themselves from white feminism(s) by invoking the struggle against racism as well as that against patriarchal violence.

Engaging politically with the notion of the family also involved support for alternative family structures. Central to most of the black women's organisations studied was their support for black single mothers. While African Caribbean women were able to choose single parenthood for economic reasons without fear of community sanctions, South Asian and Chinese women raising children alone after leaving a violent relationship were often ostracised. In addition, all single mothers were felt by the respondents to be under attack by the state and stigmatised by the media and politicians. This view is well supported by academic studies (Omolade 1995; Solinger 1994). Organisations were active in creating alternative visions of single parenthood which recognised the strength and loving within many families with one resident parent, and opposed this to the often dysfunctional nature of some two parent families. Women also found important support in creating networks of adults with whom their children could interact.

However, one parent families were not the only alternative families under construction and contestation. Black lesbian women were involved in creating healthy family structures despite opposition from many heterosexual women and a paucity of models on which to base black lesbian relationships. The lesbian women interviewed described their experiences of 'coming out' as an experience which frequently led to alienation from mixed sexuality women's groups. One of the women involved in the establishment of a London-based black lesbian group described a traumatic experience at the 1981 OWAAD conference where women demanded a lesbian-only space:

> The room erupted, it really did. Women started shouting mash 'em, I'm telling you. And I'm thinking 'Oh my God, this is terrible, I'll just sneak out'. I don't know where these women found their courage from, but individual women from isolated parts of the country, can you imagine what it feels like to stand among two-hundred black women and know that what they're shouting against is you.

(Adiola, African, black organisation)

By the 1990s the overt hostility of the early 1980s had in some cases given way to a more complex reaction from heterosexual women. Christian and Muslim women shared religious convictions against homosexuality, however, this was expressed within the context of a contradictory desire to respect and support all black women:

> Because many of us go to church, many of us are Christian and we don't really say much around lesbians. . . . There are a couple of lesbians in the group and some of us know about it. It's not

known publicly. But we don't go into details or treat them with disrespect, or so on.

(Natalie, Caribbean, African Caribbean organisation)

This desire 'not to judge' lesbian women has led many women's organisations to have a 'don't ask, don't tell'[5] policy whereby lesbian women are known to some members as lesbians, but do not openly discuss their sexuality at a group level. This stance, while ideologically contradictory, is nevertheless an indication of the political gains made by lesbian women in making overt expressions of hostility less acceptable within the context of mixed sexuality black women's organisations. This muted tolerance was echoed by one interviewee: 'On a personal level, as long as they don't promote it in the centre, it's OK. We do a lot of casework with clients and that would be confidential between the member of staff and the client' (Mai, Chinese, Chinese organisation). Two of the women's organisations had taken a more proactive stance against homophobia and in recognition of the specific experiences of black lesbian women. One women's refuge worker described the organisation's struggle to get lesbian women's experiences recognised by other domestic violence organisations:

[Sexuality is] not talked about in the women's movement, here actually it has been. We've been one of the very few who have campaigned about the whole issue of abuse not being just about male perpetrators, but also women against women violence. We looked at mother in law abuse, daughters in law. Mothers who have abused their daughters. We weren't popular but the Scottish Women's Aid had to change the whole definition of violence.

(Balwant, Asian, black organisation)

This work is also revealing because it illustrates a willingness to look at an issue which has frequently been seen as taboo within the [white] women's movement – women as perpetrators of violence. This insight is quite probably linked to an experience of white women as perpetrators of racist abuse. Having recognised the possibility of women as abusers in one context, it becomes credible that black women could abuse one another (see K. Bhavnani 1988).

What is notable in the discussions of the family as a site both of affirmation and of resistance is the relative absence of discussions about relationships between black women and white partners. It is clear that many of the women interviewed had a dichotomous view of black and white community interactions which precluded the inclusion of 'mixed' relationships as a valid family structure. This meant that when relationships were discussed, most of the women presumed that the question concerned black on black relationships. Even those interviewees who I knew to be in relationships with white partners tended to make this assumption. However, some of the women were willing to transgress boundaries. One interviewee challenged the assumption that she had more in common with a black woman with whom she had split up than with a white partner:

> It was like, 'look what you've done to this woman, she's a righteous black woman' and whatever. And actually, the reality is that I am middle class. I know that Britain doesn't see that and it's hard to be middle class as a black person, but I am. Me and this woman had a lot more in common than the woman I'd left, even though ostensibly she was black and I was black.
>
> (Adiola, African, black organisation)

Another woman who had been in a relationship with a white man when she first became involved in black women's organisations, but subsequently had relationships with black men only, claimed that 'mixed' relationships were a topic of great contention in the groups she had been involved with:

> In some black women's organisations ... there's always been issues like if the women are involved in mixed race relationships, what that means for them, and how easy it is for them to talk about it or to join in with black women, because in a sense they feel a contradiction and a split.
>
> (Brenda, Caribbean, African Caribbean organisation)

This debate indicates the far-reaching use of the personal as political by black women's organisations. Many of the women interviewed were determined that all women should be accountable for their personal choices. In an environment in which black men and women are under threat, black families undermined and belittled and healthy black on black relationships rarely represented in the media, these relationships, whether same sex or heterosexual can accurately be seen as a political, affirming choice. This affirmation becomes problematic when it translates into hostility towards and ostracism of women choosing white partners.

The third arena in which black women were highly active was that of awareness raising within local communities. This was seen by many of the organisations studied as a logical next step in creating a black woman-centred politics. The emphasis of the consciousness raising varied over time and in different organisations, as did the conception of 'community'. One interviewee summarised her multiple experiences of community:

> Sometimes I perceive myself as part of a community of black women, sometimes as part of a community of single parents. Sometimes, I'm part of a community of people of African heritage. They're all important to me, I have many different experiences of community.
>
> (Sonia, Caribbean, African Caribbean organisation)

For the organisations which catered for more than one ethnic or racialised group, there were also multiple communities with which to communicate. The Sheffield Black Women's Group was an example where women related to a number of discrete communities – Somali, Pakistani, African Caribbean, and so on. In this instance, there appeared to be very little interaction between the different communities in the city and the group focused on educating the different communities to recognise the similarities of their struggles and to resist 'divide and rule' tactics by the local authority (see Mukherjee 1988: 222):

> Responding to the divide and rule is my little bit. . . . It is not to play the system. Sheffield is a tiny place with a tiny grant aid budget. If you divide it between the different black communities, what you do is you make us keep busy fighting each other about the crumbs. The little there is. Instead of looking at the real issue which is lack of funding and resources for black community groups.
>
> (Mona, Middle Eastern, black organisation)

Operating with a more unitary sense of community, the African Caribbean women's groups focused their educational campaigns around a limited concept of community. One such group utilised the relative homogeneity of the community to their advantage in performing theatre which spoke to the community's experiences of gendered racism. The group, based in south London, utilised very specific stereotypes about African Caribbean single mothers and well known localities, such as Brixton, to create an 'insider' critique of community dynamics. Another group resisted the expansion of their 'community' when white mothers of black children of mixed origins attempted to join the group. They were allowed to attend for the sake of the children, but were not welcomed into the black women's 'reasoning' sessions. The group's wish to educate the 'community' did not in this instance encompass white women, who, it was suspected, would 'take over' the organisation. Given the limited and hard-won resources available to black women, this policy of partial exclusion was necessary in order to protect the group's focus on black women's concerns.

Relationships with local communities, whether utilising a broad or narrow definition, were not always easy. Many of the groups had been accused of attempting to 'split the community'. This accusation was usually made by black men involved in community organisations which had failed to address black women's needs. It was a corollary in many ways of the accusation of 'splitting families' and was intended to discourage women from organising autonomously. Ironically, many women described defending their right to organise as a highly politicising experience. It was an experience which coalesced their politics and forced them to take a stand on sexism within black communities. An interviewee involved in setting up a black women's group in a small town in the mid 1980s described her experience thus:

> They didn't like the implication that black women needed space from black men, they really refused to accept that black men also can abuse women or abuse children. It was a time of political idealism where black people could do no wrong, you know, the real enemy out there was the white state and white people: that's who we must focus on. Even if things were happening within black families you shouldn't speak about it, you shouldn't make it public and by making this public, by breaking away and forming our own group, it was making a public declaration.

> (Hilda, African, African Caribbean organisation)

However, it was not only black men that questioned women's right to organise autonomously, black women too were wary of the implications of such action. Discussing the rationale behind autonomous organisations therefore created the space to break the silence about racialised gendered oppression:

> A lot of women actually saw it as separatism and didn't think one should organise separately from black men and indeed one shouldn't; it was wrong to set up something separate from white

women. A lot of people believed that and were ambivalent about joining and when they heard racism discussed as well, they left. There were a lot of unpleasant realities in their own lives that they couldn't face.

(Hilda)

Encounters with hostile communities led some women's organisations to turn inwards. This was often a feature of those organisations most under attack because they dealt with a contentious issue such as male violence or anti-lesbian homophobia. The need in these cases to create a safe space for women was seen by one interviewee as preventing these organisations from community education which might bring about long term changes in attitudes:

> In our type of work you can become insulated, that's my experience of the refuge movement, you become really introspective, things happening around you in your little area. . . . Community development, at the end of the day you're not just there to provide a service, you want them to change. . . . I hate to use the word 'attitude', but that's the only one I can think of.
>
> (Balwant, Asian, black organisation)

However, this position was countered by other women who felt that educating men about sexism or heterosexual women about homophobia was not their responsibility. The 'community' is therefore a contested political arena where black women assert their right to self determination in the face of considerable hostility.

FROM LOCAL TO GLOBAL: MAKING THE CONNECTIONS

I have looked at forms of political activism directed internally to the black community. In the final three arenas of this six point schema, black women's organisations seek to influence the power-brokers: in particular, the multiple manifestations of the state in women's lives. The fourth arena is local government. Black women's organisations play an important role in equipping women with the tools, knowledge and confidence to challenge their treatment by officials. For many women the experience of making group representations on issues affecting their lives was an important part of their political growth:

One of the things a lot of us are scared of is talking to local authority, whether it's housing or whatever, because it reminds us of school days. . . . So, when you get women at the place where they have the confidence to go off and talk to any white person in authority that's brilliant and lots of women, they do it.

(Natalie, Caribbean, African Caribbean organisation)

Groups were actively involved in campaigns in their local community, such as those against racist assaults, deportations and police violence. In challenging local agencies, black women often gained skills and knowledge which were valued in the community at large. One interviewee described how they had became organic advocates in relation to the local authority after their success in a number of cases became known:

It just grew from people saying, 'can you do this and that?', and what happens now is that we operate a vigilante group. So, someone will ring up and say: 'I'm having a serious problem with my child in school around racism and can you support us?'. And two of us would go and sit with them and work out a strategy and support them at school or in court.

(Sonia, Caribbean, African Caribbean organisation)

At other times, black women's organisations were incorporated into less challenging consultation processes. Incorporation also brought with it validation: 'We will say things and people will listen, people will take notice and we are valued for our opinions and our expertise, even though people wouldn't overtly always say, we are' (Manjit, Asian, Asian organisation).

It is clear that the niche of 'expert' is one which offers both recognition and the promise of a more secure funding base. However, reframing black women's protest as a consultative inter-action between two groups with different sets of expertise, can also gloss over differences in power and access to resources between the two sets of actors. The consultation mechanism can then become an alternative to changing the way in which main-stream services are delivered. One interviewee pointed out how the designation of 'expert' was abused, so that staff of black women's organisations were expected to be experts on all black community needs. Having been designated as the sole experts, black women's organisations would also be expected to be the main service providers for black women, thus providing an escape route for local authority workers wishing to pass complex cases to an outside agency:

> That's something we're looking at now in terms of the housing, the social workers and stuff like that, perhaps it's worked to our disadvantage because we've actually done too much for people ... service providers, they've looked on us as being 'experts' and they wanted us to become experts in one particular area to absolve them of responsibility.
>
> (Balwant, Asian, black organisation)

However, the organisations involved in consultation mechanisms actively resisted this marginalisation of their concerns on two levels. They did this by criticising the practices and policies of service delivery agencies:

> We actually advocate on behalf of women all the time, and we're constantly challenging these people. ... And not just at a grass-roots service delivery level, it's on a campaigning policy level, in terms of challenging institutions and organisations about their understanding of Asian women and domestic violence.
>
> (Manjit, Asian, Asian organisation)

They also engaged in more direct and less easily contained forms of protest. When consultation and dialogue were seen to have failed, organisations would frequently utilise direct action such as sit-ins, marches and demonstrations. For many women, their encounter with grant aid mechanisms introduced them to direct political engagement with the local authority through pickets of council meetings where grant allocations would be decided.

Accessing funding became a highly political statement of black women's right to self determination which in turn spoke to the inadequacy of mainstream services. Most organisations had to counter arguments about separatism in order to become part of the grant aid programme. This opposition often took the form of an alliance between black men who had been given the status of 'community leaders' and the local authority. One organisation was threatened with closure by an Asian male councillor if they continued encouraging women to leave violent homes; another group were undermined by letters written by male members of the local Community Relations Council to the local authority, claiming that they were splitting the community. This dual jeopardy was described by an interviewee:

When it was first being set up, one there was all this internal stuff in the community, seeing it as a direct threat to family life, and then of course this whole thing from the white community about why is there a need for a special, as they called it, a special Asian women's service, why can't it be done from an existing white organisation?

(Manjit, Asian, Asian organisation)

Despite this opposition, local authority funding was often the only option for organisations wishing to acquire premises and the increased visibility offered by a centre or office was also seen as a highly political symbol. This sort of symbolism is an essential part of changing ideological constructions of black women in specific localities. For black women in Cambridge, a small town, where black people were usually assumed to be transient foreign students, it was a matter of stating 'we are here to stay'. For women in an inner city area of Coventry, where black women were highly visible in local media portrayals and folklore as prostitutes and inadequate single parents, the women's centre created a powerful counter-image of black women reviving the local community.

The fifth arena is national government. While most of the women's organisations studied engaged extensively with the local state, most of them reported only occasional attempts to create a voice at a national level. This was explained by one interviewee who described the difficulty for many women involved in daily struggles for survival, to appreciate the relevance of national issues: 'It's no point jumping to national or party politics when you actually haven't handled your local politics. . . . It's important to start where people feel confident and at the moment local politics is quite tangible' (Mona, Middle Eastern, black organisation).

Nevertheless, where national issues had an evident impact on black women's lives, the organisations studied had made interventions. Overt attacks on black communities would often elicit a public statement in response. One organisation responded to Norman Tebbit's 'cricket test' in a radio interview.[6] Other women described campaigns against racist immigration rules which particularly affected black women and mobilised in protest over the Child Support Act which was seen to attack poor single mothers.

In contrast to the highly localised concerns of the majority of the organisations, three organisations had a national brief. The Organisation of Women of African and Asian Descent (OWAAD), was highly effective in bringing together local black women and black women's organisations to create a national agenda in the early 1980s. However, OWAAD's unfunded status meant that the women involved were drained emotionally and financially to maintain its momentum. This lack of resources was one important factor in the organisation's failure to survive after the founder members moved on.

The National Association of Women of Afrikan Descent (NAWAD) was established in 1989 as a result of the lack of national coordination of issues which affect 'Afrikan/Caribbean women' (NAWAD leaflet, undated). The organisation received some local authority funding and was able to establish offices in east London. NAWAD held a number of national events and made public statements about issues affecting the Caribbean community in particular. However, it was unable to expand far beyond the initial membership of Caribbean women based in the southeast. When a founder member passed away in November 1995, the organisation lost momentum and at the time of writing was no longer active. Finally, Black Women for Wages for Housework (BWfWfH) have a national campaign brief pressing for recognition of black women's unwaged work and improved rights to benefits. BWfWfH are unfunded and yet produce copious campaign literature and educational packs and are frequently cited in the press. However, despite their national networks and clear political perspective, the organisation is not well known with the other black women's organisations and therefore does not enjoy broad national affiliation.

The importance of effective national structures was emphasised by an interviewee who had become involved in national issues via her involvement with the committee of Sia: the National Development Agency for the Black Voluntary Sector, a relatively well resourced black umbrella organisation which has established a National Network of Black Women's Organisations (Sia 1996a, 1996b). This involvement had enabled the interviewee to envision the establishment of an independent black women's aid network which would be able to coordinate and mobilise around black women and violence at a national level:

> There were black women's networks, but there was never the funding of the people to facilitate that; it was always voluntary, on top of everything else they had to do. But I think there's a real

opportunity now, real potential for that to get underway. I mean I would like to see a black WAFE, the Women's Aid Federation of England, who absolutely deny the issues to do with black women.

(Manjit, Asian, Asian organisation)

However, the difficulties of maintaining a broad based national body representative of the geographical, racialised and ethnic diversity of black women in Britain and which is well resourced, but independent, have yet to be overcome.

Moving beyond national boundaries, many black women's organisations express a desire to make contact with women's struggles in other parts of the world and to create an agenda which puts the experiences of black women in Britain within the context of global trends and movements. This constitutes the sixth arena of black women's activism. While life experiences, from employment to the environment, are shaped at a global level, local organisations seldom have access to influence policy at that level. One interviewee expressed the contradiction at the centre of many organisations, that while they recognise the importance of international struggles and networks, they are nevertheless hard pressed to look farther than the local level:

In a way we don't have the luxury to put our heads above the waterline, but we can't keep our heads buried and just survive. We have to network; we have to link; we have to have world solidarity, but it's very hard to have world solidarity when you're scared, you're vulnerable, when you've been abused and I think that dilemma is one that black women have always faced and one that black women are facing more acutely now.

(Brenda, Caribbean, African Caribbean organisation)

Nevertheless, most of the interviewees expressed interest in the situation of black women outside of Britain. All of the organisations had members born outside Britain, which led to a continuing interest in their countries of origin. Many of the women emphasised that they were 'international people' in contrast to white people who were seen as parochial and insular. In several organisations, this awareness had been heightened by the participation of members in an international exchange with black women from other European countries, or at an international conference. Three of the organisations studied had sent a delegation to the United

Nations World Conferences on Women in 1985 in Nairobi, or in 1995 in Beijing. One organisation had been active in preparing the agenda for the Beijing conference leading to the incorporation of some of their concerns in the resulting 'platform for action'. The platform was later signed by 189 countries committing them to a programme of action to reduce illiteracy, sexual exploitation and other forms of abuse (*Ms* magazine January/February 1996). The Beijing conference was seen as a victory for women's ability to work together to create an international agenda for change and the women who attended expressed their excitement and renewed commitment:

> One of the things we decided was looking at the world through women's eyes and that women are good decision makers. . . . We don't just make tea or coffee or make the beds or do the work in the house. We can make decisions, we can do policy, we can make recommendations, the sky's the limit. Cut poverty, education, stop using young girls as prostitute trafficking, stop treating women as if they haven't any commonsense.
>
> (Natalie, Caribbean, African Caribbean organisation)

The conference also served as a catalyst in bringing together a number of black women's organisations in preparation, under the umbrella of the International Network of Women of Colour (INWOC). INWOC received no funding for its work and most of the women had to pay their own fares and accommodation at the conference. Organising at an international level was therefore poorly resourced and yet benefited from the international contacts and experiences of the women involved.

BARRIERS TO POLITICAL ACTIVISM

The preceding sections have given a fresh interpretation of the breadth of political activities undertaken by black women's organisations, ranging from individual consciousness raising to influencing international forums. Despite ample evidence of a commitment to activism among the women interviewed, there were also indications that this role was internally contested and externally opposed. In order to maintain political awareness and translate that consciousness into action, women had to negotiate a number of barriers. At any one moment in the history of an organisation, one or other of these might take precedence, and the balance of politicising and de-politicising forces could swing in either direction.

One of the key barriers to maintaining a critical stance to gendered racism was the attitudes of some of the members themselves. Many of the women preferred to talk about painful or frustrating experiences at work, school or the benefits office, rather than looking at how these experiences might be challenged. Other women experienced the groups as a form of escape from the harsh realities of their lives. Black women's organisations were seen as offering a space where gendered racialised oppression did not exist and where life affirming cultural practices such as cooking, hair-plaiting and discussions in Urdu, Bengali or black vernacular could take place:

> Having a refuge just for Asian women meant they could relax and not have to live up to expectations. Because when you're with other communities, you can't always be yourself and say, speak in your own language. You always have to put up a front.
>
> (Anita, Asian, Asian organisation)

Members often did not wish to be reminded of the daily challenges to their humanity:

> A lot of the women, they can't be bothered with politics. They just want to get out and come and hear what's going on where they can feel good. Sometimes, they say it's too political for them, it's too much of issues. It's like the education don't get them to that standard and they're tired and knackered to come in from work and to come out and listen to politics and they want something that make them laugh.
>
> (Natalie, Caribbean, African Caribbean organisation)

This escapism would sometimes take the form of denial of the existence of gendered racialised inequalities. Black women who established organisations in the early to mid eighties described this attitude as particularly prevalent:

> If you talked about somebody being racist towards you, it was like you were being political, and they didn't want to join a polit-ical group. What they really wanted was to get together and cook and knit. They really were very much into separate gender roles and how women can learn to be better wives and mothers. They really thought that was what the organisation ought to be about,

not facing issues like sexism, when you talk about the city council, and kind of racism or anything like that, they defined that as political and they weren't comfortable.

(Hilda, African, African Caribbean organisation)

This attitude was more prevalent in smaller towns such as Coventry or Cambridge, where the black population had developed less organisational infrastructure and where access to black media such as the *Asian Times, Voice* and *Caribbean Times* newspapers, which were likely to highlight evidence of racism, was restricted:

The mentality in Coventry was much more of a challenge so that if you were able to put up an argument in any way referring to the system as racist, you were seen as almost on the level of revolutionaries.

(Pat, Caribbean, African Caribbean organisation)

It is a commonplace that white people are less likely to believe that racial discrimination affects the life chances of black people than black people are themselves. It is also a common stereotype that black people 'have a chip on their shoulder' which leads them to cry 'racism' where it does not exist. What has received less attention is the evidence that black people in Britain are unlikely to identify the presence of racial discrimination even where they have been the victims of it (Fryer 1988; C. Brown 1984: 265).

bell hooks in her recent examination of 'black rage' argues that there is a form of denial which enables black people to avoid the pain of facing their experiences of oppression. Part of this avoidance strategy is that of ridiculing the oppressors, masking painful experiences with laughter. In this way, separate spaces, far from nurturing critical thinking, can become spaces for unhealthy laughter and escapism:

In the past, separate space meant down time, time for recovery and renewal. It was the time to dream resistance, time to theorise, plan, create strategies and go forward. The time to go forward is still upon us and we have long since surrendered segregated spaces of radical opposition. Our separation now is usually mere escape – a sanctuary for hiding and forgetting.

(hooks 1995: 6)

hooks' insightful analysis goes to the core of the dual role of autonomous organisations as a site both of resistance and escape.

However, in positing a chronological regression whereby the separate space has changed from a nurturing ground of radical resistance to a haven of escapism, hooks fails to capture the contested nature of these spaces. Black women's organisations allow respite and relaxation, the moment of forgetting that gives one the strength to carry on in a soul destroying job, or in the face of racist stereotypes. They are also sites for the creation of resistance strategies. Women who attend them have varying needs and this will influence how the organisation responds at any given time.

The second potential barrier to activism was the manipulation of funding. Many scholars have identified a close relationship between state funding of black community organisations and the inability or unwillingness of these organisations to take on a political role (Ben-Tovim *et al.* 1986b; Solomos and Back 1995). Funding has been seen as a strategy to coopt grassroots struggle into more manageable forms of activity, by turning activists into service deliverers, black working class struggle into ethnic enclaves and creating a tier of 'race relations professionals' to control black youth energies (Anthias *et al.* 1992; Gilroy 1987). There is evidence that censorship and an overload in paperwork has the potential to restrict the activities of funded black women's organisations. One interviewee identified potential sanctions by funders as a barrier to criticising statutory agencies: 'People get caught up in the safety of what they're doing and they don't want to challenge. Because if they challenge it might affect their funding' (Balwant, Asian, black organisation). An interviewee with previous experience of allocating GLC funds to community organisations characterised the situation as follows:

> If you want to do political work, if you want to do work around consciousness raising . . . around resistance to the state, don't ask the state for money. For one thing, in order to get it you'll have to tone down what you do. You also spend such a lot of time in meetings and monitoring that there actually isn't time to do the business that you set out to do.
>
> (Faith, African, black organisation)

The potential loss of independence was a factor in the decision of one case study organisation in not seeking funding from the local authority, even though they had been invited to apply:

> I think that's why we were so successful was that we said what we

liked. And I don't think you can do that once you've got the master who's playing the tune above your head all the time and is calling the tune in terms of what you call yourself, what you can say and that it's not OK to say that.

(Alekiri, African, African Caribbean organisation)

This organisation felt that officials were responding to their popularity by attempting to bring them under their control. The organisation, which performed consciousness raising drama, was very wary of the possibility that their highly critical material would be compromised if they accepted funding. Such examples seem to support the case against funding.

However, the idea of a simple causal relationship between funding and political censorship fails to explain the existence of the funded organisations studied which were highly politicised. Such organisations stated that claiming their right to local authority grant aid and central government funding under programmes such as Section 11, Urban Programme and subsequently the Single Regeneration Budget, was in itself a political act. It also fails to explain the track record of many local authorities in refusing to support black organisations which are challenging their hegemony at the local level. In other words, if funding did indeed follow political activism, the pattern in most local authorities of substantial allocation of funds to highly professionalised white voluntary organisations and limited funding for black organisations would be reversed (Wenham 1993). Finally, the argument fails to take into account the differentiation of the state. Receiving funding from central government often puts black organisations in a strong position to be able to challenge the local authority. In this study, several organisations which had obtained central government funds in the form of Urban Programme funds were able to mount significant criticisms of the local authority. Their strong resource base made them both less likely to be the object of local authority reprisals for such criticism and more able to survive cuts in funding.

The relationship between funding and political censorship is not static and changes over time. One organisation was quite adamant about their refusal to allow local government to influence the way their organisation operated when they first started receiving funding in 1985 and would not allow the authority to place a representative on the management committee:

One of the things that we made very clear to the local authority was that we did not want them to dictate how we were going to organise and how we were going to do what we were going to do . . . if we break the law in so doing, yes you can do something about it, other than that we don't want any conditions.

(Hilda, African, African Caribbean organisation)

Ten years later, the same organisation had a white council officer on the committee and appeared to be more closely controlled stating 'the city doesn't want us to be political' (Ngozi, African, African Caribbean organisation). The change in relationship was also linked to a period during which the chair of the organisation was also a council officer and was under pressure from her line manager to take a less oppositional stance. Nevertheless, the organisation, which had initially focused almost entirely on local politics, had recently become very involved in international politics and had sent a representative to the United Nations fourth World Conference on Women in Beijing. Furthermore, the organisation had begun to channel their local concerns through an umbrella group called the Ethnic Community Forum. The shift in relationship with the local authority had therefore led to greater networking and coalition building with other racialised groups as well as making other political horizons more attractive.

Attempts by local authorities to use funding as a form of control were actively opposed. The organisations which did receive funding invented strategies to avoid this control. In some cases, this took the form of overt non-cooperation as in the case of one organisation which refused to complete new monitoring forms which reduced women's experiences of violence to misleading statistics. In other cases, women created imaginative strategies which avoided overt confrontation:

We're thinking maybe we have to work a certain way internally and project a certain image. So we will project the image they want to see, but internally we will carry on working the way we always have. . . . And that's how it's going to have to be, for survival's sake. And the groups which are folding and are disappearing are groups that haven't been able to adapt in that way as much.

(Manjit, Asian, Asian organisation)

These organisations were creating parallel worlds which offered the local authority what they wished to see, but enabled the organisation to continue behind closed doors with activities which might be opposed by officials. This dissimulation was mentioned by many organisations in relation to the local authority and is an approach which may not be evident to the researcher who is not seen as 'one of us'. It takes varied forms: editing minutes sent to council officers, using other organisational names or umbrella groups to send critical letters and organise campaigns and encouraging women with young children to picket the town hall on an 'individual' basis. This research indicates that funded black women's organisations, far from being coopted, often act as subversive political agents.

Closely linked to the ability to access funding is the decision of whether or not to apply for charitable status. Charitable status enables organisations to avoid property taxes and to apply for some restricted funds. While charity legislation ensures that registered charities do not utilise their funds to support activities which could be viewed as party political or to present 'biased' information, many black organisations interpret this to mean that they cannot be involved in political activities or campaigns. This has been exacerbated by the Charity Commission's refusal for some years to recognise the terms 'racism' or 'black' in charitable objects (Sia December 1995). One organisation which had considered the option stated: 'That's part of why for ages we hadn't become a charity as such because really you can't be too political' (Ngozi).

Few of the organisations studied had become registered charities due to their fear of control and censorship. However, those which had, while experiencing frustrating delays and difficulties in achieving their registration, once registered had little interaction with the Charity Commission. There is no evidence therefore that the organisations suffered from any external restrictions because of charity legislation. Fear of such action is far more likely than actual intervention by the commission to have a censorial impact.

The containment of fear is a little studied factor in black political mobilisation, yet it constitutes a third barrier to organising politically: 'I think Chinese women are afraid of stirring things up. They are frightened and don't know what is likely to happen' (Mai, Chinese, Chinese organisation). This perspective was not unfounded or based on unjustified anxiety. Black women were frequently the victims of hostility, from both black and white people. One interviewee described the trauma of being verbally attacked by black men involved in the local Community Relations Council when she attempted to set up a black women's group: 'We were made to feel like traitors, that we were undermining the black community with our actions, that we were rampant feminists' (Hilda, African, African Caribbean organisation).

Fear is therefore a critical weapon in controlling black women and preventing them from organising. In this case, it was fear of rejection from a community which provides protection from racial discrimination and violence. Protection by black males from racism and protection from male violence are often incompatible. Black women working in refuges experienced rejection and occasionally physical threats when male partners discovered that they were offering shelter to their spouses, as was the experience of a refuge worker:

> In one sense we are ostracised and we are treated with suspicion, but it's the same for us because we don't want to become too easily identifiable. . . . We've had people calling up and saying: 'we want to know where such and such is' and we say: 'sorry, who?'.

> (Balwant, Asian, black organisation)

The threat of violence, however, comes most frequently from the white community. One organisation found that opening a new centre attracted the attention of a skinhead who repeatedly physically threatened the volunteers on reception. This sort of event was so recurrent that the organisation was forced to put on a course on 'dealing with aggression' for the staff and volunteers. On occasions, women received anonymous phone calls, or premises were exposed to racist graffiti or were damaged. The police response to these incidents was minimal.

A study of abortion clinics in the United States suggests that the experience of overt hostility from the outside community, while contributing to emotional exhaustion, also fuels a sense of resistance (Simonds 1995). In the organisations studied, it appeared to create a form of close bonding against common opponents and a renewed resolve. However, Simonds does not analyse the affect on women not involved in organisations for whom the threat of ostracism and possible violence may be a significant deterrent. The ability of organisations to present themselves as apolitical may be a significant factor in avoiding such hostility and may in turn enable the involvement of greater numbers of women. Once again dissimulation emerges as an important factor in the survival of black women's organisations.

CREATING ALTERNATIVE VISIONS: BLACK WOMEN CATALYSTS

These barriers to political expression mean that 'coming to voice' is not simply an organic process which occurs whenever black women are gathered together. The translation of common experience into collective action requires some additional impetus. That impetus frequently comes from one or more pioneer women (Essed 1996: 96). These women have a catalytic impact on the women in a given community or locality and begin the process of awareness raising and mobilisation. Omolade (1995) likens this role to that taken by Ella Baker in the Student Non-Violent Coordinating Committee in the United States, the 'woman in front', the visionary and initiator: 'The woman in front "puts her body into the movement". She, like Ella, is found working long hours, squeezing in family obligations and sacrificing personal pleasures. Policy, programs and work evolves from and is most often initiated by her' (Omolade 1995: 175).

Like Jayaben Desai, inspirational leader of the 1976 Grunwich strike, these 'women in front' are non-hierarchical and are therefore able to exchange their role at any time for that of 'sister in the circle', utilising a more collective form of decision making (A. Wilson 1978). However, it is these women who initiate organisations, intervene when organisations are at a standpoint, and reactivate those that have become de-politicised. The organisations studied revealed various types of 'woman in front'. Women shaped and educated by their access to international political struggles played a key role. Women in this category were involved in anticolonial and independence struggles in Africa, Asia and the Caribbean and came as adults to Britain. These women have developed oppositional ideologies and are able to draw on skills and experience not readily available to black women in Britain. These skills include experience of non-hierarchical ways of working and women's involvement in decision making. One interviewee pointed out that women's active roles in the governance of her home village in India were a formative influence: 'I was brought up with my father and my grandmother [in India] . . . and that's why I remember women working together and coming into the house with discussion and decision making' (Sophia, Asian, black organisation).

Women involved in movements against white rule in the former

Rhodesia and South Africa played a key role in the establishment of the Organisation of Women of Africa and African Descent (OWAAD), the first national black women's political body. The tactic of non-violent protest utilised by the Indian Home Rule movement was also a source of inspiration for women involved in picketing and demonstrations.

Another group of women in front with origins in anti-colonial struggle are Rasta women.[7] A focus by academics and media on the supposed rebelliousness and criminality of Rastafari has masked the way in which it synthesises lived experiences of racialised and class oppression with religious and spiritual symbolism to create a radical alternative vision of social organisation (Cashmore 1979; Campbell 1985). Rastafari advocates living in harmony with nature, it refutes hierarchical and bureaucratic forms of organisation, materialism and artificial drugs and foods and aspires to an equal and just society, 'Shashamane'. In this sense Rastafari is both the successor of Garveyist Pan-Africanism and a pre-cursor of popular protest movements such as the Green Movement, Band Aid and the Anti-Nuclear Movement. This alternative vision placed many Rasta women at the forefront in the late 1970s and early 1980s when black women's organisations were emerging.

Rasta women have largely been absent from sociological studies which have replicated the media construction of Rastafari as male. For example, Cashmore's influential study of Rastafari in Birmingham was simply entitled *Rastaman: The Rastafarian Movement in England* (1979) and Small's report on Rastafari in London subtitled 'A group of young black people' (1983) focused entirely on African Caribbean men. Where there has been some interest in women, they have been accorded an exalted but socially circumscribed role as 'queen' and mother (Churches Commission for Racial Justice, in Greater London Council 1984: 14; see also Yawney 1994). This view of women's role in Rastafari communities has been reinforced by dominant views of traditional head coverings and dress and the acceptance by some of biblically defined gender roles (Greater London Council 1984: 14). It is important, however, to appreciate the gendered components of Rastafari in the context of the rise in African nationalist sentiment in Britain in the 1970s. Covering the head and body was seen by many women as a form of opposition to the sexual commodification of women's bodies characterising capitalist society and to the degradation of African women's bodies in particular. Furthermore, the nationalist belief that African Caribbean men received the brunt of state brutality led some women to declare their deference in the hope that this would restore 'black manhood'.

Despite this public face, Rasta women were involved in community organising in the form of the 'Twelve Tribes' events which occurred throughout the 1970s bringing together Rastafari followers nationwide. This experience would be critical in developing the skills and commitment necessary to build early black women's organisations:

> In a lot of cases, it tended to be Rasta women that were involved as well in the early stages as well . . . if you think about the time, it would have been the seventies when they were starting which was obviously when Rasta was at its highest – and those women would have been more ideologically placed and structurally placed to create those sorts of networks. . . . You can compare it to the Church in that you have that structure there provided by Rasta ideology and physical networks that Rasta women had.
>
> (Lynette, Caribbean, African Caribbean organisation)

Rastafari was and continues to be an important resource for community struggles. In addition to providing practical resources, networks and skills, it functions 'as a catalyst for a new consciousness and of reordering the world in the minds of the people' (Garrison 1979: 27). The creation of non-hierarchical, 'ital'[8] black women-only space is one way in which Rasta women could express their visions of utopia. These spaces subsequently became the basis for the creation of a new politics which integrated a Rasta analysis of a 'Babylon' system with black women's experiences of gendered oppression to create a new and unique oppositional vision. This new vision has been called 'the new Rastafari':

> The new Rastafari has emerged through a process whereby black feminisms have garnered the weight and media access necessary to enable them to appropriate Rastafari and redefine its content. This has also been a process of rediscovery of the history of women in struggle and an excavation of global gender, class and race relations.
>
> (Turner 1994: 55)

While scholars have noted a decline in the influence of traditional male dominated Rastafari from the mid 1980s, the new Rastafari, embodied in musicians such as Tracy Chapman, is a powerful radicalising force which lives on in the cultural and political practices of black women's organisations in Britain and in resistance movements worldwide (Gilroy 1987; Turner 1994: 15).

A further group of 'women in front' are those who are in some way 'displaced' from their communities of origin. This displacement has a liberating impact in that it frees women from the fear of ostracism experienced by many black women who take a pioneering role. One interviewee describes a group of women who came together to establish the first black lesbian group:

> We were mainly displaced women, so you would get [African] American women, women from Scotland, who it wouldn't matter what [group] they were from. . . . I tell you what else, a lot of people who have been fostered, in care and were a long way away . . . my theory is actually if you've fought that hard, I mean I was in care for a long time, if you're fostered or adopted, it's hard. You get used to being different and you learn to deal with it.
>
> (Adiola, African, black organisation)

The women's experiences of displacement were more fundamental than the shared experience of 'being black in a white society', they spoke to more profound experiences of isolation. Similarly a Sikh woman whose partner was Muslim provided the strength and radical vision necessary to establish an Asian women's refuge in the late 1970s without bowing to community pressures to prioritise marital integrity over women's safety:

> The staff make the organisation because they're there at the cut and thrust of it day in day out and if your staff are vocal and political and radical then the organisation will be automatically. . . . The [first] worker was extremely radical. Here was a Sikh woman living with a Muslim man. So it was really progressive and serious.
>
> (Manjit, Asian, Asian organisation)

The worker's rejection from both communities had prepared her for the hostility that the refuge would face.[9] Women who were brought up outside of established black communities and were the only black child in their school, women who were taken into the care system or brought up by white foster or adoptive parents, women who had come out as lesbians, women who had defied cultural expectations by dating 'out', all had experienced social ostracism and had become emotionally strong in the face of rejection.

The important role of these women has frequently been erased in the oral history of black women's organisations. In one case, a black women's organisation which had been founded primarily by lesbian women was trying to disown that history in order to attract a wider membership.

> One of the co-founders was a lesbian woman and the organisation had a reputation for being predominantly lesbian women by the time I was there. I use the word reputation, but it was a reputation in the sense that proved to be problematic because a lot of women who had heard of it didn't want to get involved because they thought it was a lesbian organisation.
>
> (Lynette, Caribbean, African Caribbean organisation)

In other cases, women who have been in institutional care as children are unwilling to share their experiences and are assumed to have been brought up in black families. This erasure of the role of 'displaced' women prevents us from recognising the fundamentally diverse nature of black women's organising in Britain. Nevertheless, these often hidden histories are a testimony to the contributions of women who have been considered 'not quite black enough'.[10]

CONCLUSIONS

This chapter has illustrated the wealth of political activism which becomes evident when the blinkers of commonsense notions about the political realm are removed. Drawing on black women's perspectives, I have redefined political activism to acknowledge its roots in personal experience, while retaining a focus on the communal action which grows out of such experience. I have also emphasised the multiple sites of political action and highlighted some arenas which have previously been ignored. In so doing, I have shown that black women's organisations are at the forefront of empowering black women, challenging inequalities and abuse within black families and communities, as well as creating broad based demands for change at local, national and international levels. While acknowledging the many obstacles to black women's involvement, I have also challenged assumptions which have been made about black women's inability to overcome the barriers which would seek to keep them from political activism. Finally, this chapter has located some agents of change who have been central to the development of black women's organisational agendas but who are hidden from view when scholars focus attention only on those political actors who have received status and recognition from the mainstream political system. These black women catalysts have mobilised alternative visions of socio-economic relations which are essential in the creation of any radical agenda for change.

NOTES

1 'Political activists are urging black people not to opt out of the main-stream political system. The call comes after figures showing that as many as one in four young black people are not on the electoral role.' ('Would-be Voters Urged to Register', *Voice* 12 December 1995: 2)

2 Since black women also experience the family as a site of male violence, black women's refuges must balance the oppositional and oppressive aspects of family life. This tension is reflected in Chapter 5.

3 'Reasoning' is a term which originates in the Rastafari practice of attending lengthy discussion sessions often based on bible study which aim to educate and uplift. In common black usage the term normally refers to a non-religious discussion in which serious issues are addressed (S. Small 1983).

4 The Muslim Parliament was established in 1995 as an alternative to mainstream party politics for Muslims of all nationalities in Britain. Its legitimacy has however been contested.

5 A policy introduced by Clinton as a compromise position on anti-gay discrimination in the US army.

6 Norman Tebbit, the former Conservative cabinet minister, argued for a particularly limited vision of Britishness when he claimed that Asians did not feel allegiance to Britain if they supported a cricket team from Pakistan or India (Brah 1996: 194).

7 Although most sociological works use the term 'Rastafarianism' and 'Rastafarian', I prefer using the terms which are used by followers of Rastafari (Ras – King; Tafari – name of Haile Selassie).

8 'Ital' is a Rasta word which translates roughly as pure or 'kosher'. It originated in reference to food, but is used more broadly to signify any attribute which adheres to the principles of simplicity, naturalness and consciousness.

9 Desai (1963) gives a vivid description of the process of 'outcasting' which accompanied marrying out of traditional communities.

10 A concept taken from Marlon Riggs' groundbreaking documentary *Black is, Black Ain't* (1995).

Chapter 4

Talking across difference

In the previous chapter, I identified diverse experiences which have enabled black women to take on the role of catalyst. In so doing, I began to unpack the notion of 'The Black Woman' as a unitary identity (Mama 1995). There is a tension, however, between embracing a differentiated notion of black womanhood and talking meaningfully about black women's collective action. It is this tension between the desire for unity and the equal but sometimes contradictory desire for a celebration of difference that I shall unravel in this chapter. To this end, I shall challenge the presumption that racialised ideologies provide the primary marker of identification and solidarity for black women at all times and in all locations, and suggest other markers, such as regional and sexual identities which have largely been overlooked.

The term 'identity politics' was coined in the 1970s to describe a new form of engagement which legitimated personal empowerment as part of political activism. Black women were at the forefront in celebrating this new and personally liberating politics which meant that multi-layered experiences of gendered racism and class oppression could be challenged simultaneously. In the United States, African American women in the Combahee River Collective which began meeting in 1974 stated:

> We realise that the only people who care enough about us to work consistently for our liberation is us. . . . This focusing on our own oppression is embodied in the concept of identity politics. We believe that the most profound and potentially the most radical politics come directly out of our own identity, as opposed to working to end somebody else's oppression.
>
> (Combahee River Collective 1983: 16)

In Britain, black feminist groups such as Brixton Black Women's Group (BBWG), established in 1973, developed their own politics based on their racialised, gendered and class positions:

> The status of black women places us at the intersection of all forms of subjugation in society – racial oppression, sexual oppression and economic exploitation. This means that we are a natural part of many different struggles – both as black people and as women. . . . It is in the context of an understanding of our oppression based on sex, race and class, and the recognition of our struggle being part and parcel of the greater struggle for the liberation of all our people from all forms of oppression, that black feminism is defined for us.
>
> (BBWG 1981, in Mama 1995: 4)

Organisations such as Southall Black Sisters and Brent Asian women's refuge were also concerned to address the specific oppressions arising from Asian women's relationship to religious and caste ideologies (Brah 1996: 83; Sahgal 1992). Yet, almost as soon as it was defined, 'identity politics' was under attack from a variety of quarters. In Britain, among the most fervent detractors were members of the Race and Class collective who saw identity politics as a form of false consciousness distracting black people from class-based analyses and struggles. These scholar activists criticised this shift from the community to the individual at a time when black communities were under attack from racist immigration laws and hostile policing:

> Identity politics is all the rage. Exploitation is out (it is extrinsically determinist). Oppression is in (it is intrinsically personal). What is to be done has been replaced by who am I. Political culture has ceded to cultural politics. The material world has passed into the metaphysical.
>
> (Bourne 1987: 1)

While some feminist consciousness raising groups may have been as introspective as Bourne suggests, it is a travesty to suggest that the majority of feminist activists were indulging in no more than personal therapy (Ferree and Martin 1995; Bondi 1993). When the wealth of political activism by black women's organisations explored in the previous chapter is made visible, it becomes clear that this analysis tells us little or nothing about black women's organisations. Far from losing sight of community-based class struggles, early black feminist groups placed battles over immigration, policing, schooling and reproductive rights in the context of struggles against capitalism:

> The black women's movement is an important part of the movement throughout the world for change and the destruction of capitalism. In that movement women are coming forward to take part in the struggle for personal and finally political emancipation. Advances for us can be made only if and when our organised attacks contribute to the erosion of the capitalist system.
>
> (BBWG 1980: 3; see also OWAAD 1979, 1980)

Black women in these London-based groups embraced a Marxist framework which posited gendered racist oppression as a tool to divide working class struggles against capitalist imperialism. What was challenging to the Race and Class school of thought was that these black women did not need a black male leadership, nor did they welcome white women into their ranks. It is perhaps the experience of being excluded from a movement which they had thought to be 'theirs' which most determined the way in which black feminism would be received by anti-racist socialists. Yet this re-conceptualisation of anti-racist praxis was profoundly radical in that it posited the indivisibility of racialised, gendered and class identities, the interdependency of the individual and the communal and connectedness of the social and the psychological. The failure to listen to this new politics means that the potential to pre-empt and bypass the paralysing dichotomy between political economy and cultural politics was shortchanged.

The accusation that 'identity politics' is naive and misguided masks a conceptual contradiction. As Bannerji (1995) points out, a politics which is engaged in by a group of actors sharing the same racialised or gendered identities, is only ever defined as identity politics when that group of actors is also a subordinated group. Gays and lesbians and black women engage in identity politics. When white women get together to 'do' politics, we call it 'feminism', when political events, such as the Conservative and Republican leadership struggles, are made up entirely of white men, it is simply called 'politics'. This conceptual sleight of hand serves to normalise the status of 'white heterosexual', so that it is not even considered an identity. Yet, it is clear that while white people do not usually identify their political groups in racialised terms, a shared 'whiteness' is nevertheless the unspoken bond which forms the basis of much of their politics (Frankenberg 1993a; Bannerji 1995: 20). If mobilisation around shared racialised and gendered identities is not unique to subaltern groups, identity politics becomes stripped of its descriptive power and is revealed to be a rhetorical tool utilised to discourage oppressed groups from organising autonomously. Joining the arsenal of terms such as 'reverse racism' and 'political correctness', it disparages any political project which does not recognise the inflated universalist claim of white-led politics. Engaging in black feminist politics reveals the hidden 'white male' behind general usage of the term politics. It is this that opponents of identity politics fear, to be revealed in their specificity, their 'we' of Empire stripped down to the 'we' of a small island.

Perhaps the most significant interrogation of identity politics has come from quite a different source. Poststructuralist writers have criticised such groups for reinforcing myths of a unitary identity, such as 'black woman', 'lesbian', as if such categories held an essential meaning: 'To the degree that identity is a radically destabilizing force and not at all a stable guarantee of a coherent politics, the current tendency to base one's politics on a rather vague and imprecise notion of identity needs to be rethought' (Fuss 1989: 105).

If, after Derrida, the 'self' is only ever constructed by reference to the 'Other' and thereby expresses 'differance' even as it speaks of sameness, a project which is based on sameness is only ever a reflection or repression of that which it seeks to oppose. In decentring the 'self', Derrida empties out the notion of identity, even as we seek to utilise it as a unifying force. If, after Lacan, 'black woman', 'identity' are mere tropes, signifiers which we fill or empty of meaning through the acts of speaking and writing, then the notion of identity is far too contingent, too slippery a form on which to build a political movement. Feminist scholars who utilise poststructuralist tools, hope to transcend the potentially divisive barriers of 'race', class and gender by proclaiming the inherently fragmented and contingent nature of these differences. Decentring the Cartesian subject, it is hoped, will undermine the very foundations of universalist humanism upon which hierarchies are constructed and legitimated. Such hopes are overblown, however, as they contain no strategies for challenging the material social relations between groups constructed as essentially different. As Bondi (1993) has remarked in her critique of poststructuralist feminism:

Taken to its logical conclusion, the category 'women', upon which feminism is based, becomes a free-floating sign apparently able to take on any meaning we give it. The materiality of social relations is, in effect, ignored, in favour of a domain of representation in which structures of power are treated as illusory.

(1993: 94)

Analysts who wish to utilise poststructuralist insights but resist the freefall into relativity implied by Derrida and Lacan have found a compromise in the notion of shifting and multiple identities. This theory allows a self definition of 'black woman', but warns us that this in itself is barely descriptive. Instead, our identities as black women must be examined at different moments in time, in different geographical locations and in different social situations. At each moment any given term may take a range of meanings and encompass a range of experiences. What is common to such writers is the desire to remove the idea of a unitary self, a core which represents our authentic being, from concepts of identity. To this end, many have moved towards 'subjectivity', a concept:

> that does not assume a unitary, static subject at its core but instead conceptualises subjectivity as multiple, dynamic and continuously produced in the course of social relations that are themselves changing and at times contradictory.

(Mama 1995: 2)

This conceptual framework calls into question truth claims about black women made by black women's organisations. Using this framework, the following statement by Brixton Black Women's Group would have to be interrogated: 'It is only by coming together and analysing our situation as black women in this society that we can make an effective contribution to the struggle' (BBWG 1980: 2). The proponent of shifting and multiple identities would have to ask, 'which black women?', 'whose struggle?', 'effective for whom?'. While this approach may be useful in clarifying the specificity of this statement – it originates from a small group of women, primarily of African Caribbean descent in London in 1980 – it does little to explain its broader appeal, for example, to black women outside London in the 1990s. In other words, while it speaks to the particular, this approach has few tools to deal with the general and universal, and it is precisely the latter which are utilised by movements to mobilise political activism.

RECONSTRUCTING BLACK WOMANHOOD

If 'identity politics' leads us into conceptual confusion, how should we talk about identity in the context of autonomous organisations? Rather than relying on static notions of identity, many black women's organisations emphasise the need to explore, analyse and redefine identities. Autonomous organisations do not simply allow black women to 'be' true to some inner core: rather, they provide a space within which one can 'become' a black woman. A Zimbabwean woman summarised this emphasis on 'building an identity':

> I'd come from a country where I wasn't black, I was a 'coloured'. That was the terminology. It took me a while to learn that in this country I am black. And so I couldn't automatically give it to my kids, that sense of black identity. I had to learn it and then I had to pass it on.
>
> (Hilda, African, African Caribbean organisation)

Black women's organisations offer the space to nurture 'identity and black consciousness' (Alekiri, African, African Caribbean organisation), to develop oneself and others as 'powerful women' (Natalie, Caribbean, African Caribbean organisation). They are spaces in which black women can create oppositional and empowering narratives of self.

Empowering notions of the self are not given, nor are they easily constructed: they are struggled for against a backdrop of hostile and dehumanising discourses on black women. The fight to maintain sight of our humanity despite the barrage of negative images and discourses about black women was a constant theme of the interviews. Much has been written about the construction of black womanhood in anthropological and quasi-scientific writings written to justify and normalise black women's treatment under slavery and colonialism (Davis 1981; Mama 1995). Less has been written about the specific ways in which these discourses have infiltrated current representations of black women in Britain or on the latter's impact on black women's mental and emotional wellbeing (Marshall 1996). It is these unquestioned and so 'commonsense' notions about black women's identity which shape our interactions with white people on a daily basis and which infuse media portrayals of black women (Essed 1990). Significantly, such representations do not only remain in the discursive field, but actively structure black women's experiences in the fields of education, employment, immigration, criminal justice and welfare (Cheney 1996; Carby 1982).

Rejecting such representations, making the mental space to create alternative self definitions was seen by the interviewees as a process of coming into 'consciousness'. This notion of consciousness is prevalent in black women's organisations. It is 'conscious' black women who are perceived to have developed radical and empowering discourses of self and community:

> X was a Rastafarian woman and had already done a lot of self evaluation work around her identity and black consciousness. And because she was the one who actually got the women into the group, most of the women were of that same type of thinking.
>
> (Alekiri, African, African Caribbean organisation)

> Black women came to a consciousness of themselves as black women where they gained support and they share that indefinable something that just happens when black women get together and connect at a deep level.
>
> (Brenda, Caribbean, African Caribbean organisation)

Consciousness is indicated via choices, whether this is reflected in the rejection of damaging hair and skin treatments which accentuate European beauty standards, in language and lifestyle or in political activism. It also implies a level of confidence gained, it is assumed, by shedding the negative self image associated with the internalisation of gendered racist notions of black womanhood.

The discourse of consciousness is double edged. In defining some black people as embracing oppositional mentalities, it implicitly defines others as 'coconuts'.[1] Gilroy (1993) describes the process of separating out what is Eurocentric from authentic black practice as a form of 'ontological essentialism' (1993: 32). He criticises this project for its authoritarian tendencies and reliance on notions of authenticity invoked to justify the censorship of non-conformist voices and minority interests. Mama (1995) has reiterated this finding in her interviews with African Caribbean women in London. Her study of the interaction between Mona, a light-skinned black woman and Claudette, a darkskinned Rasta woman revealed that women defined as conscious could be perceived as threatening and undermining to women whose claim to 'blackness' was more tentative:

> Mona refers to 'certain' black women, and, as we have already noted, elsewhere she describes them as 'conscious' black women – women to whom she arrogates the right to define what is and is not 'black'. As a Rastafarian, Claudette is probably a great deal more dedicated to being rootsy.
>
> (Mama 1995: 139)

Interviews with women involved in black women's organisations in the 1970s and 1980s indicate that the battle to define authentic black womanhood was an integral part of many women's experiences:

> There were those who felt that to be black was a rather pure and narrow definition and I didn't experience those women any differently in a way to that which I felt towards the white women, they had a very narrow definition of what it meant to be a feminist. Although I felt more love towards the black women. And in some senses the pain was worse as well.
>
> (Faith, African, black organisation)

This 'pure and narrow' definition of blackness was personified in the 'ital black woman', a phrase which came to indicate a range of characteristics and behaviour from dark skin and natural hair, to 'traditional' attire and avoidance of processed foods. Ital originates in Rasta dietary terms and refers to foods which have not been contaminated with items forbidden by the Old Testament, including pork and shell fish (S. Small 1983):

> There were some other things going on between ital black women. . . . I thought 'ital' was when you don't put salt on food. But no, ital black women and lightskinned black women. . . . I remember clearly that if you're ital black women then you should relate to other ital black women them, and the mixed race women them should relate to other mixed race and the white women to other white women . . . and that's what finished the group off really, I mean what's left? There was too many criteria to be fulfilled.
>
> (Abiola, African, black organisation)

The use of ital in reference to definitions of black women indicates the extent to which notions of authentic black womanhood are shaped by the racialised characteristics of Caribbean women, suggesting that Asian women are considered peripheral to definitions of black womanhood. I shall discuss this point further later in this chapter. Abiola's statement exemplifies a simple reversal of the 'colour complex' associated with Caribbean enslavement and subsequent social formations in the Caribbean and United States. This reversal valorises African characteristics such as 'nappy' hair and dark skin. However, in utilising this ideological weapon, black women reified a rigid conceptualisation of distinct 'races'. They therefore failed to acknowledge the arbitrariness of racial categorisation, as well as ignoring evidence that the fundamental intermixing of African, Asian, European and indigenous peoples in the Caribbean forecloses on the possibility of a 'pure' racial origin.

Light skin was not always seen as a marker of not being 'black enough'. Mama (1995) also highlighted the way in which choices, such as natural hairstyles or political activism, can serve as compensatory elements which reassert black identity. Similarly, behaviour which is seen as being against the group interest may be used to make judgements about lightskinned women's loyalty to the group in a way which is unique to their positionality. This was indicated by one interviewee whose commitment as a founder member of a group went unquestioned until she had a significant policy disagreement with some of the African women members: 'There was a meeting right in my house at which one of the women questioned whether I was really black, after all my father was white [laughs]' (Faith).

Authenticity claims did not only relate to physical attributes, but characterised a whole array of behaviours as black or non-black. A prime area of contestation was that of sexual relationships. As I indicated in the last chapter, few of the interviewees appeared to view 'mixed' relationships as valid. This assumption was made with little acknowledgement of the characteristics which black women might share with white people, such as class or regional background, interests and professional life. It is an attitude seen in its extreme manifestation in a women's centre where one of the nursery staff refused to work with children of mixed origins. A single incident should not be seen out of context of the many centres where black children of mixed origins were welcomed and accepted, however, it does highlight that black women's centres have not been immune to the passionate emotions sparked by issues of so-called 'race mixing'.

The policing of sexual behaviour was nowhere so apparent as in the treatment of lesbian women, particularly in the early days of black women's autonomous organising. Hostility towards lesbian women can be seen within a context of narratives of authenticity which place heterosexuality at the centre of black womanhood. This positioning is in part a response to the role which black women have assumed in defending black children from the vicissitudes of mis-education and criminalisation. Indeed, black children are a key site on which debates over anti-racism and multiculturalism are played out (Sahgal 1992: 183). In this context, lesbian women are constructed as unable to play a role in one of the key battles against British racism. This conceptualisation clearly overlooks lesbian women's involvement with children, both as biological mothers and as other mothers (Lorde 1984: 72–80). Heterosexism in black women's organisations has also drawn heavily on notions of homosexuality as a disease which infuse early twentieth century European medical science: 'There were women in OWAAD, for example, who expressed the view that to be a lesbian was effectively a white woman's disease, that sort of unprogressive view' (Faith).

This analysis is relocated in the context of British imperialism to imply that homosexuality is an affliction which originates in European cultures: 'A lot of the time, we see that as part of the white culture which they introduce into our community and we're not necessarily happy with that' (Misa, Palestinian, black organisation). Discomfort with an 'out' lesbian presence was therefore justified via an appeal to pre-colonial societies which were supposedly free of forms of behaviour associated with European influences. This narrative has homosexuality imported to Africa and Asia in much the same way that syphilis and small pox accompanied the European invaders. It is ironic that the roots of this conceptualisation lie in the same tradition of explaining social deviation through medical classification that led to the 'discovery' of drapetomania, a disease which supposedly led enslaved Africans to run away (Mama 1995).

Lorde points out that homophobia sometimes arises out of fear of ostracism by black men:

Heterosexual Black women often tend to ignore or discount the existence and work of Black lesbians. Part of this attitude has come from an understandable terror of Black male attack within the close confines of Black society, where the punishment for any female self assertion is still to be accused of being a lesbian and therefore unworthy of the attention or support of the scarce Black male.

(Lorde 1984: 121)

Several of the interviewees had been accused of being lesbians by black men seeking to prevent them from organising autonomously. By maintaining the myth that black women's organisations are heterosexual spaces, some black women sought to distance themselves from such allegations. In so doing, they utilised a stereotypical image of white feminism in which white middle class women mulling over their sexuality become a foil to black women's pragmatism, heterosexuality and community orientation. This is illustrated by the comments made in the mid 1980s by black women about a white women's centre: 'People saw it as a form of lesbianism, they saw it as a form of academia. You know, people debating sexuality, people banning men from their lives' (Pat, Caribbean, African Caribbean organisation).

Lesbianism was inextricably entwined with white feminism, which in turn became the reviled 'other'. Thus, while homophobia is in part a response to external pressures, it has also been a strong bonding mechanism, which, in creating a rigid line between 'us' and 'them', built a fragile and exclusionary unity among straight black women at the cost of marginalising lesbian women's concerns and contributions.

CHALLENGING THE CENTRE

By the late 1980s the attempt to define authentic black womanhood was beginning to break down. This was in part a result of regional differences which were becoming increasingly evident as black women from outside London began to assert their unique experiences. Newly formed groups began to criticise national organisations such as OWAAD for their London-centricity:[2]

As a Black Woman with my own experiences of physical/emotional violence . . . coupled with the alienation of growing up largely outside of a Black peer group and Black Women's networks. . . . Yes I've experienced a real alienation from Black Women who I've come into contact with in London, their intolerance to children in 'their space', the exertion and influence of personal power over other Black Womyn. Deemed, less conscious, less aware.

(Akua in We Are Here Collective 1988)

Many black women outside London shared a sense of resentment towards black women from London. They began to resist the automatic assumption that Londoners had a heightened consciousness and therefore were more able to define black women's struggles in Britain. Women moving from London would be received with suspicion and hostility. Such shifts are never linear and coherent. At times, non-London organisations' attempts to resist London-based hegemony would involve a simple inversion of the notion of regional authenticity. In this alternative construction, the non-London experience was seen as more authentic because of the easier access to resources and social mobility in London. However, the early 1990s saw non-London organisations involved in a genuine attempt to invoke a more open and plural notion of black womanhood:

There are the things which have existed in the past and are beginning to be broken down. There's the whole thing about education, the acceptance of educated women (supposed) and the fact that they've never been considered black enough. . . . Or you're an outsider, i.e. not from Coventry, not from Hillfields, you've got a different accent, God forbid a London accent [laughs]. And therefore you're not [pauses] you're perhaps pseudo-black.

(Lynette, Caribbean, African Caribbean organisation)

By the mid 1990s London-based black women's organisations had joined regional groups in rejecting the constraints of limited notions of black womanhood. Above all, this movement was influenced by the suffering that this conceptualisation was causing to all women who were caught outside of its boundaries and a sense that ultimately, no black woman could fulfil the rigid and yet contradictory requirements of authenticity. Many of the interviewees had struggled to distance themselves from a narrow notion of black women's unity based on the suppression of differences between black women:

If people recognise first of all that you're a black woman and I'm a black woman and we have potential areas of solidarity but then we have different concerns, different needs, different requirements, different ambitious ideas and those are valid in their own right, but they're not necessarily going to be all the same as mine. And I must allow you those differences.

(Lynette)

Women seeking to 'allow difference' took three different paths: narrating oppositional black women's histories, celebrating diversity and deconstructing difference. The first tendency involves the interrogation of previous narratives of black womanhood, often accompanied with their inversion. This is evidenced in the displacement of London-centred ideologies locating Londoners at the pinnacle of consciousness by a new narrative which valorised harsher regional experiences. Lesbian women employed similar strategies to reclaim pre-colonial history. In tracing black women-loving women who predate European influence, they refuted arguments that homosexuality is a 'white disease': 'I don't know how many of us know our history. But certainly where I come from, women were allowed to marry women' (Abiola, African, black organisation); and: 'I think that there have always been women loving women and certainly my connections with black lesbians have indicated that there have always been women loving women in our history and it's going on in the Caribbean, it's going on in Africa. It's not public knowledge unless you're part of the in-group' (Brenda, Caribbean, African Caribbean organisation).

The problem with this approach is that it creates an alternative narrative of inclusion and exclusion. Thus, women opposing London-centredness devalue the experiences of women from London. And the legitimacy of black women-loving women in black women's organisations is balanced on their presence within pre-colonial Africa or Asia. While it is important to establish an oppositional history to that constructed by colonial scholars and those who have taken on the task of reinventing black history in ways which support patriarchal and homophobic practices, it is equally important not to base claims for women's or gay rights on the extent to which they were given those rights in pre-colonial history. The possibility of producing such divergent interpretations of pre-colonial history also indicates the extent to which all histories are necessarily partial. This is not to ignore the creative and political potential of historical narratives, but to indicate the need for an alternative way of determining black lesbian women's acceptance in a movement which they have been actively involved in building.

A second tendency is the celebration of difference, although I use this title with reservations, because it retains within it a celebration of commonality as well as a valorisation of diversity. This tendency refutes the notion of black women as an undifferentiated mass, as one interviewee stated: 'Black women don't represent one homogenous blob' (Lynette, Caribbean, African Caribbean organisation). It also involves an attempt to find something other than 'sameness' as the basis of black women's collective action and unity:

> One of the things that we have tended to overlook as black women organising as black women and that is that we are going to have differences . . . and we need to acknowledge differences and respect them. We've tended to want to unify in a way . . . to create a uniform organisation. You cannot do that with such diverse histories coming from such different places.
>
> (Hilda, African, African Caribbean organisation)

These women recognise that the failure to deal with difference, in particular cultural difference, has led to conflicts between African and Caribbean women and between African Caribbean and Asian women:

> One of the things we may not have sufficiently acknowledged, but it came up in the quarrels was that we were culturally different people. We focused so much on black and women that we forgot that some of our differences went beyond that. And so there actually occurred a split, there was a split between African and Caribbean women at one point.
>
> (ibid.)

This recognition of difference leads to the creation of 'hyphenated identities', black lesbian, black African woman, black disabled, and so on (Bondi 1993). It also invokes the possibility of fragmentation leading to the creation of organisations based on ethnic group affiliation. Scholars have attributed the fragmentation of black struggle into its constituent ethnic parts to the divisive tactics of government funders (Hiro 1971; Sivanandan 1990). My analysis points to an *internal* contradiction between emotive cultural ties and a narrative of unity which requires the suppression of difference. This tension has surely played a part in the establishment throughout the late 1980s and 1990s of black women's groups differentiated by racialised, national and religious affiliations. The next section will examine ways in which unity has been forged by black women's organisations in the 1990s utilising a notion of unity in diversity. Here, I shall simply point to the potential for the celebration of diversity to undermine the notion of a shared black womanhood based on common experiences of gendered racism, which has been a powerful mobilising force for black women's community struggles.

The third tendency which black women's organisations have shown in resisting limited definitions is the deconstruction of difference. While the concept of deconstruction has arisen out of a postmodern discourse which has consistently dismissed African, Caribbean and Asian realities, some diaspora intellectuals have attempted to salvage the tools while rejecting the Eurocentric nature of the postmodern endeavour (Rattansi 1994). I prefer to acknowledge that postmodernism has offered little more than what the black experience has been speaking of since enslavement: the fracturing of universalist narratives of stability and identity and the questioning of the dominant epistemological order (Gates 1988; Mercer 1994). Without suggesting that Derrida was the first intellectual to unsettle and question modern certainties, I use the term 'deconstruction' to indicate the process of unpacking identities which are assumed to be fixed and revealing their historically and socially constructed nature. I also imply an interrogation of borders between self and other, a sense that boundaries may be more porous than at first they appear. In this sense, some of the interviewees utilised deconstructionist tools to interrogate the category of 'the black lesbian' in black women's groups:

> You know when you talk about a lesbian woman, almost like it's printed on her head and it's something that she hasn't been through a process. . . . We didn't have labels of who you are because you go through a process and one day you're sleeping with a woman, maybe next day you're sleeping with a man.
>
> (Alekiri, African, African Caribbean organisation)

In questioning who is defined as lesbian, this interviewee implicitly defies a Manichean division between straight and gay, asserting that a woman who is today defined as heterosexual may tomorrow be seen as lesbian. This complexity is not captured simply by the concept of bi-sexuality which is the catch-all phrase used to categorise those that do not fit neatly into the dichotomous configuration of straight–normal/lesbian deviant. In refuting labels, this interviewee rejects the categorisation of sexual orientation

whether into two or three boxes. This view is reiterated by an interviewee who had been actively involved in Brixton Black Women's
Group during the early 1980s, where there was an overtly woman-
loving agenda:

> I think there are some real homophobicness [*sic*] in the black
> community, but black women connected in networking or black
> women supporting and loving each other might not be in lesbian
> relationships, might not call themselves lesbians, but might be
> doing all kinds of stuff [laughs]. There's actually a lot in a label,
> lesbian feels white, women-loving women or Zami.
>
> (Brenda, Caribbean, African Caribbean organisation)

This interviewee expands the discussion of sexuality to include two
formulations of the phrase 'woman-loving', one explicitly sexual,
the other about support and friendship, and indicates that there
may be a continuum of woman-centredness, the subtleties of which
the terms 'lesbian/straight' are unable to capture.

I have called these approaches 'tendencies' to indicate that they
are not rigidly differentiated, nor do they indicate a division of
black women into different camps. In fact, an opinion which at first
glance appears to foreground one tendency, may also be seen to
contain another. This can be seen in the final quotation where the
interviewee counters notions of rigid boundaries between straight
and lesbian black women, while at the same time subscribing to a
simple dichotomisation of black and white women's sexualities:
'lesbian feels white'. This study has shown that there has been a
general shift away from limiting narratives of authenticity and
purity towards more nuanced understandings of gendered racialised
identities. Black women have learnt from previous experiences and
have actively attempted to create more flexible notions of black
womanhood. They have recognised that identities can and do
change over time and have nurtured complex and layered notions of
self within the context of uni-dimensional images of black women.
However, we should avoid creating our own 'master narrative' of
linear progress from simplistic to more complex identifications.
Rather, we can point to the coexistence of often contradictory
discourses of identity, at times determinist, at times more nuanced,
always shaped by the contingencies of material realities and the
need to create strategies for change.

THE BATTLE FOR BLACKNESS

While black women's organisations in the 1990s have begun to forge a more inclusive conceptualisation of black womanhood, 'blackness' itself has become a contested term within the context of British anti-racism. The term 'black' has long been a site of invention and creativity in the British context. Gaining popularity in the late 1960s as powerful images of revolution and change were projected onto television screens in inner city communities, black communities adopted much of the rhetoric of the American Black Power movement. While the project of throwing off the shackles of mental colonisation was not new to those of Caribbean descent in Britain, many of whom were familiar with Garveyism's reassertion of African roots, the term 'Black Pride' resonated in a way which the 'back to Africa' movement did not. This resonance was due partly to the appeal of a diasporic politics of staying, rather than that of return. It was also due to the openness of the signifier 'black', newly invented in the American context to replace the outdated and offensive categories 'Negro' or 'coloured', which could be reinvented to fit a particularly British context. It was in this context that Asian young people were able to rally with those of African descent under the umbrella of 'black struggle' (Hiro 1971; Brah 1996).

Throughout the 1970s and 1980s, 'black' was seen as a forceful unifying term which projected an uncompromising demand for rights and an end to discrimination. Yet by the late 1980s, the term was being attacked by some community activists and social scientists as being little more than a 'coercive ideological fantasy' imposed on Asian communities by zealous anti-racist bureaucrats and leaders[3] (Modood 1988, 1990; Hazareesingh 1986). Tariq Modood (1988), at the forefront of this attack, argues that the term 'black' centres on the African experience, from its origins in the Black Power movement, to the imposition of a current 'Afro political leadership':

> Because as a matter of historical and contemporary fact this positive black identity has been espoused by peoples of sub-Saharan African roots, they naturally are thought to be the quintessential or exemplary cases of black consciousness and understand black consciousness to be at its fullest, something only achieved by people of African ethnicity.
>
> (1988: 399)

The idea of blackness including Asians, it is claimed, sits uneasily with the more 'natural' association of blackness with Africanness. This in turn is reinforced by the predominance of African American cultural production equating black identity with African descent. Modood (1988) points out instances of doublespeak, whereby writers and politicians will slip from 'black and Asian' to black without acknowledging the inherent erasure of an Asian presence. For Modood, the black political project cannot help but position Asians as 'secondary or ambiguous Blacks' (1988: 399), thus creating a new hierarchy even as it seeks to depose the existing racist ordering.

Interviews with members of black women's organisations appear to reinforce some of Modood's findings. Two interviewees stated their view that 'black' did not fit easily with their constituents: 'In the past equal opportunities policies just had white and black, now people prefer to be classified by origins. If we are trying to signify unity, we use Asian' (Mai, Chinese, Chinese organisation). Some of the Asian women who defined themselves as black also referred to the struggle to maintain an open definition of blackness in the face of increasing African American cultural influences:

> When I do read 'black', it's Afro-Caribbean, when I read books and stuff. bell hooks is a classic example, her experience is Afro-Caribbean people [sic], people from Africa in America. But I can still relate to those things. . . . There needs to be more discussion of how to encompass all the differences and not just think, black is that people's property.
>
> (Misa, Asian, black organisation)

Many of the women of African Caribbean origins used the term 'black' to reference women of African descent. This usage was predominant in organisations which were limited in membership to women of African origins. The perspective of some African Caribbean women in an organisation with very few active Asian women members highlights the way in which blackness was sometimes claimed as an exclusive commodity:

> There are a few women who say, well 'Asians say they are not black' and of course a lot of Asians say they are not black. Black is a political term. I tried hard to get the women to use the word 'women of colour', meaning if you identify as black, then, yes, you are part of the group.
>
> (Natalie, Caribbean, African Caribbean organisation)

In a symbolic incident in the mid 1980s, the dominant grouping in this organisation voted to eject the only Asian woman member. In this case, it was clear that some of the African Caribbean women saw the Asian woman as maintaining an ambiguous relationship to blackness. Their acceptance of her while she took a backseat role, quickly turned into intolerance when she became more assertive:

> This is one situation where African and Caribbean women were united in saying 'she's trying to take over'. She's quite a strong woman, very forceful and was too comfortable with being black I think. She had no angst with just being black and being one of the women. I think people resented that: this is an Asian woman, what is she doing taking such as active part in the organisation, she ought to be part of the background.
>
> (Hilda, African, African Caribbean organisation)

However, while the dominant grouping refused to acknowledge the Asian woman's entitlement to full membership, it is notable that many of the members, not least the Asian woman herself, attempted to defend a much broader definition, resulting in a significant split in the organisation:

> All the young women resigned, they left en masse . . . because they said 'we have been brought up in this country, we have gone to school with them, we have fought with them against racism in schools, we do not want you bringing the history from other continents and transferring them here and making that history determine our history here'.
>
> (Hilda)

The division here was not simply between African Caribbean and Asian women, but became a division between younger and older African and Caribbean women. The younger women were embracing an inclusive definition of blackness which stemmed from their experience of a shared struggle against racism. The older women had a different perception, in particular those women who had come as adults to Britain from Southern African countries in which the Asian communities had formed a buffer class to facilitate colonial rule. Histories of bitter antagonism between African and Asian communities therefore shaped the older women's view of the impossibility of real solidarity between African and Asian women in Britain. In several other organisations, the uneasy relationship between African Caribbean and Asian women, characterised by an

African Caribbean interviewee as 'frosty', was described as a source
of tension. Some Asian women expressed anxieties about African
Caribbean women: 'Of course, there are these stereotypes within
our own communities: "Oh no, we can't go near African women,
they'll probably beat us up"' (Manjit, Asian, Asian organisation).
African Caribbean women also expressed barely suppressed bitter-
ness towards Asian women:

> I think that black women, certainly of African Caribbean
> descent have certain issues in relation to Asian women or women
> of the Indian South Asian sub-continent. That conflict is still
> there simmering under the surface. . . . [We've] not been as
> honest as we could be in the sense of how do you express your
> allegiances and wanting allies but celebrate your uniqueness,
> whatever that uniqueness is.
>
> (Brenda, Caribbean, African Caribbean organisation)

This hostility was in some cases a reflection of tensions which
developed between communities at a local level, in particular where
Asian shopkeepers were seen as representative of the Asian community:

> I think African Caribbeans have a strong love–hate relationship
> with the Asian community generally, you know there's the whole
> thing about how . . . black people used to be treated and in some
> cases still are in some Asian businesses. Mind you at [our organi-
> sation], when they had a fete and went to some of the local
> businesses, they got money from some of the Asian shops.
>
> (Lynette)

BUILDING BRIDGES

In the context of this mutual hostility, the project of creating and
maintaining an inclusive notion of blackness as the basis for
common struggles against racism is highly fraught. Yet many of the
organisations studied were involved in the struggle to build unity in
diversity. These organisations saw breaking down barriers between
Asian and African Caribbean women in order to create meaningful
alliances as an important part of their work. The coordinator of an
Asian women's project described her role thus: 'It's about making
those links and, OK, people might be a bit wary to start off with,
but then they'll get into it and they will get used to it. And that

awareness and education process begins' (Manjit, Asian, Asian organisation). Another interviewee described her involvement in an organisation which explicitly made the link between different black communities as having deep personal significance:

> It's changed me. Before, I had a narrow view about different communities and since then I've learnt a great deal. You know, I was suffering silently in what I was going through, in my community, as a Somali person. Now I know that my other brothers and sisters suffered the same. I think if we work together we can do a lot more.
>
> (Umme, African, black organisation)

Similarly, an interviewee who first stated that many Chinese women did not relate to the term 'black', also recognised the strengths of building on the commonalities suggested by blackness:

> I would like to link up with other black organisations. In the past we did not have the manpower and may not have recognised the common experiences of others. Some of us were afraid to expand. The second generation are more open and are trying to respond.
>
> (Mai, Chinese, Chinese organisation)

It has been argued that this process is one of reductionism, whereby Asian people are required to give up their rich heritage, histories and cultures in favour of an identity determined only by their resistance to racism (Modood 1988: 399). This is far from the process described by interviewees who were aware of the need to celebrate differences while maintaining an awareness of the value of organising together. A member of an Asian women's group expressed her position:

> I think African Caribbean communities get on with your work and how you perceive it to be and the best way to be delivered, Asian communities you get on with that. There's no harm with differences, there's no harm with doing things separately, but I think at a certain level, things should be done jointly. And that is the only way to move forward.
>
> (Manjit)

This organisation balanced the tension between black unity and cultural autonomy by organising separately as Asian women, but embracing a black identity as a basis for shared struggles with other organisations, at both the local and national level. They also emphasised the importance of sharing cultural events with the African Caribbean women's group in the same city as a way of building commonalities which went beyond resistance to racism. The desire to maintain cultural diversity was not limited to groups which were formed along ethnic lines. Organisations which had a membership of both Asian and African Caribbean women laid a particular emphasis on working to create a diverse and open conception of blackness. These organisations started from a recognition of shared struggles against racism and imperialism:

> I have a long experience of colonialism which is an experience that I can share with a lot of African women, a lot of Somali women, Yemeni women in terms of experience of colonialism and imperialism. That's my starting-point in terms of solidarity.
>
> We come from a different culture, different heritage, different perspective, but we've got something in common, we're black women and we experience discrimination and we experience racism. What we going to do about it?
>
> (Mona, Middle Eastern, black organisation)

Yet this awareness of common experiences did not translate into an erasure of cultural difference. In this sense, the interviewees did not adhere to the either/or dichotomy promoted by Modood (1988). Many of them identified as black and Asian, black and Somali and so on. This enabled them both to celebrate their specific cultural and historical legacies with each other, and to share a sense of 'sisterhood' arising from resistance to racism:

> I'm quite proud of the fact that I'm a Tamil person, in myself. But that does not cast a big shadow over everything else. I have to look at the reality of where I'm living, where I am. And blackness and black people and living in a white society which is racist is quite important for me.
>
> (Misa, Asian, black organisation)

Brah's research has also identified similar tendencies by Asians to embrace multiple and complimentary identities:

> I have found that South Asians will frequently describe themselves as 'kale' (black) when discussing issues of racism. But since the whole social being of South Asian and African-Caribbean peoples is not constituted only by the experience of

racism, they have many other identifications based on, for example, religion, language and political affiliation.

(Brah 1996: 99)

While social scientists usefully caution us about the contradictions in much present day usage of the term 'black', they often fail to interrogate other categories with the vigour employed to question blackness. Modood is concerned that black activists reify a racist dichotomy between two oppositional 'races':

If anti-racists borrow the racists' classifications in order to defeat racism ('racists have no trouble in saying who is black, so why should we?', it is often said), then, however successful or not they may be as an interest group they will have lost their opposition to racism as a way of thinking. In particular they will have lost the ideal of a multi-racial society for a model of society as composed of two and only two 'races' which for the foreseeable future must live in conflict.

(1988: 397)

He displays no such squeamishness in his usage of racialised categories which far pre-date the post-war formulation of black and white. He therefore rejects black as a 'chimera' while reproducing Asian and African groupings as somehow authentic and natural. This reliance on three distinct 'races' is masked by reference to 'ethnicity' and to historical markers which supposedly define Asianness. Asians are therefore defined as those people who 'believe that the Taj Mahal is an object of their history'. However, as Mason (1990) has pointed out, the term 'Asian' is considered equally problematic by some people to whom it is supposed to refer. Indeed, use of 'Asian' to describe people from the Indian sub-continent is a product not only of diasporic conditions, but of social relations within a specifically British context. In America, in contrast, the term references those of Chinese, Korean and Japanese descent (Takaki 1989).

Finally, I would argue that the numerous scholars and professionals who have rejected 'black' in favour of phrases like 'black and ethnic minority', 'black and Asian', 'Asian, black and minority ethnic' are relying heavily on quasi-biological notions of difference. It is this investment in the notion of the African 'race' which leads such writers to ignore the question of how people of African descent come to define themselves as black. Modood (1988), Cole

(1993) and others (Mason 1990) assume that people of African descent map neatly onto the signifier 'black'. This research has shown that this is not the case. There are as many battles over the turf of blackness among those who share African descent, as between those of African and Asian descent. Furthermore, many people of African descent have rejected the term 'black', traditionally in favour of a national identity such as Jamaican or Nigerian, but also in favour of a continental association, West Indian or African. The rise of Afrocentric and Pan-African ideologies also means that increasing numbers of people of African and Caribbean descent are favouring 'African' over 'black', a change which in turn reflects a rejection of the increasingly dominant use of 'black and . . .' phrases. This shift was reflected in the self definitions of some of the interviewees:

I used to argue for the term 'black' to mean African and Asian, black sections had that, I would still do so. What has happened though in the last four or five years is the term 'black and Asian' has been used increasingly, and I have a tremendous problem with the term. . . . What does present me with a difficulty is that black in conjunction with Asian means effectively African. If white people mean African, they should say African. Why should we be defined by the colour of our skins and not by the rich cultural heritage we came from?

(Faith, African, black organisation)

This discussion reveals that 'blackness' is not the natural preserve of any set of actors. Neither is it likely to be embraced by all members of the diverse communities of African and Asian descent in Britain. However, this should not be a reason to give up on an inclusive definition of blackness. Rather, it is its very oppositionality, its insistence on discussion and explanation which makes 'black' a useful sign. In insisting on using 'black' to reference two groups which have been defined as distinct 'races' and today masquerade as ethnic groups with distinct and immutable boundaries, we create a dissonance which throws up contradictions in otherwise unquestioned 'detached' social scientific categorisation (Mason 1990: 131). 'Black' also refers to a particularly British experience and therefore highlights the way in which histories of oppression, resistance and cultural production have overlapped and nurtured each other in ways which are not reflected in 'black' experiences in other parts of the globe:

My blackness is very specific to living in Europe as well. You couldn't use that in South East Asia or anywhere else. You couldn't use the term Asian in America because it denotes another category of people . . . at the moment the only term I can really think of is black.

(Misa)

COLOUR, CULTURE AND 'NEW' RACISMS

Opposition to the term 'black' is also rooted in concerns about the validity of basing a group identity on the experience of racism. Central to this argument is the assertion that the 'old anti-racism' which posited 'colour-racism' as the primary axis of oppression is outmoded (Anthias *et al.* 1992; Cole 1993). The new forms of exclusion are a complex intermeshing of ethnicity, class and culture which shift the focus from 'race' to nationality, language and religion:

> The more distant an individual or group is from the norm of white upper-middle class British Christian/agnostic the greater the marginality and exclusion. The hostility of the majority is likely to be particularly forceful if the individual in question is a member of a community [which] . . . has a distinct and cohesive value system which can be perceived as an alternative to and a possible challenge to the norm.
>
> (Modood 1990: 91)

The contention that racism based on religion, dress and language is replacing colour racism as the most virulent form of discrimination places Asian communities centre stage in an artificial hierarchy of oppression. This argument lends itself to divisive policy interventions and paves the way for a return to funding regimes which created divisions between Asian and African Caribbean communities because of their emphasis on linguistic and cultural disadvantage. A coordinator of a women's refuge explains how such 'culturalist' ideologies prevented her organisation from accessing funding for African Caribbean women escaping violence:

> It was easier to get money for the Asian community, because where did the money come from? Section 11. And Section 11 was all about language and diet, those wishy washy cultural things, so

it was easier and so that was how it developed. So, African Caribbean women's needs were never addressed.

(Manjit, Asian, Asian organisation)

A more nuanced discussion of cultural racism is provided by Gilroy (1990). Gilroy associates the development of the new racism with the rise of nationalism across Europe:

> We increasingly face a racism which avoids being recognised as such because it is able to link 'race' with nationhood, patriotism and nationalism. A racism which has taken a necessary distance from crude ideas of biological inferiority and superiority and now seeks to present an imaginary definition of the nation as a unified cultural community.

(1990: 75)

This form of racism is linked with the desire to 'put the 'great' back in Britain' (ibid.: 75). Its proponents view the invasion of Britain by alien cultures as the cause of decline and rarely make overt reference to racialised categories. I refer to Gilroy's analysis as 'more nuanced' because he rejects Modood's rather mechanistic notion of culture – dress, language, religion – for an appreciation of its ever evolving nature. While Modood traces Asian cultures back in an unbroken line from 'the civilisations of old Hindustan' (1988: 397), Gilroy (1990) is alive to the creative interactions of the diasporic process which make a mockery of such an assertion. Gilroy suggests that it is black people's exclusion from or supposed opposition to the narratives of law and order, democracy and liberalism used to define Britishness that is the basis of cultural racism. Thus, 'race' is reconfigured in terms of different values, deviant family forms and rigid ethnic boundaries. In this sense, both African and Asian communities form a series of threats to English hegemony.[4]

Proponents of the new cultural racism overlook evidence that racism remains vibrant whether the victim is a highly integrated 'Liverpool born black' or a newly arrived refugee (S. Small 1994; Mason 1990). The shift from old to new, colour to culture is refuted by Small who points out the continuing impact of so-called 'old' forms of racism in fascist literature, racist attacks and institutional violence:

> Discussions of 'new racisms' – subtle, circumspect, indirect – mean that we have tended to forget historically entrenched racialised ideologies – crude, confrontational, direct – which

might, by implication, be considered 'old' racisms; right-wing
hatred, vicious attacks against Black families and homes, police
violence, and more. The belief in the survival of the fittest, and
the so-called rights of the 'white race' to obliterate the other are
far from obsolete .

(S. Small 1994: 98; see also *Voice* 23 April 1996a)[5]

Small also points out the ways in which forms of racism which have
been characterised as 'new' have actually been an integral part of
racist discourse and practice from earlier periods, exemplified by the
Commonwealth Immigration Act 1962 which deployed non-racial
markers to remove citizenship from large numbers of black former
colonial subjects. Small is joined by Rattansi (1994) who utilises a
'postmodern frame' to question the viability of the dichotomy of
old versus new:

It seems clear, on the one hand that without a very detailed
archaeological and genealogical exercise it would be impossible
to grasp the continuities and discontinuities between the two, but
also that a simple old/new binary homogenises such discourse
and delimits its field of application, effectiveness and articulation
in a singularly unhelpful manner.

(1994: 55)

A narrow focus on 'foreign' cultures as a threat to British hegemony
also fails to acknowledge the often contradictory nature of stereotypical discourse which is able simultaneously to embrace the
notion of cultures as alien and as more British than 'the British'
(Rattansi 1994: 63).[6] 'Strong' Asian cultures can shift easily from
threat to advantage, just as assumed African Caribbean assimilation
can be recast as a basis for pathology (Lawrence 1982).

A further problem with the attack on 'colour-racism' is the
assumption that black organisations which utilise 'black' inclusively
believe that racism relates only to skin colour and that cultural or
religious differences are irrelevant. Both Modood (1990) and
Anthias *et al.* (1992) make this assertion, yet these organisations
have made it clear that black is a political colour, not a description
of skin pigmentation:

This is how we define ourselves. These are the reasons, it's political, and what we mean by political is it's not to do with
physiology, it's not to do with your skin colour, your physiology

or pigmentation, it's to do with the types of oppression that you've experienced, primarily racism, institutionalised or face to face racial harassment and how it impacts on your rights.

(Balwant, Asian, black organisation)

As black people, we acknowledge that the black community consists of groups defined by culture, geographical differences, history, sexuality, class, religion and political outlook. Thus, the expression incorporates and describes a lot more than just skin colour.

(Liverpool Black Sisters leaflet 1994)

Thus people who are not phenotypically darkskinned, such as some Liverpool-born blacks, children of mixed origins and groups such as Palestinians have been included within the definition, because they too are part of the resistance movement which has re-created blackness as its signifier.

Nor does this conceptualisation of blackness preclude recognition of the increasing demonisation of Muslims as 'the West's other' (Modood 1994; Anthias *et al.* 1992). In fact, black organisations at the national level have been aware of this trend. The National Black Alliance, a political umbrella group formed in 1994, therefore has as one of its objects: 'to counter discrimination against the religious beliefs of Black communities' (National Black Alliance leaflet 1994). That is, religious discrimination is one, albeit increasingly important way in which racism against black people works.[7] This is consistent with the attempted destruction of African and Asian religious beliefs and practices which was central to the projects of colonialism and enslavement. There is nothing new about racism expressing itself through a hostility to black spiritual expression, and Europeans have cast Muslims as warlike 'infidels' at least since the Crusades. This is not to claim that all Muslim organisations embrace the notion of blackness. The Muslim women's group interviewed as part of this study rejected references to 'race' on the grounds that Islam knew no 'races': 'You can be a black Muslim, you can be a white Muslim, you can be whatever. We don't see it from a racial point of view because Muslims can be any race, any culture' (Zaheda, Middle Eastern, Muslim organisation). Despite her desire to move beyond 'race', the difficulty of talking about racism without acknowledging racialised categories was indicated by the fact that the interviewee subsequently made references to women as 'West Indian', 'black' and 'Indian'. The interviewee identified religious discrimination and racism as two different forces, the former affecting both black and white Muslims in different ways:

> I think if you are a black woman, there is a lot of discrimination. If you dress as a Muslim, there is a lot of additional discrimination. We find that a lot of West Indian sisters, yes, it's very, very difficult for them to get a job once they start dressing as Muslims. Because there is no protection on the basis of religion here.
>
> (ibid.)

The interaction of discrimination based on racialised groups and that based on religious affiliation was therefore seen as creating a point of particular vulnerability for African Caribbean women. But this did not imply, as Modood (1994) asserts, that religious discrimination is replacing that based on racialised groupings, rather than the two having a unique simultaneous effect.

Rejecting the binary, old/new, colour/culture, race/religion, does not require that we insist on the unchanging nature of racism. Rather, that we are alive to the ways in which racisms – a plural becomes essential here – utilise gendered discourses of nationhood, culture, religion and phenotype in different ways at different moments. It reveals the highly flexible nature of racist justifications, which are able to adapt to new environments and therefore alerts us to the need for ongoing re-evaluation of our assumptions and practices. I shall return to S. Small's (1994) dogged defence of 'the colour line' in the forthcoming section on essentialism. First, I shall turn to the work of Anthias *et al.* in order to illuminate the role of the state in the creation and maintenance of racialised definitions.

PLAYING THE FUNDING GAME

Anthias *et al.* (1992) bring to their analysis of anti-racism empirical research into black voluntary organisations and local government funding processes in a southeast London borough. This empirical grounding enables them to make detailed commentary on the processes of consultation and cooption which surround the local politics of 'race'. The role of the state in supporting or contesting black as an inclusive category has been noted by other commentators. Sivanandan (1990) accuses the state of utilising the age old tactics of divide and rule to split black struggle into its ethnic components by funding community organisations on the basis of ever smaller ethnic divisions. The role of local authorities in reinforcing divisions between black groups was described by some of the organisations studied as a way of weakening and diverting challenges to poor service delivery and racist grant allocation practices. An interviewee described her first experience of community organising outside London in the following terms:

> Coming from outside and seeing Sheffield which is such a small city, but yet has an Afro-Caribbean centre, a Yemeni centre, a Pakistani Muslim centre, a Somali centre, an Irish centre. It just brought up the ethos of divide and rule. . . . Sheffield is a tiny place with a tiny grant aid budget. If you divide it between the different black communities, what you do is make us keep busy fighting each other about the crumbs, the little there is. Instead of looking at the real issue which is lack of funding and resources.
>
> (Mona, Middle Eastern, black organisation)

Retaining an inclusive definition of blackness was therefore seen as a struggle against outside agencies which felt uncomfortable with the criticism of racism implicit in this inclusive usage. One interviewee felt that one of her organisation's key achievements had been:

> That we are still a politically 'black' organisation. That although there have been times when people have tried to divide us along those lines, like trying to make it an Asian women's refuge, that we still are, we do not discriminate, it's for all black women. And I think that's something that we're proud of, that we haven't compromised and we don't intend to compromise.
>
> (Balwant, Asian, black organisation)

However, not all commentators have viewed the state in this way. Modood (1988), for example, sees the state as 'confidently assuming that Asians think of themselves as "black"' and thus being party to the imposition of an 'Afro' leadership via the hegemonic discourse of blackness (1988: 402). While examples of inclusive notions of blackness being imposed on the organisations studied was rare, in one instance an African Caribbean women's group which had 'black' in their name, were coerced by their local authority to include Asian women. This was resented by the organisation since there were already a number of Asian women's groups in the city which received funding but did not incorporate women of African descent:

> We needed to be seen to incorporate more of a broader scope of women. I don't think we need it, but when it comes to filling in our grant forms it was usually asked, 'well, what group of women were incorporated?'. So, if they felt black and wanted to be a part [pauses] although they have their own groups really.
>
> (Ngozi, African, African Caribbean organisation)

The local authority's imposition was not accompanied by an increase of resources to tackle the larger constituency. It also threw up contradictions in the authority's funding policy since it recognised racialised group membership as a legitimate basis for organising in the case of Asian women, but not in the case of African Caribbean women. This, then, reinforced the notion of Asians being 'optional blacks', which unlike Modood's conceptualisation of 'ambiguous blacks', points to the benefit of being able to slip in and out of blackness. A less contradictory approach may have been to ask the group to be more explicit about their membership being of African descent only, or to increase the group's resources to enable them to cater effectively for a much bigger and more diverse constituency.

These examples reveal the material basis of the battle for blackness. When Mason (1990) suggests that we should reject the term 'black' because it is 'unnecessarily offensive' he ignores the material relations which determine whose offence is taken seriously (1990: 130). The numerous black organisations and individuals who are likely to consider 'non-white' (Modood 1994) or 'people who are not white' (Mason 1990) a derogatory reassertion of the centrality of whiteness are not considered by either writer. Anthias *et al.* (1992), in their description of 'black' as a signifier of eligibility for state funding and positions on consultative committees, usefully reinscribe power and resources into the struggle for nomenclature. They therefore point out that with local authority appropriation of the term black in the 1980s:

> Blackness stopped to be [sic] politically just a category of resistance, and became also a system of power brokery; it stopped being just a form of solidarity, and became also a divisive category in competing for and holding on to funds and other resources.
>
> (Anthias *et al.* 1992: 145)

The authors trace the adoption by local authorities of black as a signifier of racialised groups subject to racism to a generation of 'Black militant intelligentsia' which entered local authorities in the 1980s and rejected the previous regime of multi-culturalism. Blackness thus went hand in hand with state anti-racism and became the new basis of resource allocation. The 'race relations industry' is central to Anthias *et al.*'s theorising. It comprises: 'The specific laws, statutory and voluntary organizations which have been established with the specific project of fighting racism in Britain' (ibid.: 156). According to the authors, this industry has come to dominate political power and material resources in the anti-racist struggle. In so doing, it has reified the 'black community' as a self contained and homogenous entity which is unaffected by axes of oppression other than racism. Even more seriously, it has withheld jobs, political representation and funds from other victims of racism and discrimination, such as Jews, refugees and other non-black minorities.

Anthias *et al.* create a grand narrative about the interaction of 'black militants', voluntary organisations and local authorities which fails to capture the heterogeneity of local authorities or the specificities of local political processes. The above illustrations show that far from taking a unitary approach to the term 'black' as a basis for the allocation of power and resources, local authorities continue to take up diverse positions on the continuum between ethnic pluralism and anti-racism. Thus, interviewees reported that Sheffield city council has adopted a primarily multi-cultural approach to funding the voluntary sector, whereas Cambridge city council has promoted cross-ethnic alliances. Anthias *et al.*'s (1992) analysis relies on research data from London, yet they do not acknowledge the role of the Greater London Council (GLC) in creating a unique situation for black organisations in London and in employing large numbers of black people. While some local authorities emulated the GLC model, others explicitly rejected what they saw as 'loony left' funding regimes in London. This means that for many black community groups in areas such as west Yorkshire, Lothian and the northeast, accessing funds under the umbrella 'black' is a difficult or impossible process. Similarly, while some local authorities used Section 11 as an easy option to buy out black discontent, others have shown a marked reluctance to fund any independent projects and have utilised their Section 11 funds to create supplementary teaching or social work posts within departments (1992: 180).

A further weakness in the authors' argument is their unwillingness to make distinctions between local authority workers and units, white managed voluntary organisations serving black communities and black managed community organisations. In utilising the concept of the 'race relations industry' as a homogenous mass, they erase the great diversity of strategies, ideologies and practice within these different entities. In so doing, they create the false idea of consensus between local authorities and black voluntary organisations, with the latter gaining political representation via committees and consultative processes. In most local authorities, however, consultation processes are uneven at best and fail to involve the vast majority of black community organisations unless these are highly organised (Qaiyoom 1992, 1993a).

Anthias *et al.* (1992) therefore misrepresent the relationship between black community organisations and the local state by implying a greater level of collusion and congruence of objectives than actually exists. They suggest that many black projects are set up as a response to funding opportunities and therefore speak to a local authority agenda rather than community needs. The assertion that black projects are funding-led is not supported by this research (1992: 182). Rather, many of the organisations studied displayed great creativity in describing activities which they wished to carry out in terms which were acceptable to funders. The public face, whereby an activity may be described as a new project in order to access 'seed funds', should not be confused with the organisation's private agenda. Furthermore, Anthias *et al.*'s analysis fails to acknowledge the role of other funders which may have agendas which do not coincide with the local authority. Black community organisations, particularly those that have historically been unable to rely on the GLC, are skilled at juggling the demands of a range of funders, at the local, regional, national and international level, including charities,[8] regional offices of government,[9] the National Lottery Charities Board[10] and a number of European funds. Where such organisations do respond to a range of funders, these may conflict with the local authority's agenda. One case study organisation which had previously been funded by the local authority to cater for Chinese women, found with National Lottery funding that they were expected to cater for the whole community:

> In the past we always concentrated on women's issues and educa-
> tion, but because the National Lottery insists on equal
> opportunities, we have to open up to men and women. It's
> changing things because of the need for money.
>
> (Mai, Chinese, Chinese organisation)

In this case, losing local authority funding threatened the organisation's ability to stay true to their original objectives. There is
seldom much congruence between the terminology or political
projects of these diverse funders and as such, a causal relationship
between the objectives of a black organisation and any one funder
rarely develops. Finally, black community organisations have an
agenda which encompasses much more than challenging racism
within local authorities. To award them an unproblematic position
within the 'race relations industry' is to ignore the range and
breadth of developmental activities from exploring holistic remedies
for mental ill health to recording oral histories of black elders.
Anthias *et al.*'s rejection of 'blackness' on the grounds that it has
created a new hegemony in which black voluntary organisations
and professionals collude with the state in order to exclude non-
black minorities therefore inflates the power of the former and fails
to see the myriad ways in which black struggles for self determination continue to be undermined and resisted by some arms of the
state, even as it appears to support anti-racism in other arenas.

ANTI-ESSENTIALISM: A NEW ORTHODOXY

The defence of blackness is set uneasily against the backdrop of a
highly fraught debate in academic circles on the uses or abuses of
essentialism. At the forefront in rejecting essentialist notions of
blackness in Britain have been black artists and cultural critics fret-
ting at the imposition of codes about what constitutes authentic
black cultural production and chafing at the 'well-policed borders
of black particularity' (Gilroy 1993: 6; Hall 1992). Typical of this
conceptualisation of diasporic identities is Jantjes' (1993) image of
the 'cultural salmon'. Ambiguous, cunning, adaptable, the salmon's
subjectivity is contingent and fluid:

> The salmon's journey upstream is synonymous with the migra-
> tion of African artists to the centre; a transgression of cultural
> borders; an alteration of their physical, geographic and intellec-

tual positions. It is a dangerous journey which will have many casualties.

(Jantjes 1993: 105)

Contrast Jantjes' salmon with the following anecdote from Asante, taken from an African saying. Uproot a log and throw it into a lake, he says, but however long you leave it there, it will not turn into an alligator (Asante, conference speech, April 1993). Uproot an African, ship her to the United States, and she, by association, remains true to her essential self, an African.

Slippery, shifting, disappearing into the dappled shade of the water, the salmon represents the new orthodoxy on the nature of diasporic identities. That identity is no longer static, rooted, but shifting, rhizomatic[11] and hybridised (Bhavnani and Phoenix 1994; Mercer 1994). It is quickly becoming a new academic hegemony, reflected in Bhavnani and Phoenix's statement that: 'The notion of identity as a static and unitary trait which lies within human beings, rather than as an interactional and contextual feature of all social relationships, has been laid to rest' (Bhavnani and Phoenix 1994: 9). It is also reflected in Hall's pithy pronouncement of the 'end of the innocent notion of the essential black subject' (1996: 443). To go against this new orthodoxy in talking about racialised and gendered identities is to risk academic ostracism. Stating that identity may in fact be rooted and historically shaped is little more acceptable than stating that the world is flat and invites labelling as at best outmoded. While this shift originated in the desire to decentre the 'universal' white subject, it has become a whipping post on which to flagellate non-conformist black academics. In a neat sleight of hand, it is black academics seeking to resist the new orthodoxy who are labelled racist, so that scholarship which seeks to identify African diasporic cultural retentions is pushed into the ghetto, only to be aired occasionally as a straw figure, set up to reinforce an oppositional argument (Asante 1993: 1–2).

Yet at a time when Minister Louis Farrakhan, the prominent and controversial leader of the Nation of Islam, can gather audiences of thousands of young African and Caribbean people in London to listen to his powerful rhetoric, and when a surge in anti-Islamic feeling has created a countersurge of Muslim revivalism, this new orthodoxy has made few inroads into popular movements and explanations of identity. Ironically, while the number of black academics writing about identity has never been equalled, the division between black popular culture and politics and academic debates seems to have become a chasm.

One example from the organisations studied will serve to illustrate the limitations of postmodern explanations of identity in a practical context. Hall's (1992) privileging of the discursive realm is an example of the way in which postmodernism claims to release us from the strictures of identities based on the Manichean dichotomies of white/North/male and black/South/female: 'It is only through the way in which we represent and imagine ourselves that we come to know how we are constituted and who we are' (1992: 30). These divisions, it is implied, are 'in the mind' and thus we can unlearn them by thinking 'postmodern' and resisting the discourses of knowledge/power which restrict us to our racialised and gendered boxes. How this mental freedom will be translated into material reality, and who has the privilege to cross borders is less often discussed. A number of women who are supported by Akina Mama wa Afrika, an African women's organisation, exemplify this problem. These Nigerian women had sought to flee the boundaries of 'race' in a highly practical way:

> We decided to run a campaign to get those who have not started its use or are in the early stages. We sent posters to African NGOs and began a dialogue on the issue. It's more of a problem in Africa, but you still have access to the creams in the UK. It's an environmental issue, they claim the creams are for blemishes, but they should not be allowed. Women use them due to the internalisation of the hierarchy of beauty and aesthetic acceptance. Black women experience that whitening up helps in order to move up in society.
>
> (Ifi, African, African organisation)

Women in Nigeria use bleaching creams in pursuit of light skin privilege and in the hope of escaping impoverishment (Amamoo 1993). However, these women were not able to escape their socio-economic location and had in fact come to the organisation's attention because they were incarcerated in British prisons for carrying drugs, often internally as 'mules'. Once their 'liberty' to access the necessary bleaching creams was curtailed, the women experienced distressing after effects as their skin, damaged by the mercury content of the cream, began unevenly to return to its previous tones.

A postmodern frame has little to say to the material realities which structure this account of economic and power inequities between north and south, of the economic restructuring imposed on West Africa which has led increasing numbers of women to risk their health and liberty, of the biological reality of skin tone, of the continuing hegemony of European beauty standards which plagues both African and Asian communities.[12] Tackling the complex web of factors which leads to such self mutilation is far more than 'politics as a therapeutic activity' (Gilroy 1993: 188). On the contrary, a politics which fails to speak to the need for healing and the psychology of beauty as well as the material and social effects of racialised hierarchies and boundaries, is unlikely to engage the imaginations of black women in Britain.

The failure of the majority of black scholars to speak accessibly to the concerns of black communities is reflected in the ever increasing numbers of African Caribbean women who attend the annual Education of the Black Child Conference, hosted by Kemetic Education Guidance, an Afrocentric community organisation from Manchester.[13] The keynote speakers at these conferences are usually African Americans such as Molefi Asante, Leonard Jeffries and Marimba Ane. What do these Afrocentric scholars have to offer which 'homegrown' academics lack? Afrocentricity, according to Asante whose works make up a major part of the Afrocentric canon, is 'not a matter of color, but of perspective, that is orientation to data' (Asante 1993: 3, 1990). This orientation relocates Africans from the margins of European history to the 'centredness' of their own subjectivity:

> Essentially the centric perspective holds that all experience is culturally grounded, but that one is most centred psychologically when experiences are viewed from one's cultural and psychological centre. . . . Not to be centred means that you exist at the margins.
>
> (Asante 1993: 8)

Afrocentricity offers people of African descent, dislocated through slavery and colonialism, a sense of origins, of history and of belonging. It is particularly appealing to African Americans and African Caribbeans in Britain, countering the assumption that Africans in the diaspora have lost all cultural links to Africa (Asante 1990). Afrocentricity seeks to offer a 'groundedness' from which to begin rebuilding a community decimated by poverty, violence and discrimination. It creates a common ground on which

Africans in the diaspora can come together to relearn trust and build community-based strategies of regeneration:

> Black women's actions in the struggle for group survival suggest a vision of community that stands in opposition to that extant in the dominant culture.... Afrocentric models of community stress connections, caring, and personal accountability.
>
> (Collins 1990: 223)

However, this very groundedness jars with the new discourse on identity. Identity is supposed to be shifting and ambiguous, not centred and secure. Non-Afrocentric scholars question the nature of this 'centre': is it not a mythical, non-existent Africa, reconstructed and homogenised by American scholars for their own purposes; is Afrocentricity in fact the new colonialism?

> Of course, the identification with Africa, on which that Americocentricism is premised, is necessarily partial and highly selective. Contemporary Africa, as I have said, appears nowhere. The newly invented criteria for judging racial authenticity are supplied instead by restored access to original African forms and codes.
>
> (Gilroy 1992: 307)

Many of these authenticity codes are in fact gendered. A return to 'African' principles and forms of social organisation also implies a return to traditional gender roles in which men undertake responsible leadership and women carry out nurturing functions. Much is made by Afrocentrics of their opposition to 'Western' concepts of domination and disrespect for women (Kunjufu 1993; Asante 1990: 9, 1993: 8). This must be seen in the context of African American communities in which there are high numbers of single parents, male violence is prevalent and 'macho' posturing, epitomised by gangsta rap music, has often replaced the ethic of male responsibility (Omolade 1995; hooks 1994b). The emphasis on male familial responsibilities and on respecting black women is therefore more a response to a community with deep gender rifts and recriminations than a return to any historical social system. The reinsertion of 'clearly defined roles mediated by various rites of passage' (Asante 1993: 8) is seen as an antidote to the sexism and misogyny endemic in advanced capitalist societies. Afrocentrism can therefore be seen in many ways as a theory of African manhood, in which benign patriarchy is presented as a counter to the pattern of criminalisation, alienation and violence which is ripping diasporic communities apart on both sides of the Atlantic.

Afrocentricity's weakness, then, is in its positioning of traditional gender roles and sexual codes as the answer to the increasing dissolution of African diasporic family life. While strengthening family support networks as a basis for strong communities is essential in order to counter the increasing reliance on women to shoulder the emotional and economic burdens of childrearing, the implicit lack of flexibility in the understanding of what constitutes 'family' points to a politics of exclusion (hooks 1995: 244–5; Omolade 1995). In the equation of family with heterosexuality and women with childrearing, it is unclear where lesbians and gays, or women who are infertile or do not wish to dedicate their lives to children fit in.

The return to a sense of roots as the basis for building strong communities is not restricted to African Caribbean communities in Britain. As we have seen, Modood (1990) also promotes the return to a highly selective narrative of Asian history as a basis for:

> An identity which, on the one hand, is capable of fostering pride in our historical heritage and ethnicity and, on the other hand, which can earn us the respect due to us in British society by virtue of the hard work and disciplined commitment that we or our parents have made in establishing ourselves in this country.
>
> (1990: 403)

The renewed popularity of 'traditional' religious identities among Asian young people, the increase in rigid policing of girls and women in Muslim and Sikh communities, and the revival of practices such as single sex schooling, is further evidence of this trend in 1990s Britain.

In the light of the political and emotive power of racialised, gendered religious identities rooted in discourses of tradition and origins, some scholars have attempted to hold in tension the desire to be 'centred', and the desire to move beyond limiting boundaries of self. The concept of 'strategic essentialism' coined by Gayatri Spivak (1987: 205) speaks to this tension, and is explored by Liz Bondi (1993) in her discussion of identity politics:

> This conceptualisation seeks to avoid the essentialism implicit in appeals to authentic identities while acknowledging that we cannot do without identity altogether. It defines identity not in

the realm of real essence, nor in the realm of a received mythology, but in the realm of a context-dependent creativity. In other words, fictions of identity are essential, and essentialism (humanism) is deployed strategically rather than ontologically.

(Bondi 1993: 96)

Gilroy (1993) too seeks to side step the new anti-essentialist orthodoxy by proposing 'anti-anti-essentialism', as a more acceptable positioning. However, his fervent opposition to any project which builds on the idea of centredness reveals the difficulty of turning such a position into practice. S. Small (1994) returns the debate to practical ground in his writing on black organisations. Rather than describing black community politics as naive and misguided, he seeks to learn from the strategies which black organisations have learnt to deploy. Thus, Small advocates the strategy of embracing racialised identities in a way which recognises and utilises their strengths:

> By racialised identities, I mean building on the strengths of Black organisations, mobilising Black people around common goals, and forming alliances with other racialised groups on the basis of our terms and priorities.
>
> (1994: 199)

The notion of 'embracing' implies a much more knowing mediation of notions of identity than has been ascribed to black community organisations. Similarly, this study indicates that black women's organisations are selectively utilising histories and narratives of 'race', gender and the black struggle in order to create a common basis for resistance. Thus, exclusive notions of ethnicity and nationality will be interwoven and interchanged with inclusive notions of black struggle to create identities which enhance specific struggles.

LEARNING THE LANGUAGE OF BLACK WOMEN ORGANISING

If we cannot identify a unitary basis for black women's organising, how can we capture the commonalities of black women's organisations in different spatial and temporal locations? The extreme reductionism which would have us talk about 'women's organisations which are not white' (Mason 1990), does not satisfy the desire to see black women's organisations directly, rather than through the refraction of what they are not. S. Small's notion of embracing 'racialised identities' does not delve beneath the surface to inform us what the identities to which we refer are made up of. How can we move beyond what we are not [white] and what we resist [racism] to what we are and what we do?

I suggest that blackness is neither created by racism (that is, non-white), nor is it the expression of an essential racial self. Instead, we need to acknowledge that blackness within the British context has been formed by thirty years of political thought and community activism and stands on a legacy of anti-colonial resistance. Radical discourses, while not passed on intact and unchanged, are nevertheless not forgotten (Mama 1995). Ideas and beliefs are passed on via books, newsletters, conferences, the black press and through meetings and discussions. These discursive media have combined to give black women in autonomous organisational contexts a unique language[14]. A review of literature and interviews with black women's organisations reveals five distinct codes within a larger narrational framing shared by black women organising autonomously.

The first code is an organic commitment to the creation of empowering structures and avoidance of top-down decision making. The organisations studied were all invested in working in non-oppressive and non-hierarchical ways. This was viewed by some of the interviewees as unique to black people:

> I think we are a very creative people and it is white people that impose structures and hierarchies and doing things in a particular way. They compartmentalise everything into slots. Whereas we are a creative people and don't need to take on that type of structural organisation
>
> (Alekiri, African, African Caribbean organisation)

and was thought to have originated in the women's countries of origin:

> Collectivism itself is an alternative to male patriarchal perspectives, isn't it. It's togetherness, equal participation and equal distribution of information and decision making. . . . Collectivism has been working for many years in what some people may call Third World countries. I'm a Tamil, so I recognise my roots in that.
>
> (Misa, Asian, black organisation)

However, the desire to avoid hierarchies did not necessarily evolve into overtly feminist models of organising. Of the twelve organisations interviewed, only two utilised collectivist structures whereby all staff were paid the same and shared decision making. Both of these had evolved out of white women's refuges and identified the pressure imposed by the Women's Aid Federation[15] to retain such structures as criteria for membership. Despite this pressure, one organisation was in the process of adopting a pyramid staffing structure. A worker from this organisation questioned the relevance of formal collective systems to black women who were not seen as having the luxury of giving up power. Several interviewees pointed to the failure of collective working to provide dynamic leadership and decision making: 'In a collective the buck doesn't stop with anybody in particular, it just goes round and round and round. Until you just get fed up and say "I'll do it"' (Balwant, Asian, black organisation). And an interviewee who had worked in a primarily white collective questioned the reliance on formal structures rather than on deep felt mutual respect as the basis for equality:

Having worked in a women's centre for eight and a half years, the kinds of conflict which I saw arising over the most basic decisions and even their notion of collective working created so many problems. There never seemed to be that fundamental, kind of, is it sisterhood? There wasn't that fundamental togetherness that enabled them to respect each other's views.

(Sonia, Caribbean, African Caribbean organisation)

For these organisations, ideals of empowerment and equality coexisted comfortably alongside the need for leadership. These organisations developed fair and equitable leadership, the 'strong black woman' who uses her power to nurture other women, rather than to impose authority. One such woman described her role thus:

I perceive it in the sense that I think that people look to me for direction and I do have quite a lot of power and I do have quite a considerable control over the organisation. But what I try to do is to be equitable with that and actually distribute and empower other members in also having a role and taking part. And I really don't mind taking a backseat and watching somebody else sitting at the front making a speech.

(Manjit, Asian, Asian organisation)

The refusal of many black women's organisations to take on explicitly 'feminist' structures, has led to the assumption that they are less willing to challenge patriarchal ways of working. This analysis reveals that black women are in fact tuning into a far more nuanced understanding of power, a discourse which recognises its 'two faces'. Rather than rejecting all overt manifestations of power, they attempt to balance the need to oppose abuses of power with the desire to enable women to experience control and authority: 'We are claiming back your power, it was yours in the first place and you are just reclaiming what was yours and use it well' (Natalie, Caribbean, African Caribbean organisation).

The second code which is central to black women's organising is the foregrounding of pain and the need for healing. A focus on the material basis of black struggle has led scholars and activists to ignore the emotional damage inflicted by racialised hostility, and to condemn the politics of therapy (Gilroy 1993, Bourne 1987). However, black women's organisations have continually stressed the emotive and the spiritual. The need for healing was seen by interviewees as a pre-requisite to engaging effectively with any external political struggles or campaigns: 'We have to network, we have to link, we have to have world solidarity, but it's very hard to think about world solidarity when you're scared, you're vulnerable, when you've been abused' (Brenda, Caribbean, African Caribbean organisation).

Healing did not only occur through counselling and prayer, but was often considered to be present in music, celebration, poetry, cooking and laughter. Thus, black women sharing space with white women's organisations were often brought into conflict because of their supposed rowdiness, or as Natalie said: 'it's the spiciness'. In asserting that all black women need the space to heal at some point in their lives and in asserting that healing can take place outside of institutional settings, black women's organisations have begun to break down the dichotomy between health and sickness, sanity and madness. In this sense, sickness is seen as a normal response to the economic exploitation, physical violence and emotional abuse experienced by many black women (hooks 1993: 54; M. Wilson 1993).

The third code shared by black women's organisations was the valuing of nurturing over other attributes such as wealth or status. Whereas white feminist organisations were viewed as having rejected the assignation of these characteristics to women, many of the interviewees stressed the capacity of black women to care for each other, and for their communities:

For me that was the biggest difference in being involved in a white women's organisation and a black women's organisation. That community and vibe, we do it our way. I don't think you can easily put your finger on what is doing it our way because each black women's organisation is unique in itself. But we do it with love and care and our gender and race perspective that is unique among black women.

(Brenda)

The role of carers is, of course, problematic; it also involves hours of unpaid, undervalued work. The demand for formal recognition and payment for this unrecognised work was made by one of the organisations studied (Black Women for Wages for Housework 1995; James 1995). While most do not perceive the issue as one to campaign on, in placing a premium on caring, black women's organisations are able to create an ethical base which counters the individualism, greed and materialism characterising 1990s Britain.

The fourth code describes gender relations between black men and women. While attitudes towards men varied, with notable differences between, at one extreme, cultural and social organisations which often took part in mixed gender activities and, at the other, refuges which maintained separate women's spaces, there was nevertheless a shared understanding of the need to challenge sexism in a way which did not pander to racist stereotypes of black masculinity. Interviewees were aware of the risk of being 'used' as ammunition by white feminists in particular who were perceived as hostile to black men:

What they want to talk about is integrating with black women but still having real problems with black men. It felt like they wanted us to support white women against black men which is clearly something that black women are not prepared to do on any level at all.

(Sonia)

An organisation which supported Muslim women was equally keen to distance itself from feminist representations of Islam as an inherently patriarchal religion. The organisation carefully attributed sexist practices to a cultural (mis)interpretation of Islam, leaving the 'true' Islam uncriticised: 'A lot of our clients for example have no idea that they can ask for a divorce and some of them suffer for years thinking this is Islam. We say no, this is culture' (Zaheda, Middle Eastern, Muslim organisation).

Black women who defended black men in the face of attacks from white feminists, saw black women's organisations as a safe space where they could challenge sexism away from the hostile eyes of outsiders. An interviewee who had been active in OWAAD stated:

> I think we have to challenge mindful of the extent to which critical things you say will be used against African men. And we've always done that.... I think we need to ensure we have opportunities for dialogue which are away from the gaze of white people, who like nothing more than to demonise black men.
>
> (Faith, African, black organisation)

I shall investigate the often contradictory relations between black women's organisations and black men in Chapter 6. For now it is adequate to highlight their unique position in resisting, on the one hand, racist pathologisation of black masculinity and, on the other, black male dominance and aggression. This tension has led black women's organisations to reject accusations of 'airing dirty linen in public' while nevertheless countering attempts by white people to coopt their dissent in ways which undermine black communities as a whole. It is a delicate balance which draws fire from both sides (Fernando 1993: 8).

The final common thread is the drawing together of womanist histories and mythologies of emancipation into a narrative of inspiration and hope. Black women celebrated freedom fighters and inspirational figures such as Jayaben Desai, Begum Rokeya, Claudia Jones and Yaa Asantewaa in posters and T-shirts.[16] Buildings were named after Sally Mugabe and Maya Angelou. Many Asian women's organisations also drew on religious icons embodying female strength such as Mahishasura Durga and Shakti[17]. In this way, historical and spiritual figures from diverse temporal and geographical locations were remembered and celebrated. The importance of naming was exemplified in the history of one group which had fought with white women's organisations over the name of a shared building. The white women wished to name it 'The Women's Centre'. The African Caribbean women challenged the supposed universality of this name and instead fought successfully to have the building named after Mary Seacole. Naming was not the only way of celebrating the contributions of black women:

many organisations had courses on black women's history and creative writing. And interviewees frequently mentioned the inspiration of women like Angela Davis, Audre Lorde and bell hooks (United States), Sistren Posse (Jamaica), Amrit Wilson and Kiranjit Ahluwalia (Britain), as well as goddesses such as Isis (Kemetic), Oya (Yoruba) and Kali (Hindu). The invocation of those who have been before us as a source of inspiration and strength is the basis of libation ceremonies, a resurgence of which can be noted in African Caribbean women's organisations which participate in Afrocentric celebrations and conferences. This vital connection provides a transmission of radical thinking and a remembrance of activism which reinforce present day struggles.

In characterising these common strands as codes within a socially and culturally constructed and transmitted body of knowledge, rather than as the immutable characteristics of black women's organisations, I hope to imply their narrational, visionary quality. That is, not all black women's organisations succeed in actively empowering their members, and certainly few can claim to have achieved such a goal uniformly with all women. However, the ideal of empowerment is common to all of the organisations studied. At different times, these narratives will interact with the lived materiality of voluntary sector politics or economic disenfranchisement to create outcomes which were never intended. At other times, women become entangled in the very contradictions of their own narratives. Women spoke of the ways in which these ideals turned sour. Resistance to bureaucracy could mask hidden codes and silent sanctions:

> I compare and contrast with trade unions where they've got twenty standing orders that they use and if they don't like the secretary, then they vote no confidence in the secretary and people put their hands up and you know which bastards are against you. OK so we don't buy into those structures, that way of working. . . . Women's collectives [have our] own set of rules, you just have to guess them first. And I think that's even more scary.
>
> (Abiola, African, black organisation)

The desire to empower all black women could lead to a failure to manage conflict or deal effectively with staff inadequacies:

> Black women don't get rid of other black women. So there was a whole big issue around sisterhood which split the committee in

terms of us doing something that was right for the organisation and the community which flew in the face of the politics of black women organising. It's about another black woman that ain't that good and do you look at the greater good or not.

(Brenda)

The ideal of strong black women 'doing right by their communities' could impose impossible pressures on women who were expected both to lead and to nurture, reinscribing the mythology of the 'superwoman' and reinforced by narratives of black heroines who always 'did the right thing' (Wallace 1978; Omolade 1995). These narratives could lead to 'burn-out', exhaustion and unrealistic expectations (Essed 1996: 96):

We talk about Nzinga, Yaa Asantewaa and Harriet Tubman and I'm thinking, well, did these women ever mess up? Did these women ever say something that seemed outrageous in terms of black women? I'm sure they did and we need to search that out, so that we can use that more effectively as role models and learn to handle our own differences and our own weaknesses and failings.

(Lynette, Caribbean, African Caribbean organisation)

Women who turned to black women's organisations for healing, sometimes found that they needed time away from these very organisations in order to heal from the painful arguments and hostilities which could develop. Some saw these painful conflicts as a necessary 'birthright' for women trying to break the mould in the context of immense opposition and limited resources:

There was a lot of fighting and that's my memory of how things happened. I don't mean physical fights, but disagreements, arguments and quarrelling. I think it had a lot to do with a completely new idea in Cambridge. We had never been a part of this and it was part of the development, part of the birthright almost that we had to go through this kind of fire in order to establish what it was we were about.

(Hilda, African, African Caribbean organisation)

Finally, women spoke of the difficulty of handling the disappointment when the ideal is not attained, when other black women act in ways which undermine our humanity, when the desire for personal empowerment becomes a destructive hunger for power.

They spoke of the difficulty of recognising that black women can fail to be what we might hope them to be without succumbing to disillusionment:

> Black women have been my best friends and my worst enemies and maybe some part of the problem, of overcoming, is to allow for difference. Not having a list of expectations of what black women are supposed to be ... and to allow for our weaknesses. Because I think we come together and we're bowing to that kind of stereotype of ourselves that we're supposed to be super-woman, we're supposed to have it together.
>
> (Lynette)

Handling disappointment, balancing the tension between the ideal and the reality of black women's organising, rejoicing in those moments when the two appear to gel, is the common language of black women's organisations in Britain.

CONCLUSIONS

Black women have come together to explore shared experiences of gendered racism and class exploitation and have created a new politics which does not demand the artificial separation of integral threads in the web of their oppression. In speaking 'as black women', they have revealed the hidden 'white male' behind universal projects of social organisation, the silent 'white' behind feminism's universal 'woman'. Yet in creating a standpoint 'as black women', a new tension arises. When we place the black woman at the centre, new margins are formed. Those women who do not quite fit the mould of the conscious black woman, women who are betrayed by phenotype, behaviour or sexuality, remain decentred. This is the new contradiction of black women's organising. The empowering discourse of black womanhood risks replacing the universally centred white woman with an equally unattainable image of the conscious black woman. African Caribbean women set themselves up to follow in the footsteps of a mythical Nzinga, the omnipotent, compassionate African queen. Asian women are expected to embody the spirit of Kali, strong, assertive and indestructible.

Black women organising have not been unaware of the problems inherent in this failure to allow for human diversity and frailty. From the late 1980s they have attempted to challenge the notion of the 'ital' black woman, to allow for difference and to celebrate diversity. Central to this project has been the commitment to re-building unity between women of different ethnicities, nationalities and experiences on foundations not of a unitary black womanhood, but of similar histories of imperialism and experiences of gendered racism. 'Black' has been a critical signifier in this project. It signifies not only a shared experience of racism(s), but also a common history and language of organising as black communities in Britain. This common language is often ignored by scholars who focus only on the experience of being 'non-white', as if there were no concomitant history of survival, joy and pain. This research has identified discourses which characterise black women's organising in Britain. They enable us to recognise the commonalities of black women's organisations, while recognising that differing socio-economic, political and ideological environments will lead to new interpretations of these themes. They lead us to look with honest eyes at black women, without the need to idealise or essentialise, but in recognition of the unique spaces of resistance, nurturance and creativity which they have made as they attempted to walk in their foremothers' footsteps.

NOTES

1 The coconut, white inside and brown outside, is used in Britain as a metaphor for black people who embrace English ways of speaking and behaving and act in ways which support the dominant society against black interests. The North American equivalent is the 'oreo', a chocolate biscuit with a cream filling.

2 In the 1991 census, of a black population of just over 3 million, 1.33 million lived in the Greater London Area (R. Bhavnani 1994). The dominance of London-based organisations is therefore based partly on numerical advantage. GLC funding also played an important role in establishing a strong black voluntary sector in London.

3 Despite this attack from some academics and activists, early signs of success by 'Operation Black Vote', a campaign to increase black voter registration, in mobilising Asian communities in London and the Midlands indicates that 'black' continues to be a rallying term well into the 1990s.

4 Black women are constructed as a particular threat: 'First because they are seen as playing a key role in reproducing the alien culture, and, second, because their fertility is identified as excessive and therefore threatening' (Gilroy 1990: 75).

5 In his book *The g Factor*, Edinburgh University lecturer Chris Brand claims than: 'it is a scientific fact that Black Americans are less intelligent that white Americans and the IQ of Asians is higher than Blacks'. Despite protest by Black students, Edinburgh University

upheld the lecturer's right to express his views and declined to take any action in relation to the book ('Book is Withdrawn after Race Row', *Voice* 23 April 1996a)

6 Rattansi quotes the *Daily Mail* headline 'Britain's traditional family is now Asian' as a sign of this ambivalence about Asian cultural values.

7 It is notable, for example, that while vast areas of land in the Midlands and west Yorkshire are owned by Quaker family firms, there is no accompanying panic about this primarily 'white' religion.

8 A number of charitable funders have portfolios of black community projects. These include the Barrow Cadbury Trust which has a racial justice programme and the Rowntree Charitable Foundation which funds over forty black organisations in west Yorkshire.

9 The regional offices of government coordinate the allocation of funds under the Single Regeneration Budget, a fund created in 1992 when a wide range of central government funds to promote inner city development, including the Urban Programme and Section 11 were amalgamated and devolved to the regional level.

10 The National Lottery Charities Board (NLCB) is one of five bodies which distribute the proceeds of the National Lottery introduced by the Conservative government in 1994. The NLCB prides itself on its independence from government and has alienated itself from ministers with its first programme of funding which prioritised anti-poverty initiatives.

11 The term 'rhizomatic' has been adopted by Gilroy (1993: 28) and others from Gilles Deleuze and Felix Guattari (1988: 3–25) to reference the development of cultural knowledge which, like the ginger root or 'rhizome', is not true to any fixed code, but grows in unexpected and unmapped ways (Jantjes 1993: 105).

12 For a discussion of the desire for fair skin among Punjabi women, see Bains (1988: 229).

13 See also Ackah (1993) for an example of Afrocentricity being embraced by a community organisation in Liverpool 8.

14 This assertion owes much to Gilroy's exploration of discourse analysis in the 'vernacular cultural and philosophical formations dispersed through the musics of the black Atlantic world' (1993: 83).

15 The umbrella and support network for women's refuges which was founded by white feminists.

16 Jayaben Desai, who lead the Grunwich Filmprocessing Strike in Brent, 1977 became a symbol of Asian women's militancy; Begum Rokeya Sakhawat Hussain (1880–1932) was a Bengali writer and campaigner for women's education.

17 'Mother' Durga is a Hindu goddess who is featured riding on a lion and slaying the buffalo-demon (Chatterjee 1995: 98); Shakti is a Hindu goddess who personifies collective energy.

Chapter 5

Articulating 'race', class and gender

One of the most contested issues within contemporary sociological theory is the relationship between 'race' and class. Less frequently addressed, but of critical importance is how gender articulates with these two axes of dominance. In the last chapter, I illustrated the importance of recognising difference and differentiation within the category of black women. Class divisions, perhaps more than any other axis of difference, are often obscured within black community organising. Yet class is at the centre of heated debates regarding the validity of autonomous black political organisations versus working class solidarity, the claims that have been made regarding the class allegiances of black professionals, especially women, and about those employed in the 'race relations industry' in Britain. All of these debates require serious interrogation if we are to gain a full understanding of black women's collective agency.

Recent academic research has demonstrated considerable interest in social stratification within black communities in Britain. Previously considered a homogenous 'underclass' experiencing practically universal disenfranchisement from political representation and material resources, 'the black community' is now being divided along ethnic lines. While Chinese, East African Asians and Indians are accessing further education, gaining professional employment and starting up enterprises, African, Caribbean, Bangladeshi and Pakistani communities remain at the bottom of the socio-economic pile (Modood 1994; Anthias 1990: 36). Within the groups located in lower socio-economic positions, some members are progressing into professional and entrepreneurial positions (Jayaweera 1993; Daye 1994). While theorists have indicated the dangers of drawing conclusions from the available data without considering the role of hidden and domestic labour, there is a general consensus that black people are becoming increasingly differentiated along socio-economic lines (S. Small 1994; Miles 1988).

The significance that theorists accord to this increasing stratification varies and is dependent as much on their ideological grounding as on empirical data. Theories about the black middle class tune into an overplayed debate about the determining power of class versus 'race' in structuring relations of dominance. They also tend towards tautology since to discuss the relative primacy of class implies an acceptance of Marxist analysis to the extent that society is divided into 'classes' which have distinct relations to capital[1]. To argue, therefore, that 'race' overrides class can lead to the type of conceptual confusion evidenced in Sharon Daye's claim that the black middle class are a 'class fraction of a racial group', but not a 'racial fraction of a class group' (1994: 287). We are left with the question of what it is that gives this group their 'classness' if they are not a part of the British class system?

'RACE' AND CLASS: FROM ARTICULATION TO FORMATION

This confusion suggests that we are perhaps asking the wrong set of questions (Anthias 1990: 20). Miles (1988, 1993) has suggested that the question of whether class or 'race' ultimately determine social relations is a false one, since while class is an objective category, 'race' is merely an ideological construct with social effects and therefore cannot be given the same analytical weight as the former. From this position, he shifts the focus from the articulation of 'race' and class (S. Hall 1980, Centre for Contemporary Cultural Studies 1982), to how processes of racialisation and ideologies of racism are developed and sustained within the capitalist world system (Miles 1993: 49). While I support Miles' rejection of the term 'race' (except in inverted commas) because of its unavoidably ahistorical and biologistic resonances, I differ from his conclusion that class and not 'race' is a viable category of analysis. This position accords Marxism with the status of a 'privileged science' (Gilroy 1987: 23) which enables the critic to perceive the objective reality behind the Kantian veils of appearance, or in the words of the former, the 'illusions of naturalness' (Miles 1988: 432). As the critic equipped with Marxist tools chips away at the unformed mass of gendered and racialised subjectivities, the pure form of class is revealed. The problem, of course, is that the form was not there waiting to be discovered, but was actually painstakingly created by the sculptor.

A number of scholars have questioned the notion of class as an objective fact. At the forefront of this analysis have been poststructuralists who have portrayed Marxism as a 'grand narrative' based on a realist epistemology which has lost its validity in the (post)modern era (Lyotard 1984; Spivak 1990b). Class cannot therefore be understood outside of the discursive practices which create it. This analysis positions Marxism as 'just another' narrative among many, one that affords primacy to certain actors and erases others. As Spivak points out, Marxism leans always on its origins as a theory of the European working man[2] and thus tends to universalise the experience of white male workers (ibid.: 27). Other political agents may have 'other kinds of dreams' (Parmar 1989). The limitations of poststructuralist analyses have been discussed in Chapter 4. However, placing Marxism alongside other narratives which seek to explain social organisation has been utilised effectively to create a less dogmatic approach to the idea of class. Building on this insight, Anthias points out that neither 'race' nor class can be understood as given, rather, both are constructed within the context of broader social relations (Anthias 1990: 20).

To suggest, as some scholars have, that all Marxist theory posits the working class as a ready made unitary agent is of course a simplification (Gilroy 1987; Ben-Tovim et al. 1986a). Even according to classical Marxist theory, the working class is formed as a political agent through a process of consciousness raising, hence the importance of the Labour movement in creating the working class as a political force, acting in its own interests (Marx and Engels 1965). Hence, also the distinction between the 'class-in-itself' as 'an objective structural phenomenon which exists independently of a consciousness of class position' and the 'class-for-itself' as 'bonded, organised and collectively consciousness agents' (Phizacklea and Miles 1980: 4). Responding in part to allegations of narrow economism, some Marxist scholars have acknowledged the importance of ideologies of racism in the creation of working class actors by suggesting that 'classes' are formed at specific historical moments and will therefore be shaped by the prevailing conditions (Miles 1988; Wolpe 1986). Black political consciousness will therefore be shaped by experiences of racism both within and outside the Labour movement, as well as by black people's experiences as wage labourers (Carter 1986). And in a context in which racism is used to divide the working class, eliminating racist ideology may in fact become a form of class struggle, leading to Stuart Hall's insight that: 'Race may, under determinant conditions, become interiorised in the class struggle' (Hall, in Wolpe 1986: 123).

The problem lies in the limitations of the structure/agency dichotomy which underpins this distinction between the class 'in-itself' and 'for-itself'. The distinction suggests that the closer any form of political action comes to a unified working class struggle, the closer it is to an authentic expression of structural positioning. The priority for praxis must therefore be to remove any barriers to black participation in the (white-led) Labour movement (Castles and Kosack 1985: 505). This position pre-judges black community organisations even before their effectiveness and outcomes are analysed. The question becomes not what the struggle has achieved in itself, but:

> In what way and to what extent do forms of organisation and struggle about race have consequences for the class structure; or, to put this more accurately, do they tend to sustain or to undermine the conditions of existence and reproduction of fundamental classes of capitalist society – capital and labour – and the relations between them?
>
> (Wolpe 1986: 111)

Autonomous action is thus described as an early form of political action which will increasingly cede to class consciousness as black migrants become more invested in the political processes of their adopted country of residence and as the Labour movement rids itself of racist elements (Phizacklea and Miles 1980: 40, 227).

Gilroy (1987) has rejected this 'coat of paint' analysis of racism and has made an important contribution to rethinking the structure/agency dichotomy. He suggests that class formation is determined by a complex and contingent interaction of causalities. While the economic system may determine the field of play, it is the players who determine the outcome of the game:

> The range of possible outcomes within the formation of any particular class may be determined primarily by economic considerations but 'in the last instance' it will be rooted in the results of ongoing processes of conflict. Class in concrete historical conditions is therefore the effect of struggles.
>
> (Gilroy 1987: 30)

In foregrounding agency in this way, Gilroy dissolves the boundary between the class in and for itself by suggesting that class has no meaning outside of struggle. Rather than seeing classes as always objectively there, regardless of how the political actors thus described view themselves, Gilroy suggests that classes are 'only potentially constituted' (ibid.: 31). This 'potential' indicates the retention of some measure of economic structure which thus sidesteps political relativism. But it also demands that we interrogate any project which insists on black and white working class unity as its starting-point. Gilroy thus usefully asserts the radical potential of other kinds of political formation.

SOCIAL STRATIFICATION IN BLACK COMMUNITIES

The class formation problematic is particularly relevant when we seek to understand the role of black people who are beginning to access political power and material wealth. Depictions of the impact of socio-economic stratification in black communities have tended to operate from an often unstated ideological framework. Seldom do they address the particular circumstances of black women, or acknowledge activism which cuts across differences in socio-economic status. Theories of social stratification in black communities in Britain can be divided into four broad categories: liberal, Marxist, those which subsume class to racialised identities and those which are more alive to the articulation of 'race', gender and class. Scholars operating from a (stated or unstated) liberal democratic framework tend to view access to material and political resources by some members of the black community as a sign that black people are becoming accepted as 'equals' (Anwar 1986; Goulbourne 1990; Layton-Henry and Rich 1986). Such studies look at three areas as evidence of socio-economic mobility in black communities: incorporation into the formal electoral process, access to institutions of higher education and the establishment of 'ethnic' enterprises.

According to liberal pluralists, the black middle class plays a key role in first, refuting the damaging image of all blacks as angry, radical and alienated, second regenerating inner city communities and providing employment and third providing 'role models' to inspire underachieving black young people (Jayaweera 1993: 386; McLeod 1991). In this sense, they are perceived as a boon to the black communities, as well as representing the possibility of advancement for all blacks in British society. The limitations of this analysis are clear. These scholars fail to acknowledge the structural barriers of institutionalised racism and economic exploitation, they have an unjustified faith in the political goal of enabling black people to access the existing system and they provide no empirical evidence that the advancement of a small elite actually makes any difference to the vast majority of poor working and unemployed black people. Furthermore, they fail to question the pay and conditions that accompany employment in these 'ethnic' enterprises or to acknowledge the vast amount of unpaid labour by women family members which underwrites the success of many small scale 'ethnic' businesses (Phizacklea 1990). Critically, these writers are undermined by their failure to analyse the gender implications of their data and their failure to investigate in what ways the advancement of black men in political and entrepreneurial positions will translate into gains for black women.

Marxist scholars reject this belief in individual socio-economic progress and look instead to the processes of production for an explanation of the genesis and role of black elite classes. Utilising Marxian definitions, these scholars distinguish between business owners who own capital and the 'petit bourgeoisie' which, like the working class, sells its labour but receives higher material reward because of its professional status. This intermediary class is likely to be coopted in order to support and justify the capitalist machinery and is the model for a plethora of commentaries on black professionals, particularly those that have been employed by the state or by state funded agencies to promote anti-racism (Marx and Engels 1965: 64; Daye 1994: 3–5). Critics have viewed the formation of a black 'petit bourgeoisie' as a deliberate tactic by the state, working as an agent of capital to defuse black struggle (Sivanandan 1974; Emecheta 1986: 141–2). Sivanandan's uncompromising rhetoric on the emergence of this 'class of collaborators' has been particularly powerful:

> There have been protestations that the [Race Relations] Board has failed. Failed for the masses of blacks, yes. But it has succeeded in what the state meant to do: to justify the ways of the state to local and sectional interests and to create, in the process, a class of collaborators who would in time justify the ways of the state to the blacks.
>
> (Sivanandan 1974: 118)

Sivanandan's portrayal of the black 'petit bourgeoisie' appears to owe much to the damning portrait by E. Franklin Frazier (1965: 85) of the black bourgeoisie in the Unites States. Borrowing heavily from Frazier, Sivanandan portrays the British black petit bourgeoisie as shamelessly assimilationist, coveting the wealth, lifestyle and status of the white middle classes (Sivanandan 1990: 119). But in the face of the absence of any evidence to support his claims, Sivanandan's portrayal becomes little more than a caricature, based on some limited observations with a large dose of ideology.

An incisive analysis of the link between black people's class positions and political practice is provided by Miles (1988). Miles acknowledges the significance of racism but denies that these common experiences will be sufficient to cause the black 'petit bourgeoisie' to side with black workers since their interests are ultimately structured by their economic positions:

> Thus, to rephrase a much-quoted passage from Hall, it is not 'race' but racism which, for Asian and Caribbean people, can be the 'modality in which class is "lived", the medium through which class relations are experienced, the form in which it is appropriated and "fought through"'. But I would add that the specificity of this modality is always contextualised by a universality of experience and interest that derives from a common class position.
>
> (Miles 1988: 447)

Miles thus suggests that the growth of the Asian bourgeoisie and petit bourgeoisie is likely to lead to greater affiliation to the Conservative Party and rejects the possibility of an 'Afro–Asian unity' which cuts across class positionalities (1988: 448). He is particularly alive to instances where black workers, particularly women, may be exploited by members of the bourgeoisie in their capacity as employers, although this perception of gendered dimensions to class struggle does not lead him to analyse how the Labour movement may also exclude and marginalise women. Moreover, Miles, like other Marxist writers, is reluctant to deal with instances of black unity which cross class lines. Critics have provided evidence that black small business owners in urban areas will support black community struggles through a common commitment to defeat racism (S. Small 1994: 141, Gilroy 1987: 24). Similarly, black lawyers, teachers, probation officers and social workers have all variously been active in progressive black struggles. For example, the Society of Black Lawyers was active in the campaign against the intimidation and harassment of black people in impoverished areas of east London after the election of a fascist British National Party candidate in 1992; the Association of Black Social Workers and Allied Professions led the campaign to end transracial placements of black children and the pathologisation of black working class families, the Association of Black Probation Officers consistently highlights and campaigns against racism in the criminal justice system and numerous teachers have been involved in the establishment of Saturday schools and in campaigns against 'sin bins' and exclusions. Finally, black women professionals have been involved in the wide range of political activism by black women's organisations examined in Chapter 3. The case is argued effectively by Brixton Black Women's Group: 'Since when did access to education and the fact that we may occupy "middle class" jobs automatically lead to petty bourgeois politics?' (Brixton Black Women's Group 1984b: 88).

The perceived resistance of many Marxist scholars to acknowledging the validity of forms of political activism which are not determined by economic relations is countered by anti-racist scholars who assert the autonomy of 'race' struggles from class conflict:

> We are not convinced that an analysis of racism and/or racial inequality which takes economic laws of capital accumulation, migration, declining rates or profit etc. as its starting-point can contribute very much to the struggle for racial equality. The economy does have a place in the political analysis of race, but its role should not usurp the significance of the political processes to which it is subject.
>
> (Ben-Tovim *et al.* 1986a: 132)

Ben-Tovim *et al.* highlight localised black community struggles around issues which the Labour movement has been slow to acknowledge. They also provide evidence of political strategies which bring together black workers, unemployed and professionals in common opposition to local authority racism. However, their analytical isolation of the political sphere falsely positions racist ideologies within a vacuum, detached and therefore empty of economic content. They thus tend to downplay the material manifestation of racist exclusion. The authors reduce the content of black struggle to anti-racist campaigns directed at local authority resource allocation and limit the goals of such activism to changes in policy. As other scholars have pointed out, this approach homogenises the diverse experiences of black actors and ignores the complexities provided by other axes of oppression (Miles 1988; Anthias 1990). The authors therefore fail to acknowledge the specific experiences of black women and the role of gender in shaping racialised ideologies.

Increasing numbers of writers are undertaking the necessary task of moving beyond the reduction of black political agency to either a narrow state anti-racism, or the expression of 'objective class' position. These scholars do not take a view on the universal primacy of 'race', class or gender, but seek instead to identify how different historical moments will lead to different sets of allegiances taking the fore (Allen 1982; Brah 1996). Thus, Allen recommends 'an agnostic approach to all embracing theories' (1982: 171). Similarly, S. Small seeks:

> To investigate when and where various factors (economics, politics, class as compared with racialised ideologies, stereotypes and hostility) are important (and in the light of the interplay between local, national and international contexts), rather than assuming whether or not one is more important than the others at all times and in all places.
>
> (S. Small 1994: 108)

This approach does not reject economic structures, but places them in the context of other axes of oppression. It is embraced by Marxists, who seek to 'ruthlessly modernize' class analysis and who reject the notion of black middle class actors acting universally in the interests of their socio-economic group (Gilroy 1987: 19). Noticeably, writers in this new tradition display a greater and more consistent awareness of the central role of gender in structuring experiences of racism and class exploitation. Indeed, it is black feminist writers who have been at the forefront in proposing this 'moratorium on producing a global solution' (Spivak 1990a: 30; see also Parmar 1990). Thus, Brah argues that:

> The search for grand theories specifying the interconnections between racism, gender and class has been less than productive. They are best construed as historically contingent and context-specific relationships.
>
> (Brah 1996: 110)

As Bhavnani and Coulson suggest: 'This leads us to examine how "race", class and gender are structured in relation to one another. How do they combine with and/or cut across one another?' (Bhavnani and Coulson 1985: 89; see also Bannerji 1995). It is also important to note that these scholars acknowledge that racism, class exploitation and sexism do not simply add up to a triple whammy or hierarchy of oppression, but may 'cut across one another' (Bhavnani and Coulson 1985: 89). While it is clear that under certain conditions sexism can serve to reinforce other structural conditions to further disadvantage black women in relation to black men or white women, it is also possible that in particular instances, gender may mitigate experiences of racism for black women, for example in relation to police violence[3] (Phizacklea 1992; Bryan *et al.* 1985). For these writers, then, the role of the black 'middle class' will vary at different historical conjunctures and will be influenced by allegiances related to gender, racialised group membership and ethnicity, as well as economic interests.

COMPETING MINORITIES, COMPETING MODELS

While empirically-based explanations of the articulation of 'race', class and gender within the black British population have been slow in emerging from the academic community, debates within the black press and at community level have already begun to create 'commonsense' theories of stratification in which racism, ethnicity and gender play a key role. Two main sets of ideas can be identified. The first relates to differentiation between African Caribbean and Asian communities and the second to gender stratification within the African Caribbean community. The first discourse draws on three observations. First, Asian children are presumed to receive superior schooling experiences, in sharp contrast to the high number of exclusions of African Caribbean boys in particular. Second, Asian businesses are seen as benefiting both from community cohesion and support from financial institutions which are not available to the African Caribbean entrepreneur to bring material wealth into Asian communities. Finally, Asians are seen to have successfully gained a foothold in local politics and to be utilising the powerful position of Asian councillors to access funding for Asian voluntary organisations. This discourse is fractured and inconsistent but appeared regularly at community and voluntary sector conferences I attended during 1992–5. These views were also mentioned, often with an indication that the speaker distanced herself from them, by African, Asian and Caribbean interviewees:

> People say, well, Asians think they're better than us. . . . There's this perception that they have money, they have organisations, they have strong communities, so you don't need to work with them anyway.
>
> (Lynette, Caribbean, African Caribbean organisation)

> There are issues ironically [of] who are Asian workers and people who are not Asian. Very subtle, cultural differences. 'Asian people get everything, Asian people have this, they have that'. In the organisation and outside.
>
> (Balwant, Asian, black organisation)

Increasingly, African Caribbean people are represented as the 'truly disadvantaged', the victims of the most extreme forms of racist exclusion and oppression. Often this is accompanied by the belief that if only the African Caribbean community would behave more like the Asian community, that is, spend its money with African Caribbean shops, have more trust in cooperative economics, support African Caribbean leaders instead of constantly undermining them, it would lead to greater economic wealth and political power:

> In all the other communities between 80–90 per cent of what they spend they spend with their own. If a white man's got a choice of going to a black, or a white, or an Asian shop he'll choose the white man's shop every time. If an Asian man has the same choice he'll choose the Asian man's shop. But if a black man has the choice he'll go to anyone BUT the black man's. . . . So how can we ever hope to build our own economy like the Irish, the Jews, the Chinese, the Turks, the Indians and almost every other community in this country?
>
> (Jawanza 1996)

Finally, this argument questions the relevance for African Caribbean people of organising with the Asian community since the latter are perceived as interested only in their own advancement. This then resonates with the view that Asians are 'optional blacks', opting in and out of anti-racist struggle as and when funding is made available. Representations of the African Caribbean community as a homogenous disenfranchised 'underclass', and the Asian community as a coherent upwardly mobile social unit are not only promoted within African Caribbean forums and media, but find expression in both Asian and majority popular expression. That the notion of the Asian community as a 'model minority' has gained common currency is exemplified by an article in the *Sun*, a right-wing populist newspaper, presenting the Asian family as the embodiment of British values. It is also manifest in the hard-working Asian shopkeeper who has replaced the 'traditional' English cornershop (Rattansi 1994: 68–9).

This notion also underpins Modood's (1988: 403) rejection of black resistance in favour of Asian identity based on 'hard work and disciplined commitment' and building on achievements in the professions and in commerce. While the African Caribbean community is represented as resentful and alienated, Asians are presumed to benefit from the gains of a basically fair and meritocratic democratic society. In associating progress with one racialised grouping rather than acknowledging the complex picture of stratification within both Asian and African Caribbean communities, such accounts reify stereotypical discourses about Asian communities. This is not to suggest that these discourses are homogenous. Stereotypes are never coherent and consistent and Rattansi has highlighted how the same characteristics of Asians which are presented as underpinning their 'model' status can also lead to anxiety, ambivalence and hostility in white communities (Rattansi 1994: 69). The same is true of discourses within African Caribbean communities where Asian 'success' is both coveted, and resented as a sign that Asians are 'selling out'.

What light does the empirical data on social stratification within and between African Caribbean and Asian communities shed on these commonsense notions regarding Asian progress? In the sphere of education it is evident that Caribbean boys experience disproportionate rates of exclusion from schools, a phenomenon which is not shared to the same extent by Asian children (Modood 1994: 3). However, this does not mean that Asian children are experiencing universal academic success. On the contrary, 48 per cent and 54 per cent of Pakistani and Bangladeshi 16–24 year olds respectively leave school with no qualifications at all (ibid.: 3). Asian girls in the school environment are subject to particular pressures and restrictions (Brah 1996: 79; Sahgal 1992). Furthermore, African young people are far more likely to carry on into higher education than Asian youngsters (Owen 1993: 8).

Unemployment levels also indicate a more complex picture than is suggested by the myth of Asian advancement, with Pakistanis (28.8 per cent) and Bangladeshis (31.7 per cent) experiencing significantly higher rates than Caribbeans (18.9 per cent) and slightly higher rates than Africans (27.0 per cent). Furthermore, when we compare aggregate figures for African Caribbean and Asian women, it becomes evident that they share almost identical levels of unemployment (16.6 to 16.5 per cent respectively) (Owen 1993: 7). All black groups experience unemployment rates which are far higher than whites, indicating shared experiences of discrimination and exclusion from expanding employment sectors (ibid.: 1). In employment, as we have seen, African, Asian and Caribbean women are paid significantly less than black or white men. Similar proportions of Asian and African Caribbean women are employed in part-time jobs, characterised by low status and poor working conditions (21.0 and 21.4 per cent respectively) (Owen 1993: 3). The widespread practice of undocumented 'homeworking' – piece-work in the retail industry – suggests that the extent of Asian women's exploitation may remain as yet uncovered (Phizacklea 1992; R. Bhavnani 1994). There is, therefore, no unitary, socially mobile Asian community. Indeed, a gender transparent analysis reveals that considerable segments of this grouping are suffering from higher levels of academic 'failure' and unemployment than African Caribbean communities.

The entrepreneurial success of Asians in comparison to African Caribbeans can be put in the context of the economic capital and business experience which some Asian migrants brought to Britain from their countries of origin, as well as preferential treatment by financial institutions. However, despite evidence that black business owners are more likely to create jobs than whites, there is little sign that this is making significant inroads into unemployment rates in Asian communities (for example, although 7.4 per cent own businesses with employees, Indians experience similar unemployment rates to Caribbean women (Owen 1993: 5–7). Finally, while Asian groupings do show levels of self employment and business ownership which are considerably higher than both whites and African Caribbeans, it is important to note that 'homeworkers' may be classified as self employed (Owen 1993: 5; Reeves and Ward 1984). In this sense, the notion of Asian success in business, particularly the retail industry needs to be unpacked to reveal the differential experiences of male business owners and women workers paid less than a subsistence wage, working extremely long hours and incurring hidden costs relating to working from home (Phizacklea 1990: 99–102, 1992: 108). It is clear that the profiles of African, Asian and Caribbean communities are far more complex than simplified notions of stratification along racialised lines would have us believe. Furthermore, the similarities between African Caribbean and Asian women's experiences of low pay, poor conditions and job insecurity indicate that in a labour market which is structured by racialised and gendered segmentation, black women have much in common and much to gain in working together for improved conditions.

LEAVING OUR MEN BEHIND?

The second line of socio-economic stratification which is increasingly being posited within popular discussions at community level is that between African Caribbean men and women. An explicit link between class divisions within African Caribbean communities and gender is made rather humorously by an interviewee:

> I think we're in danger of leaving everybody behind that is not compromising. Which is why I think so many black women are leaving their men behind. I never thought as a dyke I'd be worried about this. But I am seriously, genuinely worried about what is happening to black men in this country. . . . I think what's happening is that straight black women are . . . making it, you can see them, they're the first ones as Assistant Director in the voluntary sector. Even though there's not many.
>
> (Abiola, African, black organisation)

Perusal of the *Voice* (5 March 1996, 26 March 1996b, 23 April 1996a) Britain's most read African Caribbean newspaper reveals numerous allusions to the assumption that African Caribbean women are doing better than 'our men'. This supposed differential is attributed to the idea that while black men are a threat to white men and women, black women are more acceptable. The idea of African Caribbean men as a threat relies on two distinct assumptions. The first is that white men see African Caribbean men as aggressive and seek to avoid incorporating them into their work environments, particularly where this would involve interaction with white women. The second is that African Caribbean men are in fact more uncompromising and therefore unwilling to put up with the everyday racist backbiting endemic to educational institutions and office environments shared with white people. Accordingly African Caribbean women's advances in the fields of education and employment are represented as the outcome of their willingness to ignore hostility in return for qualifications, status and money. As hooks (1995) points out, writing about parallel developments in the United States, this advancement is never seen as beneficial to the black community as a whole:

> All the recent mass media focus on Black males, labelling them as an 'endangered species', reinscribes white supremacist capitalist patriarchal scape-goating of black womanhood by the constant insistence that black women are to 'blame' for the dilemmas black males face and not white supremacy and/or patriarchy . . . the message is the same – black women are gaining benefits at the expense of black men.
>
> (hooks 1995: 82)

Thus African Caribbean women are represented as benefiting from the limited positions made available to black people subsequent to the urban uprisings by, in the main, African Caribbean men. This analysis is developed by right-wing black women such as Conservative councillor, Lola Ayonrinde who states in interview:

> 'Equal opportunities is not African sensitive. We have to look for male sensitive attitudes to recruitment, that way, African men will find respectable jobs'. She admits that EOPs have helped black or African women to get highly paid jobs. 'But in the process, our men have lost out'.
>
> (Yeebo 1995: 29)

It is given further support by evidence of police brutality, imprisonment, massive unemployment and proliferation of guns and drugs which suggest that African Caribbean men in Britain are sliding down the slope of American style 'ghetto' deprivation (*Voice* 12 December 1995: 10, 5 March 1996: 4; Jawanza 1996: 23; Yeebo 1995). As Ayonride (in Yeebo 1995) continues:

> There has been enough talk about the African woman, now let us deal with the African man. They are threatened with extinction. A successful black woman without a successful black man has nothing to be proud of.
>
> (ibid.: 29)

The assumption that African Caribbean women are 'doing better' in educational and economic terms is frequently meshed with gender politics to create a discourse which resonates with black male insecurities. The compliment of the professional woman who dominates the office is the single mother who dominates the household. Resentment towards socially mobile professional women can therefore be seen to build on the ambiguous feelings of men of African descent towards single mothers who are portrayed simultaneously as the 'backbone' of the community and as matri- archs denying African Caribbean men their rightful position as heads of household (Yeebo 1995; Brixton Black Women's Group 1984b: 251; for parallel developments in the United States, see hooks 1995; Wallace 1978). African Caribbean women's socio- economic progress is therefore viewed by some men through the prism of fears of emasculation. A recent edition of the *Voice* captured the complex articulation of sexual and economic relations in an article entitled 'Should women be on top?', which went on to ask: 'Do men find it difficult to deal with assertive, successful women – are they a threat in the workplace and the home?' (23 April 1996b: 4). The same edition carried another article which sought to elaborate on the problems being experienced by African Caribbean men:

> According to experts, one of the reasons why men are unable to perform satisfactorily in bed is because they feel stripped of their masculinity as women dominate the workplace and the bedroom . . . black male authors whose books investigate the new-style sexual politics agree that changes in male behaviour and increasing male resentment are becoming more apparent.
>
> (ibid.)

This 'new-style sexual politics' is more than the backlash against feminism in blackface, but draws on a long history of racialised relations (Lorde 1984). It builds on the assumption that the posi- tion of African women in enslavement was ameliorated by their ability to manipulate the master enslaver's[4] sexual attention in order to win better treatment. It also draws on popular images of the female 'house slave' who was able to wear fancy 'hand-me- downs' and eat the master enslaver's left-over food, while the enslaved men worked in the fields and plotted revenge and flight. Such depictions were steeped in sexism and have since been coun- tered by more accurate representations of the sexual coercion and rape to which enslaved women were subject, the involvement of the vast majority in gruelling work in the fields and the role of maroon and enslaved women in resistance to the enslavers in the United States and Caribbean (Davis 1981; Reddock 1995;[5] Bush 1995). Personal narratives of enslaved women have further facilitated a re-evaluation of the role of African women in enslavement (Prince 1987; Brent 1973). However, these images have remained alive within popular discourse on black sexual relations as is elaborated by Brixton Black Women's Group:

> There is a strongly held opinion that . . . black women have always been sexually liberated. This argument has its foundations in slavery and is based on the so-called 'easy' life of those black women who were forced to 'service' their white masters sexually. Their condition has historically been projected as being closer to that of white women than black men.
>
> (Brixton Black Women's Group 1984b: 251)

The idea that enslaved African women were given favours by the master enslavers finds its parallel in the notion that women of African descent in Britain and the United States are progressing because 'the man' allows them to. This assertion relies on the assumption that African Caribbean women benefit from white supremacy. In this sense, it is African Caribbean women, not the black 'bourgeoisie' who are seen as 'selling out' the black community (for an elaboration of this point, see S. Small 1994: 135; hooks 1995: 80). 'Selling out' does not necessarily involve taking political positions which actively undermine black community interests. Simply by exceeding the economic and educational achievements of their menfolk, African Caribbean women are seen as contributing to the former's emasculation and thus to white supremacy.

While progress by African Caribbean women is portrayed as problematic, accumulation of wealth by African Caribbean men is portrayed by the same media and community organisations as bene-ficial, rather than divisive. Hence, the proliferation of African Caribbean markets, and exhortations to recycle the 'black pound':

> If we help to build these businesses, then one day they will be able to pay back by creating jobs for our children, financing black causes and giving us some political clout. That's what building a black economy is all about.
>
> (Jawanza 1996)

Power in the hands of men is seen as empowering the community, but power in the hands of African Caribbean women is seen as a threat to African Caribbean masculinity and therefore to community cohesion. To a large extent this rhetoric draws on black nationalist discourse from the United States (Hare and Hare 1984; Kunjufu 1991). Indeed nationalist and Afrocentric literature is available through black bookshops in most African Caribbean communities and is widely consumed and debated.[6] There is a danger that using literature which analyses an African diasporic community with very different historical, economic and social parameters to describe the British situation will lead to distortions. It is therefore essential to examine to what extent empirical data supports these assertions.

In education, research indicates that African Caribbean young women experience significantly lower levels of school exclusions, achieve more qualifications and tend to stay longer in education than African Caribbean boys.[7] Furthermore, African Caribbean women are more likely to subscribe to a form of credentialism which suggests a belief that academic qualifications will enable them to overcome barriers in the labour market (Mirza 1992; Osaba Women's Centre 1992). These improved educational achievements enable women to access non-manual jobs in higher proportions to men: nearly two-thirds of African Caribbean women are found in non-manual work compared to just over a quarter of African Caribbean men (Modood 1994: 3). Indeed, analysts have pointed out that while African Caribbean women are disadvantaged in comparison to white women, the differential between African Caribbean and white men is far greater (C. Brown 1984; Jayaweera 1993).

However, this apparent advantage is misleading. African Caribbean women enter a labour market which is gendered as well as racialised. Thus, their representation in non-manual labour categories should not be viewed as evidence that they are accessing well renumerated positions in local authorities and elsewhere. Rather, they are concentrated in 'women's jobs' – low and intermediary-level jobs within the service and public sectors – such as clerical work, nursing, cleaning and childcare (R. Bhavnani 1994; Brah 1992b). Furthermore, when African and Caribbean communities are disaggregated, other fault-lines within this group appear. African men and women experience higher unemployment rates than Caribbean men and women (27.0 to 18.9 per cent), and

African women actually experience slightly higher unemployment rates than Caribbean men (24.7 to 23.8 per cent). Even the relatively superior situation of Caribbean women must be put in context of an unemployment rate of over double that of white women (13.5 to 6.3 per cent) (Owen 1994). And in the light of the increased burdens of childcare and household costs which fall to those African Caribbean women who have no financial contribution from a male partner, it is also likely that the relative advantage for Caribbean women in escaping unemployment will be undermined by problems of stress, overwork and exhaustion.

The predominance of women in service sector jobs and the decline of Britain's manufacturing base suggests that Caribbean women experience lower unemployment rates than African and Caribbean men not because they are less threatening, but because their labour as women is cheaper,[8] and because they are more likely to accept casualised part-time work[9] (Cross 1993: 78; Phizacklea 1992). While African Caribbean women in the 1980s and 1990s have made greater inroads into professional and managerial occupations than ever before, a recent Policy Studies Institute study reveals that African Caribbean men are still more likely to access this level of employment (Jones 1993). While 12 per cent of Caribbean and 21 per cent of African men were in these categories, only 8 per cent of Caribbean and 11 per cent of African women were at equivalent positions. Concentration in low status professions such as nursing and in 'race' specific jobs, such as Section 11 posts in the welfare and education sectors, further undermine this apparent mobility and increase black women's vulnerability to government cuts and changes in policy such as the moves away from 'race specific' funding initiatives (R. Bhavnani 1994: 76–7; Sia December 1995: 4). Thus, the visible African Caribbean women managers and heads of department are still very much the exception and cannot sustain the argument that women have benefited from equal opportunities policies to the exclusion of men:

> Equal opportunities initiatives appear to have had little impact on real change for black women's employment patterns particularly against a background on the restructuring of the labour market. Vertical segregation is still acute, and may be changing, but bringing new problems for black women. The central issue of earnings and pay has not been touched by equal opportunities.
>
> (R. Bhavnani 1994: 100)

In the sphere of business development, it is also clear that African Caribbean men and women have similarly low levels of small business ownership (McLeod 1991: 81). In the 1991 Census, only 2.6 per cent of African Caribbean women in work were self employed (R. Bhavnani 1994). Finally, there is evidence that even when they do access 'middle class' occupations, African Caribbean women display less willingness to vote Conservative than African Caribbean men in similar positions, which suggests that women are less likely than men to put their economic interest before racialised group affiliation (Layton-Henry 1984: 55; Daye 1994: 207). Cohabitation patterns also provide embryonic indications that African Caribbean women are more likely than men to put African Caribbean communities before other considerations in personal/political decision making. While two in five African Caribbean men live with a white partner, only one in five women do so (*Voice* 7 May 1996). The existence of an insurmountable socio-economic and political fracture between African Caribbean men and women is therefore largely a construct based on male insecurities. Furthermore, initial findings indicate that where African Caribbean women have made individual socio-economic gains, these have translated into gains for the whole community and not into a process of 'selling out'.

REINTRODUCING AND REVISIONING 'CLASS'

How do political analyses in black women's organisations relate to the commonsense ideas about social stratification prevalent in community debates? What light do they shed on theoretical models developed within academia? An analysis of interviews and literature from a range of organisations reveals a spectrum of approaches to explicating 'race' and class. Discourse about class struggle has changed over time and the views of women active in the late 1970s and early 1980s vary significantly from those of women active in the 1990s.

Three organisations studied, two of which were established in the 1970s and folded in the 1980s, subscribed to an anti-imperialist Marxist analysis. These organisations equated black women's struggles with authentic working class struggles. Literature produced in the late 1970s and early 1980s by Brixton Black Women's Group and OWAAD[10] emphasised that black women were part of a broader movement against capitalism:

We in the Black Women's Group see whatever activities we participate in as being part of the general struggle of black and working class people against a world wide system of exploitation. As women our task must be to take up those issues that face us at work and in the community making clear that the struggles in which we participate are linked with the general fight against international capital.

(Brixton Black Women's Group 1980: 3)

These groups focused on the state as a primary site of oppression (OWAAD 1979, 1980). 'SUS' laws, immigration legislation, deportation, 'sin bins' and other forms of exclusion were seen as coherent actions by the state in collusion with business designed to control and exploit black labour:

This proposed change in the definition of Nationality will bring Britain more into line with EEC policies on Citizenship and Nationality, where migrant workers rather than immigrants are far more common. It will also bring some welcome advantages to the government ... enabling racist measures to be carried out more effectively, like SUS and passport raids, political and police intimidation, control of the size of the black population through the use of Depo Provera.

(OWAAD 1979: 6)

These groups interpreted black women's activism as part of an international movement and looked to socialist societies such as China for inspiration and alternative forms of social organisation where 'profit does not rule people's lives' (Brixton Black Women's Group 1980: 6). Zamimass, a black lesbian group, developed their Marxist analysis ten years later. The group set the struggle against capital in the context of an 'organic crisis' in British society (Centre for Contemporary Cultural Studies 1982). Entrenched racist, sexist and homophobic ideologies were explained in the context of this breakdown:

As Black Lesbian women we feel the increased homophobia that arises as people in desperation cling to the idea of the nuclear family for security and power, blaming us for society's changing, failing character.

(Zamimass 1992: 1)

'Working class' unity was therefore seen as a difficult task in the light of the oppressive ideologies nurtured in the white working class:

> We the working class are divided against ourselves. Sections of the white working class, in attacking Black Lesbians, forgets its own suffering and rejects the black working class in favour of the Bosses power, e.g. BNP 'rights for whites' attacks.
>
> (Zamimass 1992: 1)

Women in this grouping were careful to distance themselves from white feminists' preoccupations with the concerns of middle class women and to highlight the ways in which black women's experiences were structured primarily by racialised class exploitation. In so doing, they prioritised racism and capitalism over sexism and thus perhaps understated the gender implications of black women's experiences of racism:

> Although the women's movement has highlighted many important issues, we do not regard men as the primary source of oppression [or] see women's liberation solely in terms of sexual emancipation, neither do we support the call for wages for housework. We regard all these tendencies as middle class deviations from the real issues of women's liberation.
>
> (Brixton Black Women's Group 1984b: 3)

Drawing on Marxist analysis, but with a more overt recognition of gendered aspects of racialised oppression, is the development by one organisation of a Marxist feminist analysis which utilises the concept of the international division of labour. Black Women for Wages for Housework is closely linked to Wages for Housework and a number of feminist groups, such as the English Collective of Prostitutes and Lesbians Due Wages with which it shares premises at the King's Cross Women's Centre[11] in Camden, London. Its theoretical position is based on writings by one of the founder members of Wages for Housework, Selma James written in 1973 (James 1985; W. Brown 1984). In it James redefines class to include women and children based on the unwaged labour of the housewife and schoolchild:

> So here are two sections of the working class whose activities, one in the home, the other in the school, appear to be outside of the capitalist wage labour relation because the workers them-

selves are wageless. In reality, their activities are facets of capitalist production and its division of labour.

(James 1985: 2)

Thus, the struggles of women, children and black men are reinterpreted and redefined as 'the most comprehensive *working class* struggle'. Recognition and reparations for the unpaid work which women do in the home, cleaning, caring, producing and raising children and in developing countries in the fields growing the staples for subsistence, are therefore seen as a primary site of the international fight against capitalism and imperialism:

Counting black and Third World people's contribution to every economy – *starting by counting women's unwaged work* – is a way of refusing racism, claiming the wealth back from military budgets, and establishing our entitlement to benefits, wages, services, housing, healthcare, an end to military-industrial pollution – not as charity but as rights and reparations owed many times.

(Black Women for Wages for Housework June 1994)

Although these forms of protest are defined as 'working class' struggles, James does recognise that gendered and racialised groups are fractured along socio-economic lines. This fragmentation is seen in terms of ideological commitment rather than economic status. It is therefore variations in consciousness which are at stake:

Within the movements which these form are layers whose struggle tends to be aimed at moving up in the capitalist hierarchy rather than at destroying it. . . . But this is the history also of white male workers' movements. There is no class 'purity', not even in shop floor organizations.

(ibid.: 4)

As we have seen, the black women's organisations which supported an anti-imperialist Marxist approach did not support the call for wages for housework. Rather than seeking recognition for work in the home, they sought adequate pay and conditions for the work which they undertook in hospitals, factories, public transport and the catering industry. Indeed, the call for wages for housework was seen by many black women in the early 1980s as a reflection of middle class feminists' narrow field of vision, unable to imagine women for whom full-time waged work was a necessity and the battle against unemployment more pressing (Brixton Black Women's Group 1980: 3; OWAAD 1980: 11). However, more recent developments have revealed the anti-racist potential of this argument in recognising the vast majority of rural work in developing countries which is undertaken by women (International Wages for Housework, undated),[12] the often back-breaking work which African Caribbean and Asian women carry out in caring for elders in the home and the additional burden on 'homeworkers' of caring for children while carrying out piecework (Phizacklea 1990):

> In countries of the north the case for a minimum wage, for free or low-cost childcare, for services and benefits, including Income Support, is greatly strengthened when the economic value of work women do is recognised. In the south, women's case for piped water, sustainable fuel, credit, land rights and decent wages, can be based on the contribution of their enormous workload.

> (Black Women for Wages for Housework 17 November 1995)

Following a great deal of lobbying work by these networks, recognition of women's unwaged work was made a key demand at the United Nations Conference on Women in Beijing in 1995 (*Caribbean Times* 21 October 1995; *Weekly Journal* 12 October 1995). Nevertheless, despite its appeal at the international level, the demand for wages for housework has not received widespread support from black women's organisations in Britain, possibly because of its perceived origins in white socialist feminism.

The majority of case study organisations active in the 1990s did not subscribe to a Marxist framework for understanding black women's oppression. These organisations infrequently had a written position statement. Members tended therefore to draw their own conclusions about the relevance of class. These can be split into two broad categories. First, there were those who viewed class as irrelevant to black women in Britain.[13] For some, class differences were erased by the primacy of the struggle against racism and imperialism:

> I think from my own personal perspective as a Palestinian, class means nothing to me. The national struggle, the liberation struggle is priority number one. The emancipation of my people, the important bit.

> (Mona, Middle Eastern, black organisation)

The sooner we realise that as far as the rest of society is concerned, we have no class, we are just black. . . . As far as the Man's concerned you're just black women.

(Abiola, African, black organisation)

Others placed mental wellbeing and spiritual happiness above the importance of economic wealth and therefore took a less politicised view of economic exclusion: 'We don't see class ever, we deal with different classes, different races and it's not an issue. You can be very comfortable and you have so many problems' (Zaheda, Middle Eastern, Muslim organisation).

The second group of women acknowledged socio-economic divisions, but had varying responses to this stratification. For some, 'middle class' origins were something that they had left behind in their countries of origin. All black settlers and British-born black women were perceived as sharing a common 'working class' position, although some women born outside Britain would have benefited from a 'middle class' upbringing and education:

Most of us in the group probably class ourselves as working class women, but we're not all working class women. When we think about our background and how we were brought up, we know we're not working class women, because I wasn't. . . . People like Vivian, they're not working class, they're people who had maids when they were growing up back in Nigeria. But they're working class in this country.

(Natalie, Caribbean, African Caribbean organisation)

One interviewee pointed out that 'middle class' had very different meanings in a Jamaican context and was more associated with status than with wealth. For other women, class divisions existed within the black community but these related to attitude and behaviour. Thus, a black person who wished to assimilate could reject his or her roots and access a place in the white middle class sun. However, access to education and improved employment opportunities were not in themselves evidence of class mobility:

I think Britain is one of the countries [in] which class actually dominate everything. I know people try to hide it and say because you're educated you got a degree, then you no longer working class. I don't accept that. I think there's a more fundamental thing about class which include attitude, which include way of life, which include perspective, a personal perspective and a political perspective. ... For us it depends on where you coming from, how much you're grounded. If you haven't got the grounding and you're influenced by material possessions ... you'll start speaking funny, just like the yuppies in London.

(Mona, Middle Eastern, black organisation)

Many interviewees did not believe that socio-economic advancement necessarily brings about behaviour disloyal to the group interests. A desirable goal therefore was to achieve progress while remaining true to one's origins. This perspective enabled them to mesh a commitment to enabling women to acquire education and professional employment, with a simultaneous opposition to the system. Thus, a refuge worker who spoke of her commitment to anti-racist struggles against the state, also advanced a credentialist solution to socio-economic exclusion:

I think how class impacts is in terms of poverty, how poverty will affect black women's access to different types of services and awareness. Your socio-economic group will have a big factor in whether you stay with your husband or not. ... We encourage access to education, further and higher education colleges ... and from then onwards, maybe university or college and then helping them into employment.

(Balwant, Asian, black organisation)

Thus, class is experienced by many of the black women in the case study organisations as contradictory and ambiguous. One interviewee spoke to Gilroy's call for a 'revised and reworked concept of class' (Gilroy 1987: 27):

I think that for black women the complexity of class isn't just about whether you're a single parent living in an inner city estate struggling on social or not, or whether you're one of the black people who've been educated and think you're alright. I think it's about a complex matrix of your history, your life experiences, your opportunities, your family content, your childrearing status, your sexuality, your cultural identity, your perception of self. Your cultural links are very important, whether you're multilingual or not comes into it. All of that is unique and complex and all of that is about class, but it isn't as well.

(Brenda, Caribbean, African Caribbean organisation)

This statement captures the ambiguity of a concept of class which is broad enough to contain both the structural and subjective implications of racism, migration, nationality, family, sexuality and personal relationships. Once class has been expanded in this way, it becomes pertinent to question whether it is still adequately described as class, or as this interviewee succinctly states, 'all of that is about class, but it isn't as well'.

The diversity of ideological positions taken by black women's organisations indicates that we cannot make assumptions about what sort of politics black women's autonomy will translate into. There is also some indication that black women joining organisations in the 1990s are finding a Marxist framework too rigid to explain the diverse forces which structure their life chances. Some commentators have suggested an inevitable movement towards class-based analyses as black settlers become more embedded in the British social system and the number of British-born blacks increases (Phizacklea and Miles 1980). Far from this prediction, these women appear to be moving towards more heterogenous and 'agnostic' understandings of 'race', class and gender. The black women's organisations which retain a 'traditional' Marxist analysis are therefore a small minority.

Ironically, the rejection of Marxist analyses appears to have freed women up to speak more openly about socio-economic divisions between black women. Rather than viewing authentic black women's activism as a homogenous 'class struggle', these women are beginning to acknowledge the ways in which their lives are differentially shaped by access to education and material wealth. This development can be seen as a corollary to the more nuanced understanding of 'black womanhood' which I identified in Chapter 4. Some of the interviewees voiced concerns about the ways in which women with more formal education could utilise their greater articulacy to dominate meetings and discussions:

> Class is a dividing line. In my experience, what you tend to find is that black women who are articulate and who come to the meetings are educated and have a middle class background, I'm aware of that. I'm aware that the people who are leading black women at the moment do come from a middle class upbringing. And I think it's very important that we also know what is happening to the majority of women in our society.
>
> (Misa, Asian, black organisation)

Several interviewees voiced concerns that articulate, educated women came to see themselves as experts, able to prescribe how other black women should be liberated: 'The professional women tend to be domineering and they don't listen. A lot of the non-professionals were intimidated and left. Now we have an unbalanced group. They talk about needs but don't know themselves what the women need' (Mai, Chinese, Chinese organisation):

> It is easy for women who are well read or well educated, or are feminists to think they actually have the answers, to think they know better by virtue of their education and to dictate to other women who are then silenced by the power of these women who are knowledgeable. And I think that knowledgeability needs to be questioned and analysed more closely because it silences other women for a start. It's also dictating what is good for other women, it's a class issue that perhaps isn't sufficiently acknowledged. When there's too much focus on race one forgets the issues that might be different for women.
>
> (Hilda, African, African Caribbean organisation)

The latter interviewee explored the class dynamics evident in a dispute which had arisen within the group when they had received a small grant for equipment. The university educated women wanted to buy a computer in order for the members to access skills which could help them into professional employment or further education. The women with no further education, many of whom were unemployed, wanted to purchase knitting machines so that they could make clothes and sell them. This conflict revealed the class dimensions of gendered positionalities. The 'educated' women felt that the desire to buy a knitting machine was rooted in traditional gender roles which they as a women's group should be rejecting. The women with less formal education wanted to purchase something practical which they knew how to use. In the end a compromise was made and cheaper versions of both items were purchased.

It is clear from this example, that a simple dichotomy which poses 'working class' women's aspirations as progressive and 'educated', professional women as working 'for their own interests' cannot explain the complexities of political ideology around racialised, class and gendered identities. However, it is also evident that significant differences in organisational power can arise from socio-economic and educational stratification among black women. Organisations which have a unitary notion of black women being either intrinsically 'working class' or outside of socio-economic relations, are ill equipped to ensure that the organisational agenda is not dominated by 'educated' women.

The recruitment of paid workers, some of whom are professional women with higher education, can also lead to increased social stratification within black women's organisations. Of the twelve case study organisations, eight had paid staff. While most of the interviewees in these organisations did not perceive any difficulties arising from employing staff, two interviewees highlighted some of the ambiguities which could arise. One pointed out the tension between the ideal of self help and the reality of professional women 'empowering' 'working class' women: 'I'm thinking that the workers tended to have done better in the education system, to be professional black women, the people who were volunteers may be people aspiring to that and were not quite there yet' (Brenda):

> I think inevitably a lot of women who have jobs in black women's organisations have come from different class from some of the women that they are empowering or enabling or working with. . . . There's a tension in terms of class in terms of women being done to or done for or done with and empowered.
>
> (Lynette, African Caribbean, African Caribbean organisation)

Two potential problems arise where the management committee are less qualified than the workers whom they are supervising, and where the former lack management experience. First, workers may feel that they are not receiving adequate management support. Second, the committee may keep wages at low levels and refuse to provide benefits such as childcare or pensions because they are resistant to a worker receiving significantly more than voluntary committee members who are in low waged jobs or on unemployment benefits.[14] Some organisations had resolved these problems by coopting or electing a professional black woman to undertake staff supervision and by undertaking an objective analysis of the job requirements and appropriate renumeration. However, these tactics could also lead to the development of a dominant, educated ingroup, comprising workers and officers, or to resentment from unpaid (volunteer) workers.

The relationship between members and workers is complicated by the depressed rates of pay in most black women's organisations (nursery workers, for example, are often paid little more than a subsistence wage), which means that some workers may actually be in a less advantaged position than the centre's members. Even in 'senior' jobs, pay may be low, for example, two centre coordinators with responsibility for managing a team of staff as well as several grant aid budgets were paid under £15,000 in 1994, well under the rate they would have received for a comparative job in a local authority. The evidence for a bevy of black women getting fat on the opulence of the 'race relations industry' is therefore an inadequate characterisation of paid workers in black women's organisations (Anthias *et al.* 1992; Sivanandan 1990). Nevertheless, differences in socio-economic status between paid workers and unpaid volunteers are a potential source of tension for all organisations employing staff.

It is also important to challenge hostilities which can face 'educated' women in community-based women's organisations. The suspicion towards university educated women was expressed by one interviewee:

There's the whole thing about education, the acceptance of educated women (supposed) and the fact that they've never been considered black enough. You've gone to university, you're doing a doctorate, either you think you're better than us or you're far better than us, you can't possibly relate to us.

(Lynette, Caribbean, African Caribbean organisation)

There is an internal contradiction in organisations which both campaign against black women's exclusion from the education system and view women who have achieved as suspect. This ambiguity can translate into hostility and resentment, as educated black women become both a symbol of the movement's success and of its compromise: 'It's a bit of a strange position because looking back, they probably employed me because they were impressed by my education, but at the same time, that ended up being a threat to them' (ibid.).

Speaking after its demise, OWAAD members identified the exploitation of educational divisions as a tool to undermine the legitimacy of black women's organising:

We succumbed and continue to succumb to the fraudulent and divisive analysis that 'women on the streets' could not discuss, articulate and somehow begin to fight their oppression. The argument goes that because we are organised, we are no longer 'typical' black women.... This was based on the assumption that we are middle class because we are all supposedly the recipients of higher education.

(Brixton Black Women's Group 1984b: 88)

While it is essential for professional or 'educated' black women to acknowledge that women who do not share their privilege may at times have differing and more urgent agendas, they nevertheless play an important role in black women's organisations. An ideology which equates authenticity with socio-economic and educational disadvantage but at the same time proclaims black women's right to access educational and material benefits is both contradictory and exclusionary. Listening to women's personal and political commitments, rather than judging them on the basis of their economic and educational status, is the basis for a less exclusionary form of politics. This position is essential if black women's organisations are to remain relevant to women who access higher education or professional employment.

PROFESSIONAL BLACK WOMEN: A CLASS-FOR-ITSELF?

Finally, as social stratification increases, it is evident that some black women will desert community struggles and affiliate with organisations which they feel can benefit them individually. An extreme example of this are high profile Conservative politicians such as Joyce Sampson,[15] Lurline Champagnie and Lola Ayonrinde who promote ideologies which explicitly demean black single mothers (Yeebo 1995; Olusegun 1995). The emergence of a small number of professional black women's organisations also indicates that some black women are beginning to view their agendas as distinct from those of grassroots black women's organisations. These include the Professional Afro-Asian Women's Association (PAAWA), Black Women in Research and Black Women Achievers (BWA).[16] There is also evidence that a black women's sorority from the United States, traditionally an elitist university-based movement, is attempting to set up a branch in Britain (Giddings 1988).

A brief analysis of one of these organisations will highlight some of the dilemmas involved in professional black women's organisational goals. The BWA project was launched in 1992 at the first national Black Women's Achievement awards ceremony. The event was repeated bi-annually and the planned 1996 awards aimed: 'To use the medium of the awards as a tool to publicly recognise black women in the different sectors in order that they can further advance their achievements, and 'To encourage young black women to emulate the achievements being made by recipients of these awards' (BWA August 1995). In organising the awards, BWA hoped to achieve cross-party support, thus highlighting the non-threatening and apolitical nature of their aims summarised by the founder member:

'Black women continue to make valuable contribution to many aspects of society, yet their contribution goes unrecognised and unrewarded. These awards will go someway in honouring their achievements'. Such [a] comment hopefully echoes the views of both men and women of different races, gender and political backgrounds. Nationally, these awards have been given cross-party support.

(BWA August 1995)

This approach is highly pragmatic in that it seeks common ground between vastly differing political positions and appeals to a shared ideology: that people should get due rewards for their efforts. It is problematic in that it obscures the difference between the rhetoric of meritocracy which accompanies British capitalism and the actuality of exploitation and inequality which underpins it (Hall *et al.* 1992). Black women's exclusion is reinterpreted as an unfortunate blot on an otherwise unblemished egalitarian society and structural barriers are re-drawn as a lack of encouragement for young black women to achieve. In this sense the award scheme can be viewed as obscuring the continuing effects of gendered racism and class exploitation by presenting an 'American Dream' version of British society. Unfortunately 'dreaming' must be accompanied by rigorous analysis and active opposition to racist–sexist systems and practices if black women achievers are not to be a token few. Nevertheless, the awards do play an important symbolic and inspirational role which should not be overlooked. While they cannot hope to be the solution, neither should they be considered insignificant in the struggle to redefine black women's lives in Britain.

Professional black women's organisations such as BWA ignore radical analyses in favour of a liberal approach to black women's emancipation. However, it is clear that far from opposing the struggles of 'working class' black women, these organisations view their agendas as different from but complimentary to community-based groups. Indeed, these women may be better equipped to influence national and international debates and thus to challenge gendered racism at levels at which many grassroots organisations are unable to sustain a presence (BWA August 1995). It is also worth reiterating that these organisations form a small minority of black women's organisations and that the majority of active black professional women are involved in community-based organisations. Nevertheless, the divergence of black professional women's organisations from radical analyses leads to concerns that these groups may set agendas at national and international levels which do not match the aspirations of more representative grassroots organisations. It is incumbent on these organisations to recognise where they can learn from black women who are single mothers, unemployed or trapped in low paid jobs.

NOTES

1 Rex's Weberian model attempts to broaden the concept of 'class' to include access to the legal apparatus, but does not in the end avoid this type of economism.

2 *The Communist Manifesto* is quite explicit in describing the nature of the revolutionary agency which will form the vanguard in the overthrow of capitalism. Waged workers from 'barbarian countries', women and children are left to await emancipation by the united action 'of the leading civilised countries' (Marx and Engels 1965: 57).

3 This said, we should bear in mind that police brutality against black men also puts additional pressures on black women and that police brutality against black women, while less frequent, may be exacerbated by sexual assault (Mama 1989a; South London Black Feminist 1984: 88).

4 The term 'enslaved' highlights that no one is born a 'slave', but that Africans were actively enslaved by whites. Similarly, I utilise the term 'master enslaver' to indicate that the position of 'slave master' was not accepted by enslaved Africans, who contested the 'master's' right to 'own' them through flight, sabotage, poison and the abolitionist movement. The term also emphasises the 'master enslaver's' role in brutally enforcing the enslaved Africans' status.

5 Reddock notes that by the late eighteenth century, women outnumbered men in the sugar fields of Jamaica due to their greater life expectation under similar working conditions (1995: 128).

6 A recent edition of *The Alarm* (Jawanza 1996), an African-centred publication based in London, recommended an all-American reading list to illustrate an article on the black economy in Britain, including titles like *Black Folks' Guide to Making Big Bucks in America* by George Subira.

7 Although there is a far more significant difference between African men and women with immediate roots in the continent and those with

roots in the Caribbean. In the 1991 Census, 81.6 per cent of Africans compared to 28.2 per cent of Caribbeans were in education between the ages of 16–24 years (Owen 1993).

8 Brown's finding that: 'On average white men earn substantially more than black men, whereas there is little difference between women' has been used as evidence that racism effects black men's experience of the labour market more harshly than women (C. Brown 1984:167). This analysis overlooks the significant pay inequalities which Brown found between black men and women. Later research has found that Brown's study, in ignoring evidence that black women work longer hours than white women, obscuring differences in age, qualification and location and omitting undocumented work, misrepresented the real differentials between black women's earnings and others. This research suggests that black women earn only 72 per cent of the black male hourly wage (R. Bhavnani 1994: 87–8).

9 Although black women are more likely to work full-time than white women, the 1991 Census indicated that 21.4 per cent of African Caribbean women, compared to 5.6 per cent of African Caribbean men had part-time employment (Owen 1993: 4).

10 It should be noted that OWAAD was an umbrella organisation which included both organisational and individual members. As a member, Brixton Black Women's Group played a key role in OWAAD's development.

11 After a sustained battle with a north London housing association, the organisations were evicted from the Centre in March 1996 following a massive rent increase (Black Women for Wages for Housework, 17 November 1995; *Voice* March 1996).

12 This leaflet states: 'Despite enormous differences in wealth and workload, women south and north are in the same position in their societies: unwaged for the first job, low-waged for the second, and overworked both inside and outside the home. That women do two-thirds of the world's work for 5 per cent of the income and 1 per cent of the assets (International Labour Organization 1980) is the core of our social weakness everywhere.'

13 Daye also found that a number of her respondents 'felt that the notion of social class was not a reality for Black people in Britain' (1994: 165). They considered black labour to be external to the British class structure due to the persistence of racial hierarchies.

14 By far the most common reason for low wages in black voluntary organisations is the failure of funders to provide adequate levels of funding, often offering to cover a percentage of an already trimmed bid (Wenham 1993). Here, I aim to show other internal dynamics which exist regardless of available funding.

15 After many years of campaigning for the Conservative Party during which she was made head of the Tory 'One Nation Forum', Joyce Sampson defected to the Labour Party on 13 October 1994.

16 To protect confidentiality, the latter is a pseudonym.

Chapter 6

Sisters and brothers in struggle?
Looking for coalitions

As I have illustrated in the last two chapters, building sisterhood between black women has not been easy. Divided by economic and professional status, education, ethnicity, sexuality and geography, black women have struggled to create organisations which reflect their varied and yet complimentary agendas. At their best, autonomous spaces can provide 'time to dream resistance, time to theorize, plan, create strategies and go forward' (hooks 1995: 6). Black women's organisations become safe and creative spaces, where women can nurture one another and cultivate far-reaching and dynamic visions of change.

Yet black feminists have begun to suggest that these oppositional spaces are not enough. Pratibha Parmar in her important evaluation of the lessons of black women's organising in the 1980s, suggests that we need to move from 'identity politics' to 'a politics of articulation' which acknowledges the shared agendas of a range of actors (Parmar 1990: 108). In seeking such a politics, Parmar (a black British feminist) speaks to June Jordan (an African American), who memorably states:

> I think there is something deficient in the thinking on the part of anybody who proposes either gender identity politics or race identity politics as sufficient, because every single one of us is more than whatever race we represent or embody and more than whatever gender category we fall into. We have other kinds of allegiances, other kinds of dreams that have nothing to do with whether we are white or not white. . . . I am not dismissing it but just saying that it's probably not enough. It may be enough to get

started on something, but I doubt very much whether it's enough to get anything finished.

(Jordan, in Parmar 1990: 109–10)

Speaking also about American women, Bernice Reagon questions the efficacy of black-only organisations as a long-term strategy:

At a certain stage, nationalism is crucial to a people if you are going to ever impact as a group in your own interest. Nationalism at another point becomes reactionary because it is totally inadequate for surviving in the world with many peoples.

(Reagon 1983: 358)

These women are speaking out of a very different context to that of British organisations. Indeed, Reagon's usage of the term black to reference African Americans differs from the more inclusive British usage. Unlike the British black struggle of the late 1960s and 1970s, the Civil Rights movement has been characterised by overlapping but autonomous movements of African Americans, Mexican Americans/Chicanos and Native Americans (Marable 1995b: 194–9). The alliances between African, Caribbean and Asian women suggest that black women's organising in Britain has been less a case of organising on the basis of shared racialised identification, than on the basis of shared political and personal agendas.

Nevertheless, Reagon's work has relevance to black women's organisations in Britain. Her description of the black organisation as a 'barred room' where women create a closed community resonates with the feelings of the women interviewed. Black women's organisations were viewed by interviewees as safe spaces where women could avoid some of the strife of the outside world. But, as Reagon points out (1983: 358), coming out of these 'barred rooms' becomes essential if only because if we do not, outside forces are likely to crush them. Despite this necessity, it is often easier for black women's organisations to work on specific local issues in isolation from other organisations and movements. A worker in a black women's refuge discussed this tendency:

You can become insulated, that's my experience of the refuge movement, you become really introspective, things happening around you in your little area. People think it's just issues affecting black women . . . people get caught up in the safety of what they're doing.

(Balwant, Asian, black organisation)

A member of Southall Black Sisters, an organisation which has been active in seeking coalitions with the Left, anti-racist and feminist groups, analysed the situation as follows:

> We have problems around segregation and separatism which create a very narrow-minded perspective about the world. That's not very productive. Generally, very few women's or black women's groups try to make wider connections or have a wider analysis at all, they're just busy providing services. . . . You can use the knowledge gained from casework to create wider change.
>
> (Griffin 1995b: 88)

The range of political activity mapped in Chapter 3 suggests that there is more political activity taking place in these organisations than is suggested here. However, it is also clear that many organisations feel more confident dealing with individual, family and community issues than in tackling broader political arenas. The focus on localised small scale struggles also means that these organisations will often fail to see commonalities in the agendas of other movements. Without making these wider connections, black women's organisations may become a place merely to dream about resistance rather than a base from which to implement change.

Yet the small numbers of black women[1] in Britain suggests that regardless of how effective our organisations are, we will not be able to change legislation, take political power at a national level or make macro-level economic changes through autonomous organising alone. This is not to undermine the extensive work which black women's organisations, both at the local and national levels can effectively undertake, which I think is underestimated in Jordan's analysis (in Parmar 1990: 109–10). As we have seen, black women's organisations have been significant actors at the local level. And even at the international level, black women's organisations were able to achieve significant goals (see Chapter 5). Nevertheless, achieving the full agenda of black women's organisations in the spheres of education, social services, domestic violence, benefits, immigration and health will require some attention to building coalitions with other groups:

> It's really important to have a broad based political movement that actually looks at service provision, having critical discussions with local authorities. . . . In terms of domestic violence, it's actually campaigning against legislation. It's really important

to be linked into other campaigns like the white women's movement. Because we're all separate. And movement with Black men
as well around violence, not just violence against Black women.

(Balwant; see also Siddiqui, in Griffin 1995a: 85)

For organisations that are grant aided, linking up with other black
voluntary organisations is essential to fight cuts in funding and
ensure ongoing commitment to resourcing the black voluntary
sector. Furthermore, black women's focus on transforming black
communities demands that black women's activism be undertaken
in partnership with black men.

At this point, it is relevant to make a distinction between
alliances and coalitions. A useful definition is given by Albrecht and
Brewer (1990) who define coalitions as:

Groups or individuals that have come together around a particular issue to achieve a particular goal. These groups operate
autonomously and are usually not connected to each other; most
organizations have different agendas as well. Upon completion of
the shared goal, coalitions often dissolve and organizations go
back to their own work.

(Albrecht and Brewer 1990: 3)

In contrast, the concept of alliance is 'a new level of commitment
that is longer-standing, deeper, and built upon more trusting political relationships' (ibid.: 4). The authors value the latter as a more
meaningful and profound form of working together: 'We see coalitions as short-term solutions and alliance formation as ongoing,
long-term arrangements for more far-reaching structural change'
(ibid.: 4). Coalitions therefore occur mostly between separate organisations, while alliances are likely to exist between actors with
different agendas within the same organisation.

While I concur with the authors' distinction between these two
strategies, I differ from their conclusion that alliances are intrinsically superior. On the contrary, there are a number of arguments
against the strategy of attempting to build alliances within multi-
racial organisations. First, the in depth groundwork and exploration
of personal prejudice necessary for strong alliances may lead black
women to lose the focus that they are able to maintain in
autonomous settings and to become overly introspective (Bunch
1990). Second, it is unlikely that groups with superior resources and
power will cede to demands from subordinated groups unless these

groups operate from a position of strength. The history of the white feminist movement in the United States and in Britain supports this assertion. White middle class women were content to proclaim the universality of 'their' movement during the 1970s and 1980s despite being challenged from within by black women (W. Brown 1984; Bunch 1990: 51). It was only when black women formed autonomous organisations that the feminist movement was forced to acknowledge women's diversity (Spelman 1988; Albrecht and Brewer 1990: 11–12). The intellectual challenges which were so critical in unpacking white feminism also grew out of black women's autonomous organisations, most notably the Combahee River Collective in the United States and Brixton Black Women's Group in Britain (Amos *et al.* 1984; Albrecht and Brewer 1990: 11). And it was the existence of black women's presses that enabled significant texts by black women to be disseminated to wide audiences (Lorde 1990: 207).

Third, black women have noted the tendency for power dynamics between black women, black men and whites to be replicated within multi-racial organisations. This can lead to black women being required to educate, reassure or otherwise emotionally support white women (Welch 1984: 276; Pheterson 1990: 39) or to cook for, take minutes or otherwise service black men (Wallace 1978; Brixton Black Women's Group 1984b: 252). In addition, black women and women of colour in mixed settings are seldom selected for leadership roles and, even where they are present in large numbers, tend to fulfil supportive functions (West 1990; Pardo 1995). Although building alliances between black women and other groups may not be impossible, it is evident that the creation of such alliances is a massive task which is weakened if it cannot rest on the foundations of black women's autonomous organisations. Yet these organisations do not exist in isolation and need to create effective working relations with other groups. This chapter will therefore examine the extent and efficacy of coalition building by black women's organisations.

While Reagon (1983: 358) depicts autonomous space as a barred room, other American scholars utilise less claustrophobic metaphors. For Moraga and Anzaldua (1983), women of colour reaching out to other communities of struggle become bridges (see also Albrecht and Brewer 1990). Taking this metaphor further, Anzaldua creates the possibility of choice, moving from the bridge, always open, always communicating – to the drawbridge which can choose its mode of operation:

Many of us choose to 'draw up our own bridges' for short periods of time in order to regroup, recharge our energies, and nourish ourselves before wading back into the frontlines. . . . The other option is being 'down' – that is, being a bridge. Being 'down' may mean a partial loss of self. Being 'there' for people *all the time, mediating all the time* means risking being 'walked on', being 'used'.

(Anzaldua 1990: 223)

If individual women are the drawbridge, women's organisations become castles, a refuge against the enemy bent on destruction[2]. Black women's castles have numerous drawbridges which may be opened or closed to different groups of potential allies depending on political contingency and organisational context. Yet with the opening always comes the risk that what appears to be a peace offering is in fact a Trojan horse. As Reagon reminds us, building coalitions is dangerous work:

You don't go into coalition because you just *like* it. The only reason you would consider trying to team up with somebody who could possibly kill you, is because that's the only way you can figure out how to survive.

(Reagon 1983: 356)

Black women, 'are a natural part of many struggles' (Griffin 1995b: 85). This means that we have many different potential allies. Simultaneously, it means that we have many potential oppressors. Black men, white (working class) men and white women all have the potential to be sources of solidarity, but also sources of hostility and violence. Black women are placed at the intersection of racism, sexism and class exploitation, as 'cultural mediators', the bridges between a range of political actors (N. Hall 1990: 76). Deciding when it is safe to reach out, identifying which actors will enhance particular struggles, and which, despite their stated enthusiasm to work in partnership, will be destructive or parasitical, is an essential skill if black women's organisations are to build effective coalitions while protecting their security and integrity.

UNITING AGAINST CAPITAL

In the previous chapter, I indicated that a number of black women's organisations have developed a class-based analysis of their situation. This analysis identifies racism, sexism and homophobia as ideologies promoted by the 'ruling class' among the workers in order to divide and therefore weaken anti-capitalist struggles (Zamimass 1992). As Stuart Hall has pointed out, theory always has direct or indirect practical consequences (1980: 307). In translating this class-based analysis into political practice, one might expect these organisations to focus attention on challenging divisive ideologies in socialist organisations in order to build a united multi-racial Labour movement (Wolpe 1986: 111; Castles and Kosack 1985: 505). This was in fact a stated aim of one of the organisations:

> Organizing independently, we ensure that . . . challenging sexism is not separated from or prioritised over challenging racism, and vice versa; so that we can resist divide-and-rule among Black people/people of colour, and can work more effectively with white women and Black men/men of colour and white men who share our aims.
>
> (Black Women for Wages for Housework, undated)

In practice however, this anticipated focus did not materialise. Where links with the Labour movement did exist, they were piecemeal and perfunctory. One organisation had received a brief visit from Keith Vaz, Labour MP as part of the City 2020 campaign, however, this visit did not lead to greater communication with the Labour Party. Other interviewees expressed admiration for Bernie Grant and Diane Abbott's campaign work on behalf of black communities, but saw them as having a separate agenda to that of the Labour Party as a whole. The existence of white women MPs was not viewed as significant by any of the organisations studied.[3] Several organisations had links with Labour local councillors, however, this relationship took the form of lobbying for adequate funding in the next round of grants, or for improvements in service delivery and cannot be characterised as coalition building. Furthermore, there was an emphasis on contacts with African Caribbean or Asian councillors, indicating that the expectation of support was based on the anticipation of racialised empathy, rather than class solidarity. Finally, few of the organisations had attempted to work with local branches of other left-wing organisations such as trade unions, the Socialist Workers Party, Anti-Nazi League and Anti-Racist Alliance. The difficulties documented by Southall Black Sisters in attempting to obtain support in their campaign against fundamentalism indicate the incompatibility of such organisations with a black feminist/womanist approach:

> We are criticized by elements within the Left and the anti-racist movement who say to us, 'You shouldn't be washing your dirty linen in public. You shouldn't be talking about problems in the community.' For example, we [were] criticized by some anti-racists for the way we supported Rushdie (as Women Against Fundamentalism) by counterpicketting the anti-Rushdie demonstrations which were held in central London in May 1989. Their argument is basically that we have to live as a minority in this country and if we keep talking about the issue of fundamentalism, we fuel a racist backlash. They argue that our central and most important struggle is the anti-racist struggle.
>
> (Siddiqui, in Griffin 1995b: 86)

A member of one of the case study organisations pointed to the contradiction between the tenet of black women's self determination and the way in which left-wing organisations operate: 'You very quickly lose power in wider organisations. We used to fight wider struggles e.g. SWP deportation campaigns, but they are unable to support our women who face deportation without taking over' (letter to the author, Sheriff 10 March 1996).

Numerous writers have called for a broad based progressive movement for social change, one which can encompass new social movements as well as the traditional left (S. Hall 1988; Phizacklea and Miles 1980). There is an implicit assumption in such calls that the ideological and political differences between these groups are a bridgeable river, rather than an uncrossable chasm. Often there is an implication that black organisations' unwillingness to build coalitions with the Labour movement is due to a failure to embrace a class-based critique of British capitalism. In other words, black nationalist tendencies are as much at fault as ingrained racist and sexist practices. While there have been calls for the Labour movement to check the racism of many of its members, Bourne has pointed out that left-wing organisations are extremely hesitant to criticise working class men, particularly those who are active in the movement: 'The Left has always had difficulty in facing up to the entrenched nature of British working class racism – as though it were a sacrilege to acknowledge that the agents of revolution were not entirely without sin' (Bourne 1983: 6). This research suggests that proponents of 'black and white unite and fight' working class solidarity underestimate the continuing significance of gendered racist ideologies in the Labour movement. There are a number of barriers to the creation of effective coalitions between black autonomous organisations and the traditional Left. The first involves a visceral reaction to the Labour movement. While left-wing organisations view themselves as the people's champions, for black women who have become involved in transformative grass-roots political activism, they are simply another face of the establishment. Given the choice between one group of white men in suits and another, many black women experience a paralysing disin-terest in party politics. As one interviewee pointed out, regardless of their ideological differences, none of the political parties makes a stand for black single mothers. Since the late 1980s, Labour's attempts to counter the 'loony left' image associated with the GLC's radical social programmes, has further reinforced the white middle class image of the party (S. Hall 1988: 263). The marginalisation of black MPs in the Labour Party also reinforces the idea that black people are tolerated rather than embraced within the party.[4]

Alongside these general impressions of the Labour movement, are specific histories of interaction with black communities which have become metaphors for the relationship between the two. In Liverpool, the public humiliation of Petrona Lashley, the only black woman councillor to be nominated as mayor, and the Labour Party's subsequent failure to defend her was seen by one interviewee to highlight the kind of short-lived support which could be expected from a mainly white male movement. When the *Liverpool Echo* exhumed allegations from the 1960s that she had been involved in prostitution, Lashley, by now a woman in her sixties, was deselected and her subsequent attempts to clear her name received little support from the Labour movement. The gender specificity of this allegation, building on stereotypical notions of black women's supposed promiscuity, indicates the particularly destructive ideolog-ical armoury which can be drawn on in order to undermine black women (Marshall 1996).

In London the character assassination of Linda Bellos, who in 1985 became the first black woman leader of a London borough council, serves as a reminder that black women's leadership in the

Labour movement is seldom accepted. Bellos, who was active in promoting lesbian rights as well as supporting black community initiatives, was depicted as the embodiment of the 'loony left' and her commitment to opposing racism, sexism and homophobia was caricatured. Again, while the attacks on Bellos were led by the tabloid press, little defence was provided by the Labour Party, who were more concerned with reassuring the 'traditional' [white male] Labour voter (S. Hall 1988). Finally, she left Britain to recuperate for three years. On returning, Bellos no longer sought to participate in the white Labour movement but became actively involved in the African Reparations Movement working with black MP, Bernie Grant: 'I'm back and my batteries have been recharged and I can refocus as a black woman, as a black feminist, as an African feminist' (Bellos interview, 2 December 1995). That a black woman who has held a powerful position within the Labour movement has shifted her efforts to an African-centred organisation, suggests to many black women's organisations that active involvement in the Labour movement may not be viable. Experiences of vilification, slander and hostility suggest that such involvement may ultimately be destructive.

The history of the Militant dominated council's 'war' against Liverpool Black Caucus, an umbrella body of black organisations in Liverpool 8 during 1984–6, and its attempt to impose a hand-picked leadership on the black community, illustrates that the Left is frequently threatened by black collective action (Liverpool Black Caucus 1986). The tendency to view black self determination as 'splitist (at best) or racism in reverse (at worst)', and thus to seek to undermine it, has been noted (Bourne 1983: 6). Black groups who opposed the council, including Liverpool Black Sisters and the All Pakistan Women's Association were described as 'violent', 'unrepresentative', 'criminal' and 'self-interested' and were threatened with cuts to grant aid (Liverpool Black Caucus 1986: 85, 119). Although the national Labour leadership, under Neil Kinnock finally intervened to eject Derek Hatton and the 'inner circle' of Militant leadership for financial improprieties, the collusion of non-Militant members was overlooked and local hostilities continue into the 1990s.

Nearly ten years after these events, citing allegations of fraud, the Labour Party in Manchester, Birmingham, London and other areas ejected hundreds of new Asian members, thus pre-empting attempts to get more black candidates on local parliamentary shortlists. Stereotypical depictions of the new members being coerced by authoritarian religious leaders, having sold their membership or being 'in Pakistan' led to outrage by many black community organisations at a local and national level. The Campaign Against Labour Party Suspensions (CALPS) was swiftly formed with joint leadership from Ahmad Shahzad, a Manchester local councillor and Ken Livingstone MP.[5] The panic over Asians 'swamping' the Labour Party sent a clear message to black men and women that involvement in the Labour Party is only tolerated on the terms of a white male leadership.

In the light of the onslaught against black autonomy by Labour Party branches, the defamation of a number of high profile black women who have attempted to assume leadership positions and opposition to attempts to improve black representation, it seems highly optimistic to promote coalition building with local Labour Party branches or left-wing organisations as an effective strategy for individual black women's organisations. The alternative strategy of building coalitions between black organisations in order to lobby local councillors and MPs appears to be more effective. Six of the case study organisations were members of an umbrella group of black community organisations. These included the Liverpool Black Caucus, Sheffield Black Community Forum, Cambridge Ethnic Community Forum, at a local level and the West Indian Standing Conference, Sia: the National Development Agency for the Black Voluntary Sector and the Scottish Black Workers Forum at a national level. However, since mixed organisations seldom prioritise racialised sexism, it appears likely that black women's organisations will need to rely on autonomous policy work at the national level to ensure that such issues are tackled. The Labour government's announcement that it will repeal the Primary Purpose Rule, a rule which discriminated against black women seeking to join fiances in Britain, may be an early indication that such lobbying can be effective (*Voice* 2 May 1997).

COALITIONS WITH BLACK MEN

While relationships with the traditional Left have been fraught, black women's organisations have always involved black men (see Chapter 3). From their inception, black men as partners, brothers and elders were present, organising sound systems, caring for children while women held meetings, acting as drivers, decorators and sponsors for funding applications. Few of the case study organisations had 'women only' policies or excluded black men from their meetings, refuges being the notable exception. Women emphasised that they were not organising 'away from the men' and that the fight against racism united black men and women (Natalie, Caribbean, African Caribbean organisation). This sense of solidarity was emphasised by the Sheffield Bengali Women's Support Group:

> We [women] are half of society. If we remain fallen, how will society rise? How far can a person limp, if one leg is kept shackled? The interests of men and our interests are not different, they are the same. Our aims and goals are the same ones as those of men.
>
> (Chatterjee 1995: 90)

Many of the interviewees also felt that an essential part of their work was awareness raising with black men in order to promote a more egalitarian black community struggle around a common agenda. This dual focus was explained by Brixton Black Women's Group in their position statement, first published in the newsletter *Speak Out*:

> On the one hand, we will continue to organize autonomously and address issues we face as Black women. On the other, we must bring a feminist perspective to the work of our comrades in mixed, progressive Black organisations. In this way, we will be raising the consciousness of the Black community within the totality of Black socialist politics.
>
> (Brixton Black Women's Group 1984b: 89)

BLACK WOMEN UNDER ATTACK

We have also seen the hostility and attempted sabotage that some black women's organisations experienced at the hands of black men. Not all black men were as supportive as those mentioned above and those that were at first often became threatened as women grew and developed greater confidence. These black men showed none of the uneasiness that the black women expressed in 'airing dirty linen' or pandering to stereotypes about black organisations. One organisation headed by African Caribbean men wrote to the local press and councillors denouncing a newly formed women's group. Asian councillors opposed funding proposals made by another group to the local authority. An Asian workers organisation attempted to have another black women's organisation closed down. Black women's organisations were openly accused of being 'traitors to the race' and 'dividing the community'. Women were threatened, ostracised, verbally abused, prevented from attending meetings or accused of promiscuity and sexual deviance (see Brixton Black Women's Group 1984b; Chatterjee 1995; Roy 1995; Shah 1988).

Religion was often a cornerstone of the opposition to black women's autonomy. Conservative Sikh, Muslim, Hindu and Christian Pentecostal leaders gave legitimacy to such attacks. Southall Black Sisters and other black women's organisations have highlighted the onslaught against Asian women's autonomy by conservative and fundamentalist religious leaders and the rise in their popularity in the 1990s (Griffin 1995a; Women Against Fundamentalism 1994). In theorising religious fundamentalism within black communities in the West not as an unquestioned throwback to 'tradition', but as a (post)modern response to, on the one hand, racist exclusion and demonisation of, in particular Islam and, on the other, the perceived moral turmoil of Western society, these writers and activists enable us to identify the modern day appeal of religious conservatism (Ali 1996 and Agnihotri 1987 respectively give Muslim and Sikh perspectives on this issue). As Hanana Siddiqui of Southall Black Sisters points out:

> Increasingly religious identities are being treated as racial identities. The need for certainty and for a positive identity to combat racism and discrimination has led the young, and particularly young men, to take on the new identities associated with fundamentalism.
>
> (Siddiqui, in Griffin 1995a: 80)

Fundamentalist religious identities premised on a return to traditional family values and gender roles, are increasingly being adopted by young Asian men as an oppositional assertion of cultural autonomy. Asian young women therefore become the site of a battle over the 'community's' ability to achieve self determination. Preventing young women from attaining independence, leaving violent partners or being exposed to progressive thinking is reconceptualised as protection from Western corruption. Thus, the newly invigorated militancy of groups of Asian young men, usefully employed in opposing racial violence, becomes highly reactionary and dangerous when it is deployed in finding and returning Asian women to abusive households (Sahgal 1992: 179; Patel 1991: 101).

Black women's organisations have taken various stances in attempting to tackle religious conservatism. Some, like Southall Black Sisters promote a secular approach and advocate the separation of religion and the state. Other organisations utilise religious symbolism to promote progressive thinking, drawing on female religious figures as role models. The proliferation of Shakti groups from the late 1980s,[6] drawing on the Hindu personification of collective energy, is one example of the symbolic power of such religious imagery (Mason-John 1995b: 13; Chatterjee 1995: 97–8). Black feminists who wish to assert the compatibility of women's self determination and their religious identities have emphasised that religious conservatism is only one possible interpretation of religious texts and codes:

> The Qu'ran is being re-interpreted all the time by different political systems. The Islamic fundamentalist leaders that have come to power in the region have all imposed their own interpretation of the Qu'ran. If you visit any Arab country you find that each country has a different interpretation of the Qu'ran. When you have a progressive political system then you have a progressive interpretation of religion.
>
> (Spare Rib Collective 1992; see also A. Wilson 1984: 175)

This strategy was deployed effectively by one of the case study organisations. This organisation utilised progressive male religious scholars to debate with family members who refused to allow women the right to divorce, property or education. A member spoke of the importance to their group of working in partnership with Muslim men:

> We work within the system, and work within Islam. . . . We have a lot of support from Muslim men. . . . Because what we do is to try to help Muslim women and for us it's not the issue between men and women. We have no confrontation with men.
>
> (Zaheda, Middle Eastern, Muslim organisation)

Despite the organisation's progressive agenda and interventions on behalf of individual women, their depoliticisation of gender relations in order to maintain common ground between black men and women does little to challenge systematic and structural gender inequality. These women therefore risk colluding with the ostracism of black women who promote a more radical analysis of women's oppression. Nevertheless, their position allows for support among religious Muslim women who are unwilling to choose between belonging to a religious community and self determination as women.

It is important to note that sexual conservatism in black communities is held in tension with more progressive attitudes. These attitudes are exemplified in the respect and support that some black men have shown towards black women's organisations. Several interviewees suggested that black men were becoming more comfortable with the idea of black women organising autonomously: 'I do see that increasingly these days, men of African origin are not at all threatened by African women working together as African women around the common experience of African women' (Faith, African, black organisation). This was also acknowledged by a member of Southall Black Sisters:

> What we have also noticed is that there were some shifts in attitude within the Asian community itself. The very people who tried to close us down in the 1980s because of our stance on violence against women are now at least paying lip service to the question of domestic violence, even if they are not doing much about it.
>
> (Siddiqui, in Griffin 1995a: 80)

However, the continuing hostility experienced by many black women's refuges suggests that while some black men in the 1990s may welcome black women's autonomy where the focus of the activism is tackling gendered racism in education, social services, the police and other sites of state oppression, a political analysis which includes them as part of the problem is at best tolerated rather than actively supported. Furthermore, changes in attitudes may be limited to urban centres where a diverse range of black women's activism has chipped away at chauvinistic attitudes over a number of years. Roy (1995) points out that the small numbers of 'in the flesh' challenges to community orthodoxies in areas of more dispersed black population may lead to greater intolerance of oppositional and dissenting voices:

> Larger Black communities in other parts of the country enable expression of difference both between and within communities. Outside of that environment, Black groups struggle with the

preservation of an often fragile coalition both in struggles against racism and in the task of living in a racist society. Where there are contradictions between the construction of positive collective and personal identities, the expression of so-called marginal interests can be stifled.

(1995: 103)

In these areas, black male attacks on women's emerging autonomy, cannot adequately be described as a backlash since there have been few gains from which to backtrack. Nevertheless, the rise in conservatism and fundamentalism nationally is likely to have even more harsh effects given the absence of a network of rural and shire black women's organisations which could provide a strong and coordinated opposition.[7] In this context Anzaldua's (1990) words of caution appear to be an accurate reflection on the task of building unity between black men and women: 'There is no common ground. As individuals, we all stand on different plots' (1990: 225).

REDEFINING BLACK MALE ACTIVISM

What hope then is there for meaningful coalitions with black men around the totality of black women's political agenda, including all of the aspects of oppression? This research has identified four areas where the potential for coalition building is present or where such coalitions are beginning to emerge, often in embryonic form.

(1990: 225)

The first area is the emergence of a number of progressive initiatives focusing on black men which are beginning to appear in London, Birmingham and Manchester. These organisations aim to re-think black masculinity, to question 'macho' behaviour, and to counter violence against black women and children. In London the Black Male Forum hosts debates on gender relations within the African Caribbean community. The Black Fathers Project explores the ways in which parenting by African, Asian and Caribbean men is affected by racism, sexism and the pressure to conform to perform traditional family roles[8] (Evans 1995). In Manchester, Kemetic Educational Guidance organises study sessions for African Caribbean men in prison with an emphasis on analysing the roots of abusive behaviour and embracing 'African-centred' values such as respect for women. In Birmingham, the Rites of Passage programme creates a learning environment for male teenagers to prevent destructive behaviour and challenge sexist notions of African Caribbean women as 'baby mothers'. One interviewee expressed tentative hopes that this new agenda might lead to more productive relations with male run organisations:

> We need to perhaps think about where we're going in terms of black men and what kinds of organisational links we want to make, particularly as the new thing is about black men's groups and organisations. I think we'll see that beginning to grow and develop over the next decade and so black women need to think what kinds of links they're going to have with those type of organisations which in theory are going to be progressive.
>
> (Lynette, Caribbean, African Caribbean organisation)

While the male leadership of these organisations is nothing new, these initiatives are unique in their overt focus on black masculinity, their acknowledgement of the specificity of black male experience and their willingness to acknowledge destructive patterns of behaviour by black men. This indicates two significant changes in the approach to community activism by black men. First, there is an acknowledgement for the first time that black men's experience is not the 'Black Experience' and that autonomous and focused organisation by both black men and women is valid. Rather than viewing black women's autonomy as 'splitting the community', these organisations embrace the notion of organising on the basis of gendered experiences of racism and community. Second, it differs dramatically from the insistence of many black male leaders on not 'airing dirty linen':

> I have been told many times by elders who should know better, that there are certain things about the Black communities which we must conceal, that must not be talked about, because to reveal them would be to fuel the fires of racism and state oppression. We must close ranks at whatever cost.
>
> (Bains 1988: 226)

This closure has meant keeping a veil of silence over sexism and abuse within black communities. For the first time, it is black men who are exploring problems within black communities and the impact of racism in reinforcing these problems. In overturning two stalwarts of opposition to black women's autonomy these organisations appear to pave the way for effective partnership with black women's organisations.

However, there is a danger in this new approach. The novelty of airing issues which have previously been considered taboo for many men can lead to discussion being viewed a priori as progressive, without enough focus on the content of what is being said. In the African Caribbean community in London, the success and notoriety of the first Black Male Forum debates led to a number of spin-off events. These events often became opportunities to present the 'battle of the sexes' as entertainment, outside of any real commitment to challenging sexism. With titles such as, 'Will the real Black man please stand up' and 'Do Black men really support their women?' (*Voice* 26 March 1996b: 26; Sia May 1996d), the focus inevitably turned to trivial discussions about sexual relations. The potential to discuss more 'painful' issues such as abuse and domestic violence in a serious way was therefore diminished. One interviewee noted that such debates could also become a voyeuristic opportunity for white people to enjoy the ritual humiliation of black men and to confirm stereotypes about dysfunctional black family life:

> I'd like to see more dialogue between the groups, men and women. . . . And I'd like it to be direct as opposed to mediated through white people, which is the way that it happens now. So we get a black woman writing a play about how useless black men are, and it will get an airing and it will go into the *Voice*. . . . And the message is constantly how useless black men are.
>
> (Faith, African, black organisation)

In separating discussions about gender relations from their socio-economic context, these events may empty them of their political content and promote culturalist explanations of black women's oppression. Failing to link up with black women's organisations and to learn from black feminist theorising about gender relations, these debates often reify stereotypes about black men and black male sexism. In limiting the examination of gender roles to the sphere of personal relationships, these organisations do not address broader political challenges which have emerged in black feminist and womanist thought. Furthermore, in restricting their analysis and remit to the African Caribbean community, these debates fail to engage or draw parallels with contemporary manifestations of patriarchal ideologies in Asian communities such as the policing of

Asian women's sexuality by youth gangs (see discussion earlier in this chapter). Nevertheless, the opportunity for more inclusive and less commercialised work on gender relations by black men has been created and two shibboleths about what is and is not acceptable in community organising have been fundamentally challenged. This in itself implies a possible starting-point for carefully thought through coalitions between black women's organisations working on violence and gender relations and these organisations.

A second area of potential solidarity is black gay activism. While the nascent 'black men's movement' has not yet developed a rigorous critique of heterosexism and homophobia, black gay men have long been engaged in critical thinking on gender roles (Julien and Mercer 1991; Julien 1992). Black gay and lesbian autonomous struggles have been characterised by strong alliances between gays and lesbians within mixed organisations as well as between single gender organisations (Bellos 1995; Mason-John 1995: 13).[9] As such, these organisations are a model for black men and women working in partnership around a progressive agenda, building on commonalities in the face of different gendered experiences.

This close political relationship has not been without difficulties. Black gay men have been challenged for making black women invisible. And black lesbian women have had to challenge their own ideas about black masculinity and their expectations of gay men. A black lesbian group, established in London in the early 1980s, experienced the difficulty of negotiating racialised sexualities when they invited a black gay group to discuss possible co-parenting arrangements. The suggestion was met with outrage by the men who felt that the women were commodifying black masculinity:

> They were furious, they sent us back a letter that was so hot it smoked through the envelope. They were so angry with us because we were just using them as studs, stereotyping them in the same way that they'd been stereotyped since slavery.
>
> (Abiola, African, black organisation)

In exploring the issue, the black women were forced to confront their own fears about being childless and their internalisation of patriarchal nationalist calls for women to 'breed' sons to counter white genocidal strategies. This incident indicates the entrenched nature of gender expectations and the fragility of common bonds in the face of real differences. Nevertheless, the effective political alliances which black gays and lesbians have forged indicate that there is also an opportunity for (primarily) straight black women's organisations to work with mixed black gay and lesbian organisations on issues such as re-defining black masculinity, making links between patriarchal and homophobic violence, health and HIV. Ultimately, black women's organisations that wish to forge such links will need to challenge their own attitudes and to make theoretical links between homophobia, gendered racism and economic exploitation (Bellos 1995: 69–70). The 'don't ask, don't tell' policy which many black women's organisations operate will be an inadequate basis for any real respect between such organisations.

The third arena of successful coalitions between black mixed and women's organisations has been the development of black voluntary sector umbrella organisations. At the local level, umbrella groups such as the Black Community Forum in Sheffield, the Ethnic Community Forum in Cambridge, Bath Network of Black Organisations and Bristol Black Voluntary Sector Development Unit have been established throughout the 1980s and 1990s. These forums have active involvement from black women's organisations. Several interviewees stated that their political concerns at the local level were channelled through these bodies, as they were less easily singled out for punitive action by local authorities. Support was also received when funding was cut or threatened.

The introduction of 'partnership' funding, involving group bids from statutory, voluntary and private sectors, is gradually changing the face of voluntary sector funding. It is clear that if black women's organisations are to receive any funds from the Single Regeneration Budget or subsequent initiatives which utilise a similar approach, they will be forced to form coalitions with other black organisations (Medas 1994). Attempting to negotiate as an individual organisation when large corporations are sitting at the table with their eye on million pound 'flagship' schemes, will clearly be inadequate. While two case study organisations had been involved in partnership bids, one successfully, it is clear that black women's organisations which are comfortable with local authority grant aid procedures are unfamiliar with the processes involved in accessing funds under the new central government initiative. It is also evident that those black women's organisations which already had significant links with umbrella bodies were in a better position to negotiate joint funding bids. Thus, building effective coalitions at the local level can have financial as well as political benefits.

At a national level, collaboration between Sia: the National

Development Agency for the Black Voluntary Sector and a group of black women's organisations has led to the formation of a National Network of Black Women's Organisations (NNBWO). At a national conference in Birmingham in 1993 entitled 'Agenda 2000', black women's organisations came together in a workshop and challenged Sia: the National Development Agency for the Black Voluntary Sector to include a more comprehensive approach to supporting black women's autonomy and challenging black male sexism (Sia 1994). As a result, the national network was established in 1995. Development work was undertaken by a black female project officer at the agency and the network currently involves over one hundred black women's organisations. Countering previous London-centred tendencies, the network held conferences in Leeds and Nottingham where pragmatic issues such as funding as well as strategic and political goals were examined. The network is only one of many attempts to take up the challenge of OWAAD's demise in 1982. Yet the deployment of the resources which Sia can command as a national development agency funded by central government means that women who are already over-stretched in dealing with local issues, do not have to put in the additional work of coordinating a network. As notes of a meeting of the network stated:

> Whilst it was recognised that the vast majority of Black women's organisations are out there 'firefighting' – meeting the needs within their communities on a daily basis, it is also essential for Black women to maintain a policy agenda in an attempt to stem the continued invisibility and marginalisation of Black women's concerns in the decision making forums of central and local government.

(Sia May 1996: 4)

Women's organisations which might otherwise be unwilling, are therefore encouraged to engage with broader political issues at a national and international level, and the burden on those already involved is reduced.

Fourth, black women's organisations which work on issues of violence against women may find potential allies in burgeoning racist violence projects. The link between violence against women, state hostility and racist harassment has been made by black feminists (Shah 1988: 289). The fear of racist attack is an additional burden on women considering escape from abusive households, the high visibility of a house full of black women also lays refuges in primarily white areas open to further violence. Police collusion in cases of domestic violence is mirrored by their frequent failure to acknowledge racist harassment, their unwillingness to prosecute offenders is common to both events. In addition, the failure of the courts to bring about justice in many cases of domestic violence, is matched by a paucity of successful prosecutions against perpetrators of racist murders (Mama 1989a, 1989b). Black men and women working together in a primarily Bengali community in east London have created CAPA, a multi-racialised organisation which tackles both sexist violence against women and racist violence against men, women and children. The organisation's philosophy, that violence is indivisible and that no elements of violence against black communities can be left unchallenged is the foundation for solid work with black women's organisations. Its strong stance in opposing sexism within black communities and working towards 'a strategic black unity' also creates a common ideological framework with black women's autonomous activism (Ocloo 1995).

CAPA is not the only anti-violence project to have developed a commitment to tackling sexism, the Coventry Anti-Racial Harassment and Attacks Network, which ceased to function in 1992 due to lack of funds, nevertheless developed strong links with local Asian and African Caribbean women's organisations. Similar projects in Liverpool, Newcastle, Birmingham and other parts of London should provide an opportunity for black women's organisations in these localities to create joint campaigns against all forms of violence.

It is no longer possible to talk about a homogenous black community or a unitary black voluntary sector. Black organisations express as many diverse political ideologies as white-led political organisations. It is therefore not useful to talk about sexism in black communities as if this were a monolithic force. Black men, both autonomously and in alliance with black women, are engaged in building anti-sexist and progressive organisations. Black men have also learnt lessons from black women's organisations. Embracing the notion of the personal as political, they are beginning to look at their 'dirty linen' and address themselves to the task of washing it. At a historical moment when calls for a return to traditional gender roles are rife within black communities, this re-examination of black masculinity could not be more timely. There is a need for these organisations to challenge reactionary religious and political forces which seek to reinscribe oppressive gender roles, and to work in partnership with black women's organisations that have strived to understand the interrelationship of many struggles over a period of two decades and have many lessons to offer. Black women's organisations have much to gain in seeking coalitions with such organisations.

LOOKING FOR SISTERHOOD

From the early days of the Women's Liberation Movement in Britain, black women have struggled to have their voices heard as an integral part of feminist thought and praxis (Amos *et al.* 1984; W. Brown 1984). However, it was only in the late 1970s, when black women organised an autonomous base and began a coordinated attack on white hegemony, that white feminists were forced to take note of the serious challenge posed by black feminism. From the early 1980s, black women and white feminists engaged in often acrimonious exchanges in meetings, conferences, newsletters and journals including *Spare Rib*, the *London Women's Liberation Newsletter* and *Feminist Review* (Parmar 1982; Bhavnani and Coulson 1985; Lees 1986). As black women involved in OWAAD, Awaz, Brixton Black Women's Group and Southall Black Sisters developed black feminism as 'a distinct body of theory and practice', increasingly rigorous theoretical challenges were made to the tenets of white feminism[10] (Amos *et al.* 1984: 18). On a more practical level, black women protested against racism and lack of support from white feminists, leading to the claim that: 'Black Women have to survive white feminists and then white society' (Maxine and Arati 1984; *London Women's Liberation Newsletter* 1984a).

White feminists did not take this criticism without fighting back. They made counter-allegations that black women were promoting a divisive separatism which was in effect reverse/black racism (Welch 1984). They alleged that black women were utilising aggressive, 'male' tactics which were incompatible with women's essentially peaceful nature (K. Bhavnani 1988). They accused black women of 'diverting the cause' because of their insistence on opposing racism and supporting black men against racist attacks (W. Brown 1984; Spelman 1988: 113). They claimed that black women were 'watering down' feminism and promoting an 'anything goes' approach to the family. Black women's refusal to offer unquestioning support to the call for 'abortion on demand', in the light of experiences of forced sterilisation and hostile birth control strategies, was used as evidence that they were 'anti-feminist' (W. Brown 1984). Finally, white feminists utilised an analysis of racism as a product of patriarchy created to divide women's liberation struggles thereby to exonerate themselves from any active involvement in the continuation of racialised oppression (Amos *et al.* 1984; Spelman 1988: 93). Early white feminist responses to challenges by black feminists were therefore largely those of counter-attack and denial.

Seven of the twenty-five interviewees had been involved in the [white] Women's Liberation Movement prior to their involvement in black women's organisations. These women expressed their hope on joining the movement, that it would provide answers to many of their concerns which had not been addressed by black male-led struggles and the pain and disillusionment which they experienced on discovering that this was not the case:

> I was a feminist and I identified with other feminists. It took less than a year, but I became increasingly shocked at the way that feminism wasn't as all embracing, it wasn't as encompassing as I had originally hoped and wished, it was still very much about the experience of white women.

> (Faith, African, black organisation)

A key area of disagreement was black women's relationship with black men. Black women in the early 1980s were involved in campaigns against the harassment of black men under 'Search under Suspicion' legislation, exclusions of black boys from schools and concentration in disruptive units (sin bins), and police brutality against black men (and women) involved in urban uprisings and demonstrations against far-right groups (OWAAD 1980). In the light of the onslaught against black men, white feminists' claims to be oppressed by all men were seen as false and hypocritical. Yet white feminists were reluctant to acknowledge the impact of racism on black men and hesitant to recognise the legitimacy of solidarity between black men and women on the basis of class exploitation and racialised oppression:

> At the time, it was felt by white women that the issue of womanhood kind of transcended issues of race and that we had far more in common, which we felt was blatantly untrue. Because the issues of sexism from white men was very different from the

issue of sexism from black men, because black men don't have the power that white men have. And I think that in the feminist movement, there's an inability to see that. It's just: 'men are men and men are sexist'. Our experiences were different and clearly we suffered racism from white men and women and there was enormous racism in the women's movement which was why we felt we couldn't be a part of it. Because fundamentally, it's a white middle class organisation.

(Sonia, Caribbean, African Caribbean organisation)

White feminists' racism and insensitivity to black community struggles in organising 'Reclaim the Night' marches through black areas, and in demanding an increased police presence at a time of overt police brutality towards black communities, created further antagonism between black and white women (see Bhavnani and Coulson 1985: 84):

I remember arguing in groups against white women who would say that the solution to violence against women is to have more police officers in the street. And I said, 'wait wait wait, these are the days of the SUS law. What will happen is that every black man will be harassed by the police and when you say there are certain areas where you won't go, well, you name those areas'. And they'd say 'well Brixton'. Oh you mean you're afraid of black men – you're safe with white men?

(Faith)

Black women were frustrated with white feminists' refusal to acknowledge the impact of racialised and class privilege on their lives, and of racism on the lives of black women in Britain. One interviewee pointed out that white feminists preferred to think of racism as being either historically or spatially distanced from their lives (see Bhavnani and Coulson 1985). This was yet another way of exonerating themselves from any implication in racism and imperialism. The 1984 black feminist conference in London entitled 'We Are Here' was a direct attack on this tactic:

I became increasingly frustrated with the way white feminists would talk about racism as something that was far away. They were heavily into Nicaragua and Soweto, but my reaction was to say actually 'we are here' . . . we were treated as exotic, racism was a separate subject to be bolted on, there was feminism and there was racism, but for those of us that are black and women, being black is an integral part of women and we don't want it bolted on, it's not an additional extra.

(Faith)

Finally, black women were incensed by the refusal by many white feminists to acknowledge and support their right to self determination. Rather than supporting the establishment of black women's autonomous organisations, many white women reacted with hostility, anxiety and anger. In so doing, they undermined the potential for developing constructive partnerships at an early stage in the development of a burgeoning black women's movement:

Some white women may go there and feel: 'why is it black women only?'. I suppose they're coming from a feminist perspective . . . you might feel 'we're supposed to be all women together, our struggles are the same'.

(Lynette, Caribbean, African Caribbean organisation)

Black women holding meetings in predominantly white women's centres reported suspicion, anxiety and nervous attempts to control what was viewed as inappropriate behaviour:

Ostensibly they were [supportive]. . . . In reality they were completely terrified of us, most of them at women's parties would have seen one black woman. . . . They would never have had to deal with more than one in any of their collectives, cooperatives and organisations.

(Abiola, African, black organisation)

Black women en masse refused to be integrated into feminist organisations on pre-defined terms. Their presence, their assumed and often real anger fundamentally disturbed the prevailing [white] feminist order.

Opposition to black women's autonomy is not only rooted in psycho-social dynamics. One interviewee commented on a series of letters that appeared in the *London Women's Liberation Newsletter* (LWLN) during the early 1980s:

It was in that forum which was the heart of feminist London at that time, that this debate raged about whether black women should organise autonomously. It would be black women writing as well, but actually, there were a lot more white women arguing for and against. And a lot of the time, I felt like I was just watching a tennis match.

(Abiola)

Black women organising were debunking the white feminist excuse for failing to involve black women in 'their movement', that black women were too overworked, apathetic or unskilled (LWLN 1984b). The existence of black women's organisations a priori highlighted the racism and exclusion embedded in white women's praxis and analysis. While it is important to note that some white women supported black women's right to organise, the motivation for this support is not entirely clear cut. For some white feminists the existence of autonomous organisations putting forward a separate black women's agenda could be used to relieve themselves of rethinking their political analysis (Feminist Review Collective 1986: 20; Barrett and McIntosh 1985: 23). Black women's organisations could then become a resource to be called on when a black woman was needed to give some necessary diversity to a conference platform, or to provide expertise on 'black women's particular needs' (Misa, Asian, black organisation). This approach creates a parasitical relationship between white and black women and leaves white feminism fundamentally unchanged.

The perception (not altogether unfounded) that the [white] feminist movement's focus was on expanding white male privilege to include white women, reinforced by a sense of disillusionment, led many black women to reject the term 'feminist' (hooks 1995: 100). This rejection was particularly true for younger black women who had not come to black women's organisations via the feminist movement and thus saw little reason to identify with what they saw as a platform for white women:

I do remember some tension around the fact that a lot of black women in London were very critical of feminism which was seen to be exclusively white and I and some other black women argued that it need not, we shouldn't let white women have a monopoly on something that was as important to us as to them, if not more so.

(Faith)

This tension led to increasing fragmentation between women who felt that black women's activism should be located within black struggle and those that also saw it as part of the feminist movement.

Disagreements over this issue, which surfaced at the fourth OWAAD conference in 1982 on the theme of black feminism, contributed to the organisation's subsequent demise (Brixton Black Women's Group 1984a). In the late 1980s a number of women adopted the term 'womanist' from Alice Walker's conceptualisation of the term (Walker 1985: xi) as an alternative:

> The term black feminist . . . doesn't or [n]ever will fit comfortably – 'Womynist' is definitely more me. As it more accurately encompasses the sum total of my experiences, personal, artistic and political at this point in time.
>
> (Akua, in We Are Here Collective 1988)

This term has not taken on widespread acceptance possibly because of its African American origins which do not resonate as strongly with African, Caribbean or Asian vernacular. Nevertheless, Alexander finds its revitalisation among young black Christian women in the 1990s in the form of a 'womanist theology' (V. Alexander 1995: 104). Ultimately, white British feminists' colonisation of the label 'feminist', which appears to have been more far-reaching than in the United States, has serious implications for creating an oppositional language shared by black and white women (B. Smith 1983, Collins 1990).[11]

By the mid 1980s the [white] Women's Liberation Movement was beginning to show signs of severe stress, organisations began to close, newsletters were discontinued and the sense of a central coherence and energy began to dissolve. This fragmentation was interpreted by many white feminists as the fulfilment of their predictions that black women were dividing 'their' movement. This interpretation was therefore the basis for further hostility towards black women:

> It unravelled around race primarily, it unravelled around difference, it unravelled around the inability of women to negotiate difference among us and there were some white women who felt . . . that WE had ruined THEIR Women's Liberation Movement. They would still complain that we caused trouble by raising issues of class and race, these unpleasant disruptive things which weren't really feminist.
>
> (Faith)

While black feminists had been clear that their political analysis was one which was able to unite women in a broad based alliance against all forms of oppression (Bhavnani and Coulson 1985), their stance was misconstrued as speaking only to the particular experiences of black women. It was therefore felt by socialist feminists in particular, that a broader political analysis had been diverted into small scale, fragmented and culturally specific analyses. In 1986, Michele Barrett in a round-table discussion with *Feminist Review* stated: 'I think it's true to say that within the women's movement the socialist-feminism of the 1970s has given way to feminist peace initiatives and to the specific demands of black feminists' (Feminist Review Collective 1986: 14). Barrett's analysis conceptually excludes black feminism from socialist feminism. Yet, as we saw in the last chapter, Brixton Black Women's Group, OWAAD and other groups active in the 1980s had an explicitly socialist feminist analysis. The battles won by black feminists should therefore also be victories for socialist feminism. White feminists' failure to welcome black women's autonomous achievements as beneficial for all women therefore prevented them from utilising black women's analyses to create a broader based feminist movement which could have sustained its appeal to a diverse range of women.

Recent contributions to feminist thought have acknowledged that the dissolution of the [white] women's movement was not due to the allegedly divisive tactics of black feminists. On the contrary, it was white women's racism and inability to listen non-defensively to black women's concerns which created stresses in mixed women's organisations. More significantly, there were a number of other fault lines. Lesbian and disabled women (black and white), Jewish women and other non-black minorities also accused the movement of failing to represent their interests. As Griffin remarks, 'the homogeneity, common purpose and mass mobilisation of the Women's (Liberation) Movement' is 'a myth, a nostalgic retrospective view of some golden age of feminism that probably never was' (Griffin 1995a: 4). Given the constant challenges to white hegemony by black women, the experiences of unity which some white feminists claim, were surely achieved by excluding these and other voices of dissent. These women experienced the early days of the Women's Liberation Movement in the cocoon of privilege. In failing to break out, they colluded in the oppression of women who were not able to participate in their particular safe space (see Reagon 1983).

The movement also fractured along political lines. By the mid 1980s, three separate movements: liberal feminists, socialist feminists and radical feminists (including the Women's Peace

Movement) had emerged. The differences between these approaches have been examined elsewhere (Ramazanoglu 1989; Gunew 1991). What is significant is that these positions premised different political methods, different sites of resistance and different goals. For example, while radical feminists focused on the family as the ultimate site of resistance and saw lesbianism and separatism as political strategies, socialist feminists placed an emphasis on building a broad based struggle against capitalism and were therefore willing to work with working class men. Similarly, many socialist feminists rejected the essentialism of the culture of femininity promoted by many women involved in the Women's Peace Movement (Feminist Review Collective 1986; Ramazanoglu 1989). Both radical and socialist feminists tended to reject liberal feminism for having no theoretical analysis of systems of domination in their battle for access to existing social, political and economic institutions. The chasm between women with these different viewpoints could not be bridged by any simplistic call to 'sisterhood', any more than the gulfs between black and white women would be overcome by the desire for women's unity.

MOVING ON

What significance does this recent history have for the potential of coalition building between black and white women? One important outcome of the hostility shown by white feminists has been the conceptual and political location of most black women's organisations within the black voluntary sector, rather than within the women's movement.[12] Few of the interviewees felt that they had significant commonalities with white women, while all the organisations laid emphasis on their shared experiences and organisational goals with black men and black communities, even if these common causes were limited by actual experiences of sexism. White women in the 1990s were believed, with few exceptions, to be in denial of racism, reluctant to accept black autonomy, hostile to black men and invested in a non-existent 'sisterhood'. In addition, black women utilised ridicule, objectification and scorn to emphasise their cultural distance from white feminists. Such comments represented the latter as hostile to children, unwilling to keep their community buildings or homes clean, unable to have fun, cook or eat well, emotionally sterile and culturally and spiritually barren. These characteristics were given as further reasons why black women and white feminists were essentially different.[13] This picture of white feminists, while drawing on observed trends (for example, many white women in collectives viewed housework as demeaning), is largely anachronistic, oversimplified and is informed by derogatory and homogenising media images. It nevertheless indicates the enormous barrier which must be overcome if any meaningful partnership is to be built between the two groups.

Much has been made of white feminists' progress on issues of difference and diversity in the 1980s (Frankenberg 1993a; Feminist Review Collective 1992). Shaken by black feminist critiques, white feminists in Britain began to acknowledge black women's exclusion from the political strategies of the [white] Women's Liberation Movement and to seek to rectify that exclusion in conferences, collectives and editorial boards (Barrett and McIntosh 1985). Yet these strategies have fallen short of embracing the thorough analysis of racism by black feminists. In fact it has been pointed out that many white feminists, while appearing to learn from these black feminist critiques, actually rejected their findings (Bhavnani and Coulson 1985). There have been three broad approaches by white British feminists in the 1980s. The first, which was bravely laid out by Barrett and McIntosh utilises the concept of 'ethnocentrism' to analyse 'what went wrong'. These accounts agree that white women have placed themselves and their experiences at the centre of feminist analysis, but attribute this to 'ethnocentrism'.[14] Barrett and McIntosh acknowledge that white feminist thought was premised on the experiences of white women, but reject allegations of racism on the grounds that this focus is merely 'ethnically specific':

> We do not accept that such work is necessarily racist, nor indeed that it is necessarily inadequate as an analysis of the position of women from different ethnic groups. . . . But we do accept the central point made against white feminists such as ourselves – that our work has spoken from an unacknowledged but ethnically specific position.
>
> (Barrett and McIntosh 1985: 25)

They then go on to defend their key arguments, utilising examples from black women's experiences to show that they are compatible with the authors' positions on patriarchy and the family. A detailed critique of the 'ethnocentrism' approach has been made by Bhavnani and Coulson (1985). Here it is sufficient to point out the remarkable similarity between their article and earlier white feminist rejections of allegations of racism. In keeping with the tradition of denial, they acknowledge racism, but distance it as something 'out there', which feminists should not ignore, but are not guilty of. In keeping with the history of counter-attack, they accuse Amos and Parmar (1984) of a 'militant cultural relativism' (Bhavnani and Coulson 1985: 42). Barrett and McIntosh's article is merely symptomatic of a [white] feminist movement which, even as it fragmented, was unwilling to let go of central tenets in favour of the radical transformation demanded by black women.

While Barrett and McIntosh's argument for discarding 'race' in favour of ethnicity was attacked by both black and white feminists at the time of its production (Ramazanoglu 1986; Kazi 1986; Mirza 1986), it nevertheless appears to have heralded a new direction for socialist feminism. Much subsequent work has taken a similar approach and has rejected analysis of racism in favour of a re-evaluation of ethnicity (Anthias *et al.* 1992; Gamman *et al.* 1993). Socialist feminists were unwilling to accept the necessarily simplified dichotomies of black and white promoted in much black feminist writing, which sat uneasily with their more complex understanding of white women as a group differentiated internally by socio-economic divisions. Rejecting anti-racism's homogenisation of white men and women, they instead found in 'difference' a concept which captured diversity of experience without creating dualistic and unitary categories. When in 1992, for example, the Feminist Review Collective announced their new-found anti-racist commitment, it was in the context of a theoretical and conceptual distancing from what were clearly considered the excesses of anti-racist politics:

> Our respect for the achievements of earlier antiracist policies coexists with a recognition of the need to be part of a politics and analyses which articulate difference, take on contradictions and ambiguity, avoid moralism and nurture radicalism. It is in this spirit we wish to express our commitment as an anti-racist journal.
>
> (Feminist Review Collective 1992)

The discomfort with aligning themselves with anti-racist theory and praxis was swiftly resolved by a more conclusive distancing from anti-racism via the embrace of ethnicity:

> At the political, at the popular and at the academic level, 'ethnicity' is a concept which we all need to come to terms with

and 'ethnic identities' are identities which we need to be able to grasp and understand. This understanding is necessary if we are to come to terms with ... the ways in which ethnicism (the construction of culturally essentialized groups) becomes a tool to produce and reconstitute relationships of dominance and subordination.

(Gamman *et al.* 1993: 1)

The shift to ethnicity has most consistently been advocated by Anthias *et al.* (1992), socialist feminists who argue that racism relies on ethnic boundary formation to define the out-group. Ethnicity therefore pre-exists racism; 'ethnic phenomena' are the 'axis' upon which 'race' depends (1992: 2). Anthias *et al.* reject the 'ethnic studies' approach for its unwillingness to engage in the realities of racism, yet their own analysis rejects the specificity of white on black racism, the reality of the 'colour line' which remains a key variable in explaining current socio-economic inequalities between women (S. Small 1994). The authors retain the concept of 'racism' as one form of exclusion which occurs in the context of other forms of exclusion, on grounds of ethnicity, gender and class. In their project to find a schema which speaks to the experiences of white minorities, refugees and asylum seekers, the authors position issues of boundary setting at the forefront and allow racism only a secondary importance. Their assertion that, of course, blacks can be racist, and their onslaught on the term 'black' indicate that this project, while inspired by black feminism, continues Barrett and McIntosh's tradition of rejecting the latter's findings. As Kazi points out:

Discarding racism as unsatisfactory would neither eradicate racism nor would it be acceptable to black women. . . . Focusing on ethnic terms is already regarded . . . as a fashionable weapon for depoliticising the black struggle.

(Kazi 1986: 89)

The second approach largely has been adopted by liberal feminists who sought redress for women's inequality through improved access to the education, legal, political and economic infrastructures. Finding a base within left-wing local authorities, liberal feminism adopted a 'double jeopardy' approach to black women, adding racism to sexism to locate black women as 'doubly oppressed':

Black and ethnic minority women, lesbians, older women and women with disabilities all experience double discrimination, although these groups are not mutually exclusive, and many women experience the compounded problems of several kinds of discrimination.

(GLC 1986: 20)

The absence of any over-arching theory of oppression enabled white liberal feminists, unencumbered by a commitment to the primacy of patriarchy or of class relations, and pressured by highly vocal black feminists, simply to add racism to their existing concerns. This relatively untheorised position has led to a movement to create equality of opportunity for black and white women. The solution proposed was the statist regulation of both racism and sexism and the channelling of funds to black women in order to enable them to 'empower' themselves. Black women's autonomy was therefore accepted relatively comfortably within the framework of liberal pluralism. Difference and diversity were celebrated within the boundaries of established norms and institutions were (at best) reformed, but never fundamentally questioned.

By the early 1990s the professional feminist voluntary sector, itself primarily liberal in focus, had also embraced the concept of black women's autonomy within a cultural pluralist framework. In 1993 the National Association of Women's Organisations, an umbrella organisation of predominantly white feminist groups, employed a researcher to identify 'good practice' for black women in rural areas (Goldsmith and Makris 1993). In a similar vein, in 1993 the Equal Opportunities Commission (EOC)[15] organised large conferences for 'Black and Ethnic Minority' women in Wales and Scotland with the aim of establishing 'autonomous' black women's networks (EOC 1993, 1994). The conferences were framed within a liberal pluralist framework utilising a cumulative theory of oppression:

Black women work in the most vulnerable industries and employment. They suffer from double discrimination (a) as women (b) as ethnic minorities. Their needs have rarely been researched. . . . The black woman . . . experiences the same sex discrimination as her white counterpart – an experience compounded by her ethnic origin and the colour of her skin.

(EOC 1993: 3)

There are two key problems with this (rather confused) conceptualisation of the socio-economic position of black women. First, the
writer appears to be unable to decide whether it is racism or
ethnicity which is 'compounding' black women's experience of
sexism. While it is suggested that both culture (her ethnic origin)
and racism (the colour of her skin) are implicated: an earlier
passage in the text suggests that culture is the key variable:

> According to recent research, black employment in Wales in 1991
> amounted to 51 per cent of the regional unemployment rates.
> Such barriers to work and employment exist because of the
> unique cultural and language needs of the community.
>
> (EOC 1993: 2)

This ambivalence is reflected in the use of terminology, which
shifts from 'black' as a political designation to 'ethnic minority'
implying that ethnicity is the important category. Thus, this text
appears to slip into a culturalist approach which has been much
criticised for obscuring the role of racism in structuring socio-
economic relations. Discrimination is therefore reduced to
individual acts of exclusion which are abstracted from their institutional context and as such, it is implied, can be eliminated without
fundamental social change. This analysis is clearly unable to explain
the entrenched social exclusion of black communities in, for
example, Cardiff, Bristol and Liverpool, where there has been an
African presence since the late nineteenth century.

The assertion that black women experience the same 'sexism' as
white women plus racism/ethnocentrism which, presumably, is the
same as that experienced by black men is also inaccurate. As black
feminists have been asserting for over two decades, black women
experience a sexism which is racialised and a racism which is
gendered (just as black men experience racisms which are gender
specific and white women experience sexism through the prism of
white privilege). That is, their experiences cannot be deduced from
the experiences of either white women or those of black men. This
inadequate theorisation leads to the assumption that policies and
strategies designed to facilitate access for white women need only
the addition of cultural sensitivity to be effective for black women.

The focus on working within a reformist framework with an
emphasis on educating white women can have disturbing consequences. For example, white women were included at both
conferences as 'observers', an involvement which was questioned by

some of the black women present (EOC 1993: 10). However, the critique of the EOC made by conference participants indicates that whatever the political framework of such events, gathering black women together can have unexpected and oppositional outcomes. In addition, the resources and worker time deployed by the professional feminist sector offer opportunities for the creation of a valuable infrastructure in areas where black women are geographically dispersed.

The third strategy in responding to black women's critiques, was developed from a radical feminist perspective. It acknowledges racism as a key factor in shaping the interaction between black and white women, but interprets this in the light of the tenet 'the personal is political'. In part, this approach is a response to allegations that white feminists were acknowledging racism but only as something which operated 'out there', an acknowledgment that racism was a force which had direct implications for feminist organising: 'I saw racism as entirely external to me, a characteristic of extremists or of the British State, but not a part of what made *me*, or shaped my activism' (Frankenberg 1993b: 52).

A solution to this externalisation was found in personalising racism, looking to the traditional radical feminist methodology of consciousness raising (CR) in order to tackle racism[16] (Bourne 1983). Racism awareness became a form of individual catharsis where white women purged their guilt through painful soul-searching sessions. As Bourne points out, this analysis dislocates racism from its structural context and reduces racism to prejudice. In practical terms, it shifts the focus of anti-racism from the state and institutional sites such as immigration, education and health, to the individual. It leads to white women experiencing guilt and paralysis around black women and to a desire for forgiveness:

> CR's route into anti-racism, for instance, is through the instilling of guilt into women for being white – and leads to a kind of confessional situation, with black people (irrespective of class or values) in the position of arbiters of our racialism dealing out the mea culpae.
>
> (Bourne 1983: 17)

In a study of groupwork with black and white women, Pheterson (1990) found that black women reacted to white women's desire for legitimation with frustration and annoyance. Black women were expected to absolve white women of their racism, by educating, reassuring and affirming them. Yet again, black women are pushed into a supportive role. Understandably, many black women have rejected this role and refused to dedicate themselves to educating or otherwise servicing white feminists (Welch 1984). Furthermore, many black women have become impatient with white feminists and view them as introspective, self indulgent and intellectualising. These 'white feminist' characteristics are then contrasted to black women's activism, pragmatism and 'grassroots' agenda. White women involved in consciousness raising on racism recognised white women's shared culpability in racism, but seldom moved beyond that. Thus, they limited the possibility of partnerships with black women's organisations which are largely unwilling to focus their energies on educating white women.

In opposition to these three trends, some white feminists have called for an anti-racist socialist feminism which could link black and white women in a holistic struggle against racism, sexism and class exploitation (Bourne 1983; James 1985). However, barriers of fear, defensiveness and antagonism prevented the fundamental transformation of feminist theory implied in this agenda. As feminism entered the 1990s, a decade of struggles over racism had led to some tentative gains. Black women were increasingly seen on conference panels, in journals and in edited collections (Gunew 1991; Griffin 1995a). The collective of Spare Rib became predominantly black; five black women joined the previously all-white collective of *Feminist Review*, proclaiming: 'The diversity and difference of women's lives upon which black feminists had for so long insisted – once acknowledged – changed the political and theoretical shape of feminism' (Feminist Review Collective 1992). Yet these gains were contested and tenuous, *Spare Rib*'s closure due to lack of funds coincided with a protracted argument on the letters page about whether the magazine had shifted its focus from 'women's issues' to 'world politics' and three of the five of *Feminist Review*'s black members left after acrimonious battles over the content of the journal (Feminist Review Collective 1992; *Spare Rib* 1992, 1993). Nevertheless, some white feminists appeared to have gained a new-found confidence and commitment to creating an anti-racist feminism which could serve as a basis for solidarity between white and black women. The starting-point for this transformation of white feminism was to acknowledge its specificity. White feminists began to analyse the social construction of whiteness, the meanings and expressions of white privilege and the actuality of lived relations between black and white women (Frankenberg 1993a, 1993b; Ware 1992). These works are groundbreaking, not because of their belated acknowledgement of racism and racialisation, but because of their insider's eye view of the minutiae of white privilege. These scholars draw from the consciousness raising (CR) approach, in acknowledging the ways in which racialised privilege shapes the lives of white women, but in placing this awareness in the context of an analysis of racism and imperialism, they avoid the introspection and political paralysis of CR:

> Unlearning racism, however, is not the same thing as ending it. Nor can we wait for a moment when we feel we have finished changing our 'race consciousness' before becoming active in working against racism in the world at large.
>
> (Frankenberg 1993b: 80)

In identifying the specificity of white women's experiences and acknowledging how much they have benefited from interactions with black feminists, these scholars begin to challenge the dominant response modes of denial and counter-attack. They have therefore set the precedent for re-building the link between black and white women's activism.

BEYOND WHITE DENIAL AND BLACK ANGER

> I want the white woman to own up to her responsibility in the historic part in terms of being part of the people who oppressed black people. If white women can't face that and say yeah, ... not just because we got tits and [points] it's not because we just females that makes us the same.
>
> (Mona, Middle Eastern, black organisation)

Beyond white denial lies the possibility of acknowledging that white feminists, as individuals, often silence, ignore or otherwise oppress black women and as a group, benefit from racism and imperialism. To recognise that: 'between us and white people, there's a lot of blood, there's a lot of pain' (Mona). When white feminists abandon the unsubstantiated claim that we are all 'sisters', black women will be freed up to identify where and when black and white women may have common agendas. When white feminists cease to respond to challenges from black women with counter-attack and defensiveness, black women may take a more positive view of feminism.

When white feminists support black women's struggles on a range of issues, rather than only those initiatives which highlight sexism; when they value black women's writing which challenges their theory and praxis, not just those publications which focus on what they have defined as 'feminist issues', more black women may see a value in building coalitions against racialised sexism.

Beyond black anger is the possibility of revisiting women's history to identify the moments when a different relationship between black and white women was glimpsed. The organisations operating out of the King's Cross Women's Centre offer one such example. Born out of the International Wages for Housework Campaign (WHC), Black Women for Wages for Housework (BWfWfH) was formed in the early 1970s by black women who were active in WHC. Drawing on experience of anti-Vietnam and Civil Rights activism in the United States, a small core of black women established BWfWfH and Black Women Against Rape as autonomous organisations, while still working closely with white women in Wages for Housework, lesbian, prostitute, anti-rape and peace organisations (Mason-John 1995b: 18). All of the organisations operated out of the King's Cross Women's Centre, which was run by an umbrella organisation Housewives in Dialogue and therefore, all had access to shared (if limited) equipment and printed resources. The centre was developed as: 'A base for women's organizations and projects providing survival information and services, and for continuous dialogue between women of different ethnic, social and economic backgrounds' (James 1995). Black and white women worked closely together, while respecting black women's need to formulate autonomous positions and hold separate meetings. In 1977, for example, when BWfWfH held the first black women only meeting in Bristol, white feminists defended their right to meet:

> There were rumours of threats from the National Front to break up the meeting, which was held at the Inkworks. Some white women came and stood guard outside the door of the meeting, defending Black women's right to meet autonomously; some Black men said they were available if the white women needed help. Some white women turned down our call for help.
>
> (W. Brown 1984: 57)

A critical element in the success of the coalition between these groups was white women's embrace of black women's autonomy as a strength. However, this is only a starting-point. It was equally important for the organisations to adopt a complex theoretical understanding of systems of domination. Operating from a marxist feminist standpoint developed by Selma James in the early 1970s (see Chapter 5), WHC and Housewives in Dialogue rejected a radical feminist analysis of all men as 'the enemy'. Instead, they identified men's roles in upholding systems of dominance and exploitation, but also recognised the potential for black men and white working class men to recognise their interest in dismantling these systems (W. Brown 1984). This non-essentialist view of men enabled the women involved to acknowledge that men could be allies in fighting against oppression, thus moving away from the common [white] feminist allegation that black women's choice to organise with men is a sign of a poorly developed political consciousness:

> If the military–industrial complex is the tool of men, we can bypass attacking the war machine and attack men instead. But if men are the tool of the military–industrial complex, if we organise independently of men, we can work out a relationship with them from that position of power in order to defeat a common enemy. . . . [Separatism] is another example of the feminist movement treating 'other' women, some of who don't call ourselves feminists, as though we are too stupid to make judgements about which men are acting in our interest and which are not.
>
> (W. Brown 1984: 73)

Critical to the coalition between black and white women in WHC has been the development of a theory of women's liberation which is international in scope and broad in vision. Rather than defining 'women's issues' as those which (supposedly) unite all women, such as violence and reproduction rights, WHC define women's issues as all issues which threaten the survival and welfare of any woman. Therefore a broad range of issues including racism, indigenous land rights and ecological destruction are drawn into the scope of feminist concerns (James 1995; BWfWfH 1995). In appreciating the political, economic and ecological systems linking countries within and across the north/south divide, WHC avoids the parochialism of much white feminism and enables white feminists to learn from the campaigns and writing of women from developing countries. Broadening the definition of women's struggles also creates a space for black and white women to identify their own legitimate priorities and work together where these overlap. This is not sisterhood as a goal in itself, but being sisterly in order to achieve a shared objective. It is a pragmatic approach to creating coalitions between black women and white feminists, which puts the object of the struggle before the ideal of a community of women:

> By and large, we don't socialise together, by and large we don't sleep with each other, by and large we don't live next door. So if we're going to talk about the basis on which we come together, it has to be on the basis of 'What is it that we're trying to accomplish? What do we want to do together?'.
>
> (W. Brown 1984: 81)

No strategy is entirely problematic, and the organisations clustered around the King's Cross Women's Centre have in turn been accused of a crude economism which reduces rape and sexual discrimination to tools of capitalist exploitation. Some women have also found their theoretical stance dogmatic and exclusionary (*London Women's Liberation Newsletter* (LWLN) 1984c). Finally, the centre has become vulnerable to the unsympathetic climate of the 1990s. Politically opposed to government funding and lacking a broad base of support to provide donations and subscriptions, it has been unable to maintain occupation of its central London premises. It remains to be seen whether the coalition's considerable political impact will be undermined by the failure to establish a sustainable organisational base.

The creation of Women Against Fundamentalism (WAF) is another example of black and white women coming together with very specific goals. WAF was formed in 1989 by members of Southall Black Sisters who were seeking a broader based political alliance in order to respond to the threat to women's security and independence posed by the rise of fundamentalism, 'the mobilization of religious affiliation for political ends' (Connolly 1991: 69). Identifying links between Catholic fundamentalism in Ireland, Islamic Fundamentalism in Britain, Pakistan and Middle Eastern states and Christian Fundamentalism in the United States, WAF has created the opportunity for white women to support Muslim women's rights within Islam without being intrusive or patronising. In linking different forms of religious conservatism, it counters the tendency towards the pathologisation of black religions or the focus on black cultures as patriarchal and traditionalist.

WAF's success is built on Southall Black Sisters' credibility as an organisation with a fifteen-year track record of fighting for the rights of black women and communities. Its political agenda and theoretical analysis is rooted in the organisation's practical work. Nevertheless, WAF has faced difficulties in convincing some black women that the Asian spokeswomen are not merely a front for an anti-Islamic, white feminist organisation. It has been criticised by Muslim feminist, Rana Kabbani for being Westernised and intellectual, and thereby distanced from the 'authentic' Asian woman in the street (Siddiqui 1991). It has also had to be wary of some offers of support from 'well meaning' but patronising white supporters and from liberals with a 'crusader attitude' (Connolly 1991). The threat to integrity is ever present in such juggling acts. WAF was initiated by black women and operates from the political and theoretical grounding of black women organising autonomously. The organisation's success in tackling issues which other groups have shied away from, including the Rushdie *fatwa* and Muslim schools, indicates that with these parameters, alliance building between black and white women can be highly effective. White feminists can offer resources, time, access to media, edited collections and feminist journals, used extremely strategically to highlight the work of WAF and Southall Black Sisters. However, the threat to political integrity which accompanies alliances with white women is a severe barrier to organising in partnership. In the context of a recent and painful history between black and white women in Britain, the goal of creating sisterhood between all women is at best unrealistic and at worst arrogant. As we have seen, it is a goal promoted primarily by white feminists, which is not embraced with as much enthusiasm by black women. While the ideal of sisterhood may be: 'Sisters united by shared interests and beliefs, united in our appreciation for diversity, united in our struggle to end sexist oppression, united in political solidarity' (hooks 1991: 41). For many black women in Britain the actuality involves the attempt to deny real differences of power and resources, obscure a history of racism and imperialism and places black women in the role of educator–nurturer. It also pathologises women who do not wish to pursue this role, implying that black women who refuse white women's offers of friendship are bitter or resentful. Advocating unity between black and white women at this moment in time, suggests that feminist organising stands outside of history, or that good intentions can transcend that history. This is contrary to Ramazanoglu's claim that: 'We cannot afford wholly to abandon a sense of sisterhood. Without it there can be no basis for a feminist politics' (1989: 174). It is only when white feminists shake off their essentialist belief in sisterhood between all women that the real task of identifying what commonalities may exist can begin. Unity even among white women has been an elusive goal. Coalitions between black and white women's organisations must inevitably be more modest, starting with specific goals, rather than aiming for a shared position on every issue; working towards mutual respect rather than friendship and interdependence. For black women's organisations, there is always the dilemma of whether the energy expended in working jointly, and the risk to the organisation's integrity will be counterbalanced by the support which is on offer. There will be internal divisions as some women who have had more painful experiences with white women may be reluctant to turn the other cheek:

> There are questions about white women as allies or the enemy or competition, or the sadness of being let down. I think all those feelings emerged in our organisation and in all the Black women's organisations that I've ever been involved in and they're still emerging now.
>
> (Brenda, Caribbean, African Caribbean organisation)

There is the difficulty of juggling relations with black men, who will probably be hostile to white feminists, and white feminists who are frequently mistrustful of black women's alliances with men (Ramazanoglu 1989: 189; *Spare Rib* 1992). Finally, there is the critical task of identifying when and with whom a coalition is likely to work, and when the 'drawbridge' should be pulled up, even when support is on offer.

There are a number of factors which appear to create the framework for effective joint work: first, where white feminists have an anti-racist commitment, have engaged with black feminist critiques and are able to recognise the historical and geographical specificity of their experiences as women. This commitment may arise out of the pragmatic recognition that feminist activism is weakened if it speaks only to a minority of women, or it may arise out of shared experiences of marginalisation from and therefore hostility to feminist hegemonies. Second, where women recognise and support black women's right to organise autonomously and to decide when and with whom to create coalitions without being accused of separatism. Third, where there is the replacement of sisterhood as a goal, with sisterly behaviour as a method in pursuit of a common objective. Implicit in this change of focus is a theoretical shift away from gender separatism (as opposed to autonomy) to a non-essentialist view of men, so that black women's alliances with black men are acknowledged as legitimate and necessary forms of organising against racism. Fourth, white feminist organisations must be willing to show solidarity on issues which they have not identified as immediate concerns for their constituency, but are issues for black women. This means that rather than supporting only those issues in which men's individual oppression of women is evident, white feminist organisations claiming to represent 'all' women will have to develop theory and praxis on racist violence, police brutality, school exclusions and other issues pertinent to black women. It is only with this broad understanding of women's issues that white women will be able to make the connections between their lives and the experiences of black women.

Finally, white feminists need to demonstrate 'political generosity' when working with black women's organisations. By this I refer to the practice by some white feminists of selectively utilising black feminist writings to represent black masculinity as hyper-patriarchal. This practice has the effect of forcing black women to be defensive and to keep their critiques of sexism within black communities behind closed doors. 'Political generosity' means portraying black feminist arguments in full, contextualising their criticisms of black men and avoiding the temptation to pit groups which have different perspectives on black sexism against each other. This position also recognises that the political and material resources required to sustain an antagonistic relationship with, for example, male religious leaders, may be available to a group in London, but not to one in Cardiff. Black women's organisations must therefore have the local autonomy to identify which types of political activism will be effective for their given situation.

CONCLUSIONS

This chapter has laid out a framework for the creation of coalitions between black women's organisations and other political movements. While highlighting a tendency in some organisations to be insular and to ignore the possibilities for joint working which exist in their locality and at national and international levels, I also indicated some reasons why black women should use autonomous spaces as a stepping stone to create meaningful partnerships. While alliances in which black women's activism is subsumed in mixed organisations are potentially a threat to black women's political integrity and leadership, coalitions are less problematic. Such coalitions offer the possibility of increased resources, greater media coverage and publicity, more lobbying power and access to information and networks. I then explored three potential sites of support and commonality: the Labour movement, black men and white feminists. In revealing the often painful and destructive history between black women's organisations and these sectors, I sought to caution against naivete in expecting close working relationships or 'unity' to occur easily.

Nevertheless, while relations with the Labour movement indicated a limited basis for creative partnerships, both black men and white feminists have proved supportive at specific moments in the development of black women's autonomy. Building on these moments of good practice leads to a range of suggestions for coalition building in the 1990s. Offering most ground for hope is the evidence that some black men are developing oppositional ways of viewing black masculinity and are moving against the current trend towards the revival of traditional gender roles; signs that the 'dirty linen' argument is finally being laid to rest and the examples of white feminists moving beyond denial and guilt to a new and more inclusive politics of women's resistance. Returning to an earlier point, the appropriateness of coalition building will depend on the political, ideological and structural context of the organisation and the decision of when to let the drawbridge down and to whom must ultimately be determined by black women themselves:

> I realise that enemies exist on both sides of the cultural and racial divide, as do friends. Winning freedom means the right to choose who my enemies and friends are. In this hope for the future lies.
>
> (Siddiqui 1991: 83)

NOTES

1 The 1991 Census counted 456,900 African Caribbean women and girls, 726,200 South Asian and 323,300 'Chinese and other'. Black women and girls make up 5.32 per cent of the female population (Owen 1994).
2 Black women's organisations 'create a space where women can meet

without threat or intimidation' (Sheffield Black Women's Resource Centre 1994: 1). Such threats include black male violence, racist hostility and state brutality and range 'from name calling to murder' (Shakti Women's Aid leaflet).

3   The Labour Party's landslide victory on 1 May, 1997, in which 104 women MPs including only two black women were elected, took place after the interviews for this research had been carried out. It is therefore not known whether the unprecedented number of white women now in the House of Commons and the Cabinet will translate into gains for black women.

4   Although black MP Paul Boateng was awarded a low-level portfolio in the Department of Health, black MPs have yet to access Tony Blair's Cabinet.

5   '5000 Asian members suspended by the Labour Party. A campaign against the suspensions has been launched to expose the undemocratic methods used by the Labour Party to silence the Asians in Birmingham, Bradford, Manchester, Nottingham, London and other areas. Please support our campaign for equal rights for the Black and Asian members of the Labour Party' (Campaign Against Labour Party Suspensions (CALPS) November 1995).

6   Mason-John (1995b) notes that the first Shakti was set up in London in 1988 as an organisation of black lesbians, gays and bisexuals. Since then, Shaktis have been set up in most major cities.

7   The Warwickshire African Caribbean and Asian Women's Network (WACAWN), established in 1995 is a model of community development and emerging solidarity between women of different racialised groups in a rural area characterised by scattered black communities in small towns and villages (WACAWN Constitution 1995).

8   The Black Fathers Project arose out of Moyenda, an action research project into the support needs of black parents. It builds on the anti-sexist work of the Everyman Centre, a multi-racialised group in south London which created a ground-breaking approach to working with abusive men.

9   The Black Lesbian and Gay Group, which grew out of the more male dominated Black Gay Group, secured funding for the country's first black gay and lesbian centre in 1985. Black Lesbians and Gays Against Media Homophobia, formed in 1990, has waged a successful campaign against the treatment of gays and lesbians in the *Voice* newspaper. Black gay and lesbian groups have made the 'Black Tent' an expected feature at the annual Gay Pride event.

10 I use the term 'white feminism' to reference the body of theory and practice which was developed as an analysis of the position of white women in Western societies. Not all of the women who participated in the organisations, conferences and critical thinking of the feminist movement at that time were white. The term therefore references a theory and praxis rather than the agents of that theory and praxis. Black feminists' written critiques were targeted largely at this body of theory and praxis, however, black women were also equally critical of the personal behaviour of white feminists.

11 Although hooks suggests that the term feminism has been rejected as strongly by the majority of African American women, it is notable that significant numbers of African American women intellectuals do refer to themselves and their work as feminist (hooks 1989: 179).

12 Southall Black Sisters (SBS) who claim to bring 'an anti-racist perspective to the women's movement and a feminist perspective to the black struggle' (SBS, in Wilson 1991: 194) and Black Women for Wages for Housework are exceptions to this general trend.

13 The essentialist homogeneity which many black feminists have ascribed to white women has more recently been subject to auto-criticism (Aziz 1992). It is clear that at the popular level, this tendency still pertains.

14 A similar approach in the United States can be found in Adrienne Rich's concept of 'white solipsism' which is 'not the consciously held belief that one race is inherently superior to all others, but a tunnel vision which simply does not see nonwhite [sic] experience or existence as precious or significant' (Rich, in Spelman 1988: 116).

15 Valerie Amos was chief executive of the Equal Opportunities Commission from 1989–94; her involvement has been pivotal in encouraging the commission to address issues facing black women.

16 In 'Feminist Practice Notes from the Tenth Year' (1991), British radical feminists describe CR as one of the principles of Women's Liberation: 'The "personal is political" means that our different personal experiences have a link: the oppression of all women. In WL groups we pool our experiences to find their common roots in our common oppression. This process is called consciousness-raising' (York et al. 1991: 310).

Chapter 7

Conclusions: from identity politics to the politics of transformation

Writing a conclusion to this study of black women's organisations in Britain inevitably feels premature. One work cannot hope to redress the decades of scholarly silence that have greeted black women's activism or to rectify the scarcity of research on the subject. Rather than an ending, this final chapter hopefully announces a beginning as the way is paved for further explorations of black women's dynamic efforts for social change. As the first extensive sociological study of black women's organisations in Britain, I have provided an overview of key themes and debates. The minutiae of organisational life have yet to be examined and may form the basis of further studies. Informed readers with their own experiences of black women's organisations may feel that one element or other deserved greater depth, and may thereby be inspired to write further analyses of black women's organisations in a particular location, or of those which focus on a specific sub-group. This book provides an analytical framework for such studies and offers an alternative to sociological ways of seeing which have erased the experiences and contributions of black women activists.

This research set out to achieve two goals. First, I aimed to redress the erasure of black women's collective agency in current thinking about social change. Second, I sought to explore black women's organisational responses to diversity and differentiation within black communities along lines of gender, ethnicity, sexuality, class and political ideology. In addressing these concerns, this book has suggested a number of shifts in paradigm which have arisen out of the specific experiences of black women in Britain in the late twentieth century but are applicable to the study of agency by black, migrant and women of colour in other historical moments and geographical contexts. My first shift in paradigm has been to regard black women not as passive victims of exclusionary systems and structures but as actors with the ability to undertake critical political analyses and to turn these analyses into praxis. Through listening to the everyday theorising by black women activists, I have been able to move beyond the limited conceptual framework of much current work on black people and the political arena. In Chapter 3, I illustrated that the focus on electoral trends, black politicians in the public eye and black organisations which engage with the mainstream, such as black sections, has rendered black women's activism largely invisible and is incompatible with black women's definitions of political activism which embrace a far wider range of activities. Instead, I suggested that we should utilise a conceptualisation of the political sphere which incorporates activism directed internally within black families and communities as well as that which seeks to transform the consciousness of black women actors.

My second paradigm shift has been to move from the privileging of identity as the basis for knowledge claims to a 'politics of location' (Mohanty 1992; Lewis 1996). In Chapter 2, I rebuffed the static and essentialising notions of black women which form the basis of much standpoint theory. These conceptualisations of black women's subjectivity fail to acknowledge the differences in experience, history and perspective between an African American feminist scholar and a black woman activist in Liverpool 8. I was also aware of the danger of undermining theoretical and political projects which seek to give voice to subordinated groups. I therefore suggested that we needed to look at how the location of black women in historically and spatially specific structures and systems of dominance shapes the way in which they understand and represent their experiences. This understanding formed the conceptual framework for the methodology described in Chapter 2 in which I combined the overt accountability and political commitment of a womanist standpoint with a nuanced appreciation of differences in location between myself and my research subjects.

My third shift in conceptualisation draws on the work of numerous black feminist scholars who have asserted the fundamental integration of 'race', class and gender. In Chapter 2, I suggested that black women's experiences of racism are always gendered and therefore differ from those of black men. Similarly, our experiences of sexism are always racialised and therefore differ from those of white women. I therefore indicated that we should focus not on 'racism and sexism' but on the complementary concepts of gendered racism and racialised sexism. These concepts do not permit the separation of one system of dominance from the other when referring to black women's experiences. They also remind us that building racialised solidarity with black men and sisterhood with white women are far from simple tasks since the experiences and agendas of black women are likely to be significantly different. In Chapter 5, I explored the ways in which theorists have analysed 'race', class and gender and asserted that the wish to identify one over-arching system of dominance is usefully replaced with the discussion of how these axes of dominance are articulated in different contexts. I also suggested that these should be analysed in the context of other variables such as sexuality, single parent status and ethnicity. I then explored how black women's organisations have theorised 'race', class and gender and suggested that those which had subordinated 'class' to 'race' and gender were unlikely to be able to deal with real differences in economic status, education and political ideology among black women.

My fourth paradigm shift has been to reject notions of 'race' and gender as biologically given indelible markers of difference while retaining a clear view of the power of 'race and 'sex' as social facts which limit black women's life chances. This shift has enabled me to take a fresh look at the ways in which racialised and ethnic identities are shaped and mobilised for political purposes. In Chapter 4, I explored the construction and maintenance of 'black' as a category of resistance and belonging which crosses racialised borders. The contestation over this term and the grassroots resistance to attempts by social scientists to replace it with more 'accurate' racialised and ethnic signifiers illustrates both the power of naming and the historical content of identity. I argued that many black women utilise a 'both and' framework to describe their identities, thus retaining their cultural and ethnic heritage while embracing a legacy of black struggle in Britain. I also suggested that the retention of the term 'black' by many black women's organisations is an oppositional act which asserts the primacy of histories of resistance and oppression over the divisive tactics of 'scientific' categorisation.

These four paradigm shifts form the conceptual framework for this study of black women's organisations in Britain. This framework is highly flexible and could equally be applied to other groups and other contexts. The study of black men in Britain could for example benefit from an analysis of the ways in which men's gendered experiences of racism are intricately entwined with their understandings and definitions of masculinity. Similarly, a study of the global movement of capital which benefited from an understanding of women of colour as engaging in everyday theorising would seek out the views and political mobilisation of women in multi-national factories in Indonesia, Taiwan and the Philippines. The combination of an integrated understanding of 'race, 'class' and gender formation with a nuanced understanding of identity, location and agency creates a new way of seeing which may be utilised to illuminate numerous blind-spots in the sociological imagination.

APPROACHING THE NEW MILLENNIUM

In October 1992, a conference entitled Agenda 2000: the Black Perspective hosted in Birmingham by Sia: the National Development Agency for the Black Voluntary Sector brought together black women in a workshop where the future of black women's organisations was discussed. The workshop declared: 'Black women as a force . . . must be recognised. There is no time for complacency' (Sia 1996a: 4). This conference was perhaps the first of a spate of events speculating on the role of black communities and voluntary organisations in Britain. These events, with visionary titles such as the Future of the Black Voluntary Sector, Race for the Millennium and Agenda 2001: Strategies for Change, captured the anxiety and aspiration embodied by the new century. Participants suggested that black organisations needed to make some significant changes in strategy if the exclusion and hostility experienced by black communities and black women in particular were not to continue unabated. This research has highlighted five trends which will affect the effectiveness of black women's organisations as they approach the new millennium.

The first trend is the declining power of unitary notions of black women's identity. Increasingly, black women are unwilling to obey rigid authenticity codes in order to meet the narrow definitions of black womanhood previously upheld by many grassroots organisations. Black women activists' rebellion against the orthodoxy of the 'conscious black woman' has brought into relief the diversity of black women. Chapter 3 illustrated that those women who have been considered marginal and whose identification has been declared questionable have often been radicalising elements in black women's organisations. Chapter 4 discussed the evidence that many women are learning lessons from the past and are able to identify the ways in which the denial of difference has undermined organisations. Organisations which have assumed that all black women's agendas, needs and ambitions are either the same or fundamentally compatible have found to their cost that this is not the case. These organisations have been unprepared for disputes and have had no mechanisms for resolving contestation without bowing to the most forceful voice. As Valentina Alexander perceptively remarks:

> The mythologising of the Black woman ... means that we assume a bond of sisterhood exists, without our having to work at it. It makes the assumption that simply because we have had to rely on each other for practical, emotional and spiritual survival, that we can take for granted our sameness. It does not begin to consider that human relations, even among Black women, may at times be problematic; that in 1995, stress, fear, misunderstanding, greed or power, may influence the way we relate to each other and may even destroy our bonds if we make no attempt to identify and strategise against [them].
>
> (Sia 1996a: 11)

Differences in sexuality, class, education, geography, religion and ethnicity have all created a diversity of perspectives, agendas and priorities which are only just beginning to be incorporated into organisational strategies. Nevertheless, some organisations still adhere to exclusionary notions of black womanhood. The denial of a lesbian presence is one forceful example of this adherence. The assumption that a white partner is prima facie evidence of 'selling out' is another. The belief that black women are undivided by educational attainment or class positioning is another.

This research has illustrated extensive diversity within black women's organisations which has at times been obscured by an over-emphasis of the black/white divide at the expense of internal differentiation. The strength of black women's organisations in the new millennium will depend on their ability to build a 'strategic unity' which acknowledges difference and celebrates cultural specificity while retaining a focus on the commonalities of black women's histories, experiences of gendered racism and political struggles. The history of black women's activism in Britain has shown that black women have been at the forefront in building and maintaining a strategic unity between diverse communities and this historical and politically central role is likely to continue into the twenty-first century.

The second trend which will have a significant impact on black women's organisations is the increasing religious, ethnic and racialised fragmentation of black communities in Britain. Chapter 4 highlighted a number of factors which are inducing this fragmentation. I suggested that the state's role in fracturing black struggle into its component ethnic parts has been overstated. In order to perceive the state's actual impact, it is necessary to recognise the internal differentiation between local and central government and between London-based and regional offices of government. I identified that the state's actions in this regard have been far from unitary and that some local authorities had in fact encouraged organisations to utilise an inclusive definition of blackness. However, it does appear evident that the limitation of 'black' to those of African ancestry in the 1991 Census and the embracing by public agencies and quangos such as the Commission for Racial Equality, the Policy Studies Institute and the Runnymede Trust of Asian ethnicities and a pan-Asian racialised identity, supported by social scientists who have always been uncomfortable with the political overtones of the term 'black', are both factors which will militate against the retention of an inclusive definition of blackness. In the sphere of popular culture, the rise in popularity of North American black nationalist ideologies such as Afrocentricity, and the increasing globalisation of African American film, music and literature will also encourage people of African Caribbean descent in Britain to assert their privileged position in relation to blackness. Finally, the increasing importance of religious identities, in particular via the international revival in Muslim identification, will continue to interrogate the primacy of racialised identities.

In the light of this fraught debate over the content of blackness and the preferability of different terms, black women's organisations which continue to utilise 'black' as an inclusive organising concept may be accused of being outmoded or resistant to acknowledging internal differentiation. In Chapter 4, I illustrated the existence of a common discourse which is not based on essentialist or reified notions of black women. This discourse is often ignored by scholars who focus only on the experience of being 'non-white' and ignore black women's shared history of survival, resistance and creativity. These concepts of the janus-headed nature of power, of pain and healing, nurturing and love, resistance to sexism, mindful of racist pathologisation and of a connection with those who have been before, cohere black women's organising in Britain. Recognising the common discourse of black organisations in Britain offers the possibility of a strategic unity between people of different ethnicities, religions and experiences founded not on a hegemonic notion of 'the black community', but on similar histories of imperialism and experiences of racism(s). 'Black' continues to be a critical space in this project. It signifies not only a shared experience of oppression, but also a common history and language of resistance. As black communities in Britain approach the new millennium, it is essential that we build on the struggles of the past and draw on this legacy of African–Asian unity.

The third trend which threatens to challenge black women's ability to bring about social change is the increasing social stratification within black communities. In Chapter 5, I offered a gender sensitive analysis of social stratification in black Britain. I illustrated that the assumed social mobility of the Asian community did not reflect either the differentiation between Asian communities, or the socio-economic exploitation of Asian women in a gendered and racialised labour market. Commonsense notions of African Caribbean women's over-achievement were not an accurate reflection of the different experiences of African and Caribbean men and women.

Although black women have not made as much progress *vis-à-vis* other groups as has been suggested by the media, there is evidence to suggest that more black women are accessing higher education and professional employment than previously was the case. The suggestion that black women's struggles are necessarily 'authentic working class' struggles therefore no longer holds true. This analysis means that black women's organisations can no longer be complacent about their agendas and priorities. There must be open and clear discussion about different agendas within and between organisations. These discussions should not take as their starting-point the assumption that educated or professional women will automatically have a vested interest in the status quo. This research has illustrated that education may inspire women to make more radical choices and that many black women act from gendered racialised solidarity rather than in the interests of the class allegiance suggested by their income or education. Indeed, the increasing numbers of black women in higher education speaks in no small part to the success of these organisations in breaking down barriers to social and economic mobility. Black women's organisations must therefore identify strategies for incorporating the skills, experience and knowledge of these women without compromising their priorities or alienating their more traditional constituencies.

The fourth trend which is significant for the future of black women's organisations is the shift from 'race' specific to colour blind policy interventions at the governmental level. In Britain this trend can be evidenced in the rolling back of Section 11 and Urban Programme funding, both of which were grants provided by central government to assist urban regeneration and both of which utilised racialised markers in the distribution of funds. The Urban Programme was replaced in 1992 by the City Challenge Fund which introduced two key characteristics to the regeneration terrain: colour blind social deprivation indices and competition between regeneration partnerships. These characteristics were consolidated when this and other funds were dismantled in favour of the Single Regeneration Budget introduced in 1994 which also shifted the location of decision making away from the local level, where black organisations had accessed some representational mechanisms to the regional level, where little black voluntary sector infrastructure existed (Sudbury 1995).

The 'deracination' of governmental regeneration schemes is perhaps indicative of a sea-change in funding for social and economic improvements. It is mirrored in the establishment of National Lottery Distribution Bodies in 1995 with no initial infrastructure for ensuring the access to grants by black communities and black voluntary organisations. Indeed, when the Charities Board responded to pressure from national black organisations and provided both outreach funding and monitoring of black organisations, it was met with a hysterical response from the media, Conservative politicians and from many in the white community[1] (Sia 1996c). This sea-change can also be seen in part as a response to the anti-affirmative action mobilisation occurring in the United States. Although Britain does not have a history of embracing quotas or affirmative action in pursuing racialised parity, many white politicians and lay persons have felt that black people are unfairly favoured by government (C. Brown 1984: 271). The dismantling of affirmative action in the United States therefore provides a language and conceptual framework for those in Britain who feel that equal opportunities and political correctness have 'gone too far' but do not wish to be labelled racist for saying so (Ouseley 1995).

The combination of initiatives emphasising competition and large scale projects, regionalisation of government and the increasing popularity of deracinated policy agendas will inevitably diminish the funds available to black voluntary organisations. In the cut-throat environment created by these changes, small organisations and black organisations alike will be displaced in favour of large white-led organisations which can fulfil substantial contracts. These in turn may offer small scale sub-contracts with little security or opportunity for growth to black organisations. This environment will also encourage smaller black organisations to amalgamate or grow in order to be able to offer broader services. This may lead to a two-tier system of black voluntary organisations with those which have the capital and staff to access contracts for training or community care becoming larger, more competitive and with an orientation towards service-delivery. Black women's organisations, many of which are already under-resourced, are unlikely to be in this new black voluntary sector elite and are therefore likely to see their funding base decline further.

The organisations in this study were addressing this grim prophecy in a number of ways. First, many organisations had recognised the insecurity associated with having only one funder, particularly their local authority. Those which nurtured a diverse funding portfolio were less vulnerable to political whims and could also utilise one funder's support to attract and retain others. Second, most of the organisations studied emphasised the need for consistent campaigning for the recognition of black women's right to receive resources at the local and national level. This campaigning was often done via a local or national campaign group and there is evidence that black voluntary organisations are responding to the regionalisation of government with the establishment of regional networking and campaign groups. Third, organisations are beginning to identify the need for greater self sufficiency. This means that traditional forms of fund raising such as dances, subscriptions and local events which had been superseded by government grants are being revitalised, as are new forms of income generation such as consultancy and sponsorship by black businesses (Sudbury 1994). Many black women activists are therefore becoming activist–entrepreneurs engaged in accessing a wide range of funds for their organisations. Finally, some organisations are shifting their sights away from government funding altogether. Three of the organisations in this study were politically committed to existing without funding. Others were beginning to access funds from charitable trusts and the National Lottery which were seen as being less vulnerable to local political vagaries. In summary, black women's organisations are becoming far more sophisticated and are engaging more actively in planning their financial base. Since many of the organisations which have demised have done so due to lack of funding, this is an essential part of building a movement for the future.

The final trend characterising black voluntary organisations in Britain is a shift in emphasis from political activism in the 1980s to service provision in the 1990s. This has not been a linear shift and this research has highlighted many organisations engaged in political activism in the 1990s. However, the trend away from the coordinated national activism witnessed in the late 1970s and early 1980s was also lamented by some interviewees. This shift may ironically be a feature of the success of black organisations in campaigning for improved service delivery. These organisations have now been provided with funding to provide important culturally relevant and non-racist services. In this context, some activists have become managers and have seen their energies diffused in the minutiae of quality standards, evaluation and monitoring required by funders. Other organisations have had to recruit professionally trained staff who may have little commitment to the political goals which led to the organisation's establishment.

While the provision of holistic and culturally relevant services to black communities should certainly not be seen as a mere diversion, if black voluntary organisations as a whole and black women's organisations specifically are not to lose their oppositional edge, there is a need to retain a focus on their campaigning and political elements. This may be through attention to whether users are becoming disempowered 'clients', distanced from decision making within the organisation. It may be through raising consciousness about racialised and gender inequalities or about the importance of African–Asian unity: it may be through engaging in local, national and international campaigns and umbrella groups. In Chapter 6, I illustrated that in many cases, the pursuit of such goals will require black women's organisations to become 'castles' with the drawbridge down, creating opportunities for coalition building with other movements for social change. Black women's organisations may therefore move into a new phase, utilising their analysis of gendered and racialised oppressions to identify commonalities between their struggles and those of other groups. These coalitions will not be based on idealistic calls for sisterhood or racialised solidarity, but will involve specific goals and delineated roles. In particular, the progressive elements of the new black men's 'movement' may offer the foundations for an oppositional alliance between black men and women which does not require black women to declare their loyalty to men at the expense of their commitment to black women's survival.

The survival of black women's organisations depends in part on their ability to monitor and respond to national trends in popular consciousness, governmental priorities and demographic patterns. However, their continued relevance into the next century will also depend on their ability to analyse international trends, to think globally even as they struggle locally. Gilroy's comment on black people involved in urban protest in the 1980s suggests that black grassroots activism is limited to the local realm: 'Unable to control the social relations in which they find themselves, people have shrunk the world to the size of their communities and have begun to act politically on that basis' (Gilroy 1987: 245). In Chapter 3, I illustrated that many black women's organisations have not limited their political vision to that localised domain.

Increasingly, all black women's organisations will have to respond to the reverberations of international social, political and economic trends. The rising global hegemony of North American cultural production and models of 'race relations', the alignment of mechanisms of economic and social control in European Union states and the growing political and social exclusion of black and migrant peoples in Europe are all factors which will have a direct impact on black communities in Britain (S. Small 1994; Back and Nayak 1993). Structural adjustment programmes, the devastation of natural resources and the educational, legislative and political disenfranchisement of women will affect family members remaining in formerly colonised nations as the noose of European immigration controls tightens to keep them out of Britain (Akina Mama wa Afrika 1995; Zimbabwe Women's Resource Centre 1995). The challenge to black women's organisations is to build on those elements of black women's activism which have linked the struggles of black women in Britain with black, migrant and women of colour in the West and with those in the 'Third World'. Building on visions of transformation which transcend local specificities, black women in Britain may become part of a global network of progressive organisations working for a new social order.

VISIONS OF TRANSFORMATION

This book has explored the often contested and difficult realities of black women organising. Yet all of the interviewees emphasised the hope and joy which such organisations had given them. Underlying the conflicts and disagreements is a sense of black women's organisations as an oppositional space where dreams can be remembered and visions given voice. Fundamental to black women's organising is the belief that transformation is a possibility, that black women can assert their agency and 'claim back our power' in opposing the structures of dominance which shape our lives.

Chapter 4 explored the utilisation of the term 'identity politics' to describe political mobilisation by subordinated groups. I suggested that the term had been appropriated as a way of undermining those social movements which demand a platform for previously silenced voices and has led to the assumption that all political groupings formed by subordinated groups are dedicated to introspection and personal discovery alone. The history of black women's organisations in Britain has not been limited to a narrow focus on identity but utilises what may be described as a 'broad-based identity politics' as its starting-point (hooks 1995: 203). Where they have looked at issues of identity, black women have done so with the aim of creating a strategic unity drawing on women's individual experiences but leading to communal strategies for change. This research has revealed that black women have been engaged in a comprehensive politics of transformation which engages with socio-economic structures, political mechanisms and popular understandings of 'race' and gender and which is far more complex and significant than has previously been suggested.

The politics of transformation begins with personal exploration and consciousness raising. For women who have been trapped in abusive relationships, who feel powerless before institutional abuses of power or who have internalised gendered racist stereotypes about themselves and others, this personal transformation is a necessary task. Without the confidence, awareness and political analysis which such self examination and debate brings, black women are unlikely to create meaningful change or to be able to work together without resorting to power struggles and divisive tactics. Yet this personal transformation is not an end in itself. Rather, it is a first step which enables women to see the links between the roots of their own pain and the oppression of others and thus is an essential part of building strong organisations for social change.

The second element of black women's politics of transformation is the realignment of family life. This involves challenging notions of what constitutes healthy family life, defending single parent families against social stigma and legitimising the relationships of black lesbians. It also involves challenging destructive relations between black men and women in the family. While they are conscious of the need to avoid providing ammunition for the racist pathologisation of black men, black women's organisations have demanded that black men treat women with respect, that they do not commit violence against them and their children and that they take responsibility for supporting their offspring. In so doing they have refused to be silenced by accusations of betrayal or of 'airing dirty linen' and have thus established an oppositional discourse to the nationalist legitimation of black male violence as a response to racism and emasculation.

The third aspect is the transformation of the local community. Although black women's organisations are not limited to the local sphere, much of their activism has attempted to transform local dynamics. By asserting their right to organise autonomously, black women have changed the political environment of local communities, establishing black women as a force to be reckoned with in black communities and as 'players' in the local political economy (Sia 1996a: 4). At a symbolic level, they have highlighted the inability of existing services and political mechanisms to provide for black women. At a pragmatic level, they have successfully demanded the provision of anti-racist, anti-sexist and holistic services for black women and children and have facilitated the entry of numerous black women into adequate housing, higher education and employment. Furthermore, in many areas they have established black women as a constituency which cannot be ignored by local politicians.

Finally, black women's organisations have moved outward from the local arena, utilising an analysis of the integration of 'race', class and gender to work for the lasting transformation of social, economic and political structures and ideologies. Organisations such as Southall Black Sisters have challenged the silencing and confinement of women accompanying the global rise in Muslim revivalism. Akina Mama wa Afrika has brought its analysis of structural adjustment programmes back home in its campaigns on behalf of West African women in British prisons. Black Women for Wages for Housework has played a critical role in gaining recognition of black women's invisible and unwaged work in Britain and in formerly colonised nations. These and other programmes and campaigns highlight global concerns for black, migrant and women of colour. They resist the fragmentation of black women's concerns and the artificial prioritisation of one aspect of dominance over another. They speak to the need to nurture a trained, politically sophisticated and effective black women's leadership in all progressive social movements. Above all, they illustrate the interconnectedness of black women's activism in Britain and all struggles against racialised, gender and class oppression. Black women's organisations in Britain have therefore created a fundamentally holistic politics of transformation which integrates the individual and the communal, connects the local with the global and meshes the pragmatic with the visionary. It is this philosophical and ideological base which will sustain black women's activism into the next century.

NOTES

1 Although it should be noted that a number of national white-led voluntary organisations came out publicly in support of funding for black organisations in a paid advertisement in the *Guardian*.

Summary of case study organisations

AKINA MAMA WA AFRIKA (LONDON)

AMwA is a national non-governmental organisation of African women. The organisation's name signifies 'African sisterhood' in Swahili and reflects the membership of women from different parts of Africa, including migrants, refugees, students, professionals and women of dual heritage. AMwA grew out of an International Women's Day event in London in 1985. The organisation has a two-prong approach to their work. First, they provide support, education and networking for African women in Britain. Second, they support leadership, education and community development and are involved in the women's movement in Africa. AMwA coordinates the African Women Prisoners Project at Holloway Prison (est. 1991) and is involved in educational campaigns against skin bleaching and female genital mutilation. They have a quarterly publication called *African Woman* and undertake research and policy development. AMwA has funding from a variety of sources including trusts, the regional health authority and local authorities.

BLACK LESBIAN GROUP (LONDON)

The BLG was established in 1982 following a painful experience of hostility and exclusion at the 1981 OWAAD conference. The group utilised an inclusive definition of blackness and included women from across Britain of Asian, African and Caribbean origins. The group struggled to find premises and after being ejected by Brixton Black Women's Group, eventually found space at A Woman's Space, a white feminist centre. Although meetings were held in London, a fare pool policy enabled women from the north to attend. The group focused on personal development, exploration and support as well as tackling isolation and providing opportunities for socialising. Members used their experiences to build careers in media, film and equal opportunities, however, the group, which was never funded, folded in the late 1980s.

BLACK WOMEN FOR WAGES FOR HOUSEWORK (LONDON)

BWfWfH is an international network of black women/women of colour in Third World and industrial countries organising against economic injustice and claiming reparations and recognition for unwaged women's work. BWfWfH was established in the early 1970s by members of the Wages For Housework Campaign and (until spring 1996) shared premises in King's Cross, London. The group has a policy of not seeking funding and campaigns on racism, immigration controls, economic restructuring, Third World 'debt', environmental racism and rights of sex workers, gays and lesbians. BWfWfH coordinates the International Network of Women of Colour and the Black Women's Rape Action Project which works to ensure both that the rape of black women is not hidden and that black men are not stereotyped as rapists. The group operates a political definition of blackness in the British context, although the term 'women of colour' is utilised in mobilising international campaigns.

BLACK WOMEN'S RESOURCE CENTRE (SHEFFIELD)

The resource centre was established in an unlet council house in the multi-racial and impoverished area of Burngreave in March 1994, following eighteen months of prepatory work by a city council community worker in partnership with a group of local volunteers. The centre is funded 'in kind' by the city council and has a grant from the Church Urban Fund. The centre actively works to overcome ethnic barriers and operates a political definition of blackness. Members consist of West African, African Caribbean, Pakistani, Bangladeshi, Somali and Yemeni women. The centre provides training courses including English language, computers and sewing, advice and welfare rights work and informal drop-in social events with a cross-cultural emphasis.

CAMBRIDGE BLACK WOMEN'S SUPPORT GROUP (CAMBRIDGE)

CBWSG was established as a house group in 1980 by African and African Caribbean women. Initial seed funding from Kings College, Cambridge University enabled the group to apply successfully for funds from the city council and Commission for Racial Equality in 1986. The group provides social and educational opportunities for black women and operates the Mary Seacole day nursery (est. 1990) and holiday playschemes for children. The group also participates in local authority consultations, particularly on educational issues. Their location in a relatively prosperous small town has excluded the group from most funding schemes targeting black communities. They share a building with other women's groups in a commercial area near the station. The majority of members are of African descent, although Asian women have also been involved in smaller numbers and the definition of blackness has oscillated between narrow and more inclusive usage.

LIVERPOOL BLACK SISTERS (LIVERPOOL)

Liverpool Black Sisters was established in the early 1970s. 'Black' is promoted by the group as an umbrella term to describe all those who experience racism. The group's initial concerns were lack of childcare provision, inadequate mental health support mechanisms and inadequate recruitment of black foster carers. The Sisters were also involved in campaigning against immigration legislation and deportations. In the late 1980s the group secured trust funding for a coordinator and in the early 1990s, funding for training, childcare and administration was obtained from Urban Aid, Granby Toxteth Taskforce, Children in Need and a number of other agencies. The group currently operates from a shared building in Liverpool 8 where it provides summer playschemes, after school care and training courses including black studies, computers and personal development.

MUSLIM WOMEN'S HELPLINE (LONDON)

Motivation for the establishment of the helpline came from a conference at the Islamic Cultural Centre in west London in 1987, when women shared experiences of divorce, domestic violence, sexual abuse and concerns about arranged marriage. After two years of preparation, a national helpline was launched in autumn 1989 with a paid coordinator and a rota of volunteers. The helpline provides spiritual counselling and guidance from a Muslim perspective and reached 1,145 women by telephone and face to face in 1994. The helpline receives no grant aid and relies on donations from the Muslim community for its running costs. The organisation views Islam as transcending barriers of 'race' and ethnicity and has Arab, African Caribbean, Asian and some white users.

ONYX (NEW ADDINGTON)

Onyx was initiated in 1986 by an African woman social work trainee undertaking a community work placement. The group was formed primarily of single African Caribbean mothers who were isolated in a large industrial council estate. Meeting initially in the city council community development office, the group decided to use creativity and the arts to challenge racism. They therefore organised an open day where racism and discrimination were humorously tackled through poetry, drama and music. Subsequently, the group began to act as advocates for local black families in their dealings with the local authority. Onyx decided not to apply for funding in order to retain their critical independence. However, by the early 1990s, the group lost its momentum as members moved away or started jobs. Currently, Onyx exists as a loose network of women which occasionally does performances at community events, but no longer has formal meetings.

OSABA WOMEN'S CENTRE (COVENTRY)

Osaba Women's Centre was established in 1984 by members of an African dance group with sponsorship by the Coventry West Indian Youth Council. The group aimed to provide opportunities for African Caribbean women and children in the fields of social welfare, health, education, employment, training and culture. Premises were obtained in the inner city deprived area of Hillfields, initially in social services premises and then in a former shop. Early members tended to be single mothers and Rasta women had a key role in the centre's development. In 1993 the group moved to spacious newly renovated premises purchased with an Urban Aid grant. The centre provides training including black history, personal development and job search; childcare including summer playschemes, playgroup and day care; a newsletter; cultural events and a drop-in facility. The centre has also been involved in establishing a centre for African Caribbean women experiencing domestic violence.

PANAHGHAR (COVENTRY)

Panahghar was established in 1979 when an Asian male councillor, working in partnership with Asian women council employees, obtained Section 11 funding for a service for Asian women escaping violence in the home. Initially the project was located within the Haven, a white women's refuge, however, in 1986 Panahghar obtained a house and became independent. The organisation provides services in four areas: the refuge, including counselling, legal advice and advocacy; aftercare for women resettling in the community; outreach work to support women unable to leave their homes; support groups and surgeries. The organisation also participates in policy debates and is a constant critic of the local authority. Funding by the social services department and Children in Need, Safer Cities and Orbit Housing was supplemented in 1996 with a large grant from the National Lottery Charities Board to purchase a community centre and to pay for additional staff posts. Although Panahghar provides a refuge for Asian women only, they operate a political definition of 'black' and were involved in establishing a similar service for African Caribbean women in Coventry.

SHAKTI WOMEN'S AID (EDINBURGH)

Shakti was established in 1986 by a group of black and white women. Initially, the organisation was a part of Edinburgh Women's Aid, but subsequently it became independent and obtained separate premises. Shakti provides support and safe temporary accommodation to Asian, African Caribbean and Chinese women and children escaping domestic violence throughout Scotland. The organisation provides advice on welfare benefits, legal rights, immigration/nationality, racial harassment, education and employment and has an interpreting service. Shakti also challenges institutional discriminatory practices in housing, social services, health, education and immigration and is actively involved in campaigns such as 'Zero Tolerance'. Shakti works to operationalise and defend a political definition of blackness.

WAI YIN CHINESE WOMEN'S SOCIETY (MANCHESTER)

The society was established in 1988 and in 1995 obtained European Community funding to purchase and renovate a building in central Manchester. Funding from a range of sources including central and local government, the Consortium on Opportunities for Volunteers government quango and the National Lottery Charities Board facilitates a range of cultural and educational opportunities including Mandarin, calligraphy, Cantonese opera singing, as well as training courses such as English language, interview techniques and computer training. In addition, the society provides a drop-in centre, information, emotional support and vocational guidance. The centre also coordinates involvement in celebrations such as Chinese New Year, Dragon Boat Festival and International Women's Week. The centre focuses on empowering Chinese women to overcome marginalisation, isolation and cultural/linguistic barriers and enabling children to participate in cultural activities.

Chronology of black women organising autonomously in Britain

EARLY 1950S

African and Caribbean Evangelical Christian women excluded from white services establish 'house groups', subsequently take over disused churches; despite predominantly female congregation, pastors are men.

LATE 1960S

Black Unity and Freedom Party, Black Liberation Front, Black Panthers Movement, Radical Adjustment Action Society (RAAS) and other Black Power organisations form in London, Liverpool, Manchester and the Midlands; hundreds of young black women participate, but are excluded from leadership.

[White] Women's Liberation Movement becomes active in Britain; black women's voices are not acknowledged until two decades later.

1964

December Martin Luther King visits London on his way to receiving Nobel Prize in Sweden; Campaign Against Racial Discrimination (CARD) established; folds in 1968.

1965

Malcolm X visits black communities in Britain.

1966

Confederation of Afro-Asian-Caribbean Organisations (CAACO) holds march of solidarity with Martin Luther King's People's March on Washington; Claudia Jones heads the organisation.

1967

July Stokely Carmichael meets black activists in London and speaks at rallies in Notting Hill and Brixton.

EARLY 1970S

African, Caribbean and Asian women active in youth organisations and defence committees.

Rastafari women involved in 'Twelve Tribes' gatherings in urban centres throughout Britain.

Black women's action committees formed in some Black Power organisations including Black Unity and Freedom Party.

Liverpool Black Sisters established.

1972

Muslim Ladies Circle formed in Nottingham; later renamed Muslim Women's Organisation.

1973

Manchester Black Women's Co-operative established by a group of women involved in the George Jackson House Trust, in Moss Side, Manchester.

Brixton Black Women's Group formed in south London primarily by African Caribbean women involved in the Black Panthers movement; folds 1986 due to funding cuts and condemned building.

1974

May   Asian women at Imperial Typewriters strike over pay differentials between black and white workers; the union refuses to back them and they are sustained by community support including black women's organisations.

1976

Industrial action at the Grunwich Film Processing plant in Willesden over poor conditions and union recognition is led by Jayaben Desai; black women's organisations join the picket line.

1977

April   *The Oppression of South Asian Women* magazine launched.

Black Women for Wages for Housework (BWfWfH) take part in Women Against Rape demonstration against goverment and industry in Trafalgar Square; Jayaben Desai also speaks.

First black women-only public meeting takes place in Bristol organised by BWfWfH to protest a proposed nuclear power site.

1978

February   Organisation of Women of Africa and African Descent (OWAAD) launched as a national umbrella group by members of the African Students' Union in the UK; British born women of African descent join to plan a national conference.

Winter   OWAAD becomes Organisation of Women of African and Asian Descent; focus changes from anti-colonial struggles abroad to British experience.

1979

Spring   United Black Women's Action Group, Tottenham, London, organises boycott of the test Census ethnic monitoring questions; campaign is taken up by OWAAD.

March   First OWAAD conference held at the Abeng Centre, Brixton, London; over 200 women attend the one-day event.

Following OWAAD conference, participants set up a number of local group including East London Black Women's Organisation, North Paddington Black Women's Group, Simba Black Women's Group, south London.

April   Police brutally attack demonstrators against the National Front in Southall, west London, 350 arrests are made; Southall Black Sisters subsequently established.

May   Conservative government comes to power under Thatcher; black women's organisations protest cuts in education, health and other public services.

June   United Black Women's Action Group organises public meeting in Haringey, London, on school exclusions, disruptive units (sin bins) and racist curriculum; similar initiatives follow in Camden, Brixton and other locations; Awaz ('voice' in Hindi) and Brixton Black Women's Group, in partnership with the Indian Workers' Association and Blacks Against State Harassment (BASH) organise demonstration in central London against state harassment.

July   First issue of *FOWAAD!*, OWAAD's fortnightly newsletter.

OWAAD organise a sit-in at Heathrow airport to protest against vaginal examinations ('virginity tests') of Asian women; joins the 'Scrap SUS' campaign.

Asian women strike at Futters and Chix factories; supported by black women's organisations including OWAAD.

Awaz formed by Asian women in London; joins campaign against vaginal examinations.

Brixton Black Women's Group and Mary Seacole Craft Group open Britain's first black women's centre at 41 Stockwell Rd, south London.

LATE 1970S

Gujarati women in Wandsworth, south London, initiate anti-dowry campaign.

Black women in Lewisham initiate the 'Scrap SUS' campaign.

ZANU Women's League formed in London by African women engaged in liberation struggles.

SWAPO women's campaign established in London by African women involved in anti-apartheid movement.

Black/Brown Women's *Liberation Newsletter* established in York.

Latin American Women's Group formed in London.

1980

February   Following campaign led by Brixton Black Women's Group and OWAAD against use of Depo Provera, governmental committee on safety of medicines asks for further research on the drug.

March   OWAAD's second conference, Black Women in Britain – Fighting Back, held in London over two days, attended by 600 women.

Friends of Nazira Begum Committee established by OWAAD members to support her appeal against deportation following her husband's desertion.

OWAAD and Brixton Black Women's Group campaign against proposed Nationality Act.

Hackney Black Women's Group established.

St Vincent and Grenadine Women's Association formed to alleviate the suffering caused in the St Vincent hurricane.

Asian Women's Refuge Project established in Lambeth, south London.

Women from Brixton Black Women's Group attend UN Decade for Women Mid Decade Forum in Copenhagen.

1981

OWAAD third conference held in London; members form defence campaigns for black men and women arrested during the Brixton uprisings; forty black lesbians demand separate space and are verbally abused by other women.

Brixton Black Women's Centre becomes headquarters for the Brixton Defence Campaign Legal Defence Group.

Summer   Uprisings in Southall, Liverpool 8, Moss Side, St Pauls and other inner city areas against police harassment, racist violence and discrimination; black women active in defence committees and in supporting families affected by arrests.

Peckham Black Women's Group formed in east London by women of African and Asian descent, later sets up centre; folds in 1990 due to loss of funding.

Greenham Common Women's peace camp is set up; black women protest against verbal abuse of African American soldiers and accuse the organisers of nationalism and parochialism.

1982

Wilmette Brown (BWfWfH) presents talk, 'Black Women and the Peace Movement' to GLC Women's Committee Peace Working Group promoting black autonomy; published in 1983, first edition sells out.

Inner city aid dramatically increased to £270 million under the Urban Programme to be channelled into black self help groups.

March   *Outwrite* newspaper established to cover black and Third World feminist struggles in Britain and internationally.

First Black Lesbian Group formed in London; women attend from all over Britain; refused space by black women's organisations, meet at A Woman's Place, a white feminist centre.

June   OWAAD's last conference fails to overcome differences of sexuality and political analysis; focus on black feminism receives criticism from new members; OWAAD folds.

Esme Baker wins case against Walthamstow police for sexual assault; Black Women for Wages for Housework picket the trial.

London Black Women's Health Action Project set up by African women to mobilise against female genital mutilation.

1983

January   Nationality Act, 1981, comes into force introducing two tiers of citizenship based on birthplace of parents/grandparents; many black people are deprived of British citizenship; black women's organisations protest, including OWAAD.

Black Womentalk forms, a publishing cooperative of women of African and Asian descent.

Chinese Lesbian Group launched following Lesbian Sex and Sexual Practice conference, co-organised by members of Black Lesbian Group.

Spare Rib feminist monthly is the site of a battle between black and white women with allegations of racism and counter-allegations of anti-semitism; folds in 1983.

Halimat Babamba wins fight against deportation with support from black women-only campaign organised in Leeds.

Greater London Council Labour administration declares anti-racist year; Black Women's Working Group established as part of GLC Women's Committee.

1984

Spring   First issue of *Mukti*, Asian feminist magazine.

May   We Are Here, national black feminist conference, London; attended by 250.

July   First issue of *We Are Here* newsletter; folded in 1986; later relaunched.

Autumn   'Many Voices, Many Chants: Black Feminist Perspectives', *Feminist Review* 17, edited by four black women activists; includes 'Black Women Organising Autonomously'.

October   Appointment of Sam Bond as principal race relations advisor in Liverpool provokes two-year battle between black organisations and the Militant dominated Labour council involving Liverpool Black Sisters and All-Pakistan Women's Association.

EARLY 1980S

African Caribbean women nurses and support staff initiate nine-month strike over low pay levels and privatisation in National Health Service.

Anwar Ditta is reunited with her three eldest children from Pakistan after a five-year campaign led by OWAAD to have them recognised as legitimate dependents.

Southall Black Sisters organise mass protest and picketing in Southall to protest death of Krisha Sharma after years of spousal violence.

Scottish Black Women's Group set up in Edinburgh.

1985

Successful campaign by Birmingham Black Sisters leads to re-trial and subsequent release of Iqbal Begum, sentenced to life imprisonment for killing her violent husband.

March   Akina Mama wa Afrika established as a non-governmental organisation for African women.

July   Several black women's organisations attend UN Decade for Women non-governmental organisations forum in Nairobi, Kenya.

October   Zami I first black lesbian conference held in London and attended by over 200 women of African and Asian descent; first issue of *Zami*, a black feminist bi-monthly magazine produced in Coventry; Balwant Kaur campaign formed in London to press for justice after Kaur's husband breaks into Brent Asian women's refuge and murders her; he is sentenced to life imprisonment in December 1986.

Bengali Women's Support Group established in Sheffield, later set up a bilingual book project and publish anthologies of Bengali women's writing, *Barbed Lives* (which wins the Raymond Williams Community publishing prize in 1990) and *Sweet and Sour*.

1986

April   Scottish black and white women access funds to set up a black women's refuge; Shakti Women's Aid is established in Edinburgh.

August   Afro-Caribbean Educational Project Women's Centre opened in Waltham Forest, east London.

1987

Muslim Women's Conference held at Islamic Cultural Centre in northwest London leads to establishment of Muslim Women's Helpline project; National Helpline is launched in 1989.

June   Black Womentalk publishes first book, *Black Women Talk Poetry*.

1988

March   *We Are Here*, black feminist newsletter relaunched in Leicester; folded 1989; Sheba feminist publishers launch *Charting* *the Journey: Writings by Black and Third World Women* at London Women's Centre; Universal Rasta Women and Wadada Rasta Women host one-day event in Birmingham.

1989

March   Public meeting organised by Black Women for Wages for Housework in Bristol, banned by district health authority for being political.

May   Women Against Fundamentalism formed by Southall Black Sisters in alliance with white women; picket anti-Rushdie demonstrations in central London.

June   Over 2,000 participate in demonstration in Edinburgh after racist murder of Ahmed Sheikh.

September   Manchester Bangladeshi Women's project formed; National Alliance of Women of African Descent formed in east London; fold in winter 1994 after coordinator, Babs Ashie Nikoy, passes away.

LATE 1980S

Onyx group for black lesbians formed; over-forties Black Lesbian Group formed.

1990

Zamimass monthly group established for black lesbians.

March   Strengthening Our Networks Conference held by Akina Mama wa Afrika in London.

April   Zami II second national black lesbian conference held in Birmingham over two days, over 200 women attend.

June   Cambridge Black Women's Support Group opens Mary Seacole day nursery.

August   Formerly abused wife, Rabia Janjua, facing prosecution for 'Zina' (unlawful sex) under Pakistan's 'Hudood Ordinance'; granted exceptional leave to remain in the UK; Southall Black Sisters/WAF lead the campaign.

Lightskinned/mixed race black lesbian group forms in London after workshop at Zami II; later formed MOSAIC.

Black Lesbians Brought up in Care Group formed in London.

1991

African Women Prisoners Project established by Akina Mama wa Afrika to promote welfare of African women in UK prisons.

July   WAZOBIA ('come' in three Nigerian languages) formed in London to mobilise women for the first International Conference on Women of Africa and the African Diaspora, Bridges Across Activism and the Academy, to be held in Nigeria in July 1992.

1992

July   Saheliya black women's multi-lingual counselling and health project established in Edinburgh.

Summer   Kiranjit Ahluwalia sentenced to life imprisonment for killing her violent husband; freed after Southall Black Sisters (SBS) leads massive campaign for her release; SBS receives Martin Ennals Liberty Award.

September   National Black Women's Network Planning Group formed with newsletter, *Transitions* after London Women's Forum Conference.

October   Black European Women's Network launched in London; delegates from twelve EC member states attend; Strengthening our Links: African Women In Europe Conference organised by Akina Mama wa Afrika in London; attended by women from Europe, Africa, North America and Brazil.

Northern Black Lesbian Conference held in Manchester, attended by over 100 women.

Chapeltown Black Women Writers' Group, Leeds (est. November 1991), publishes *When Our Ship Comes In: Black Women Talk*, an anthology of life stories and poetry by older Caribbean women.

Black Women Promotions' first national Black Women's Achievement awards hosted at the Trinidad and Tobago High Commission by Dame Jocelyn Barrow; subsequent awards held in 1994.

1993

Walsall Black Sisters Collective wins reprieve on funding cut following successful local media campaign.

June Making Voices Heard – All Wales Black and Ethnic Minority Women's Conference held by Equal Opportunities Commission in South Glamorgan; calls for establishment of Welsh black women's network.

July Osaba Women's Centre (est. 1984) launches new Urban Programme funded community centre in Hillfields, Coventry, Britain's largest independently owned black women's centre; Disabled Asian Women's Network (DAWN) established with support of Redbridge Asian Women's Association.

October Osaba Women's Centre, Coventry, launches appeal to find bone marrow donor for member Josephine Fishley, and to raise profile of black leukaemia sufferers.

November Equal Opportunities Commission holds Black and Ethnic Minority Women's Conference in Glasgow; Rainbow is formed as a National Forum of Black and Ethnic Minority Women in Scotland.

1994

February   Black Women's Rape Action Project, London, launches campaign in support of Sammy Davis, an African Caribbean man falsely convicted of rape and facing deportation.

March   Sheffield Black Women's Resource Centre established; *Diaspora*, a newspaper for women of colour, launched on International Women's Day.

April   Pan-African Women's Liberation Movement formed at seventh Pan-African Congress held in Kampala; branch meets in London.

June   Change Without Denigration Conference on female genital mutilation held by London Black Women's Health Action Project.

July   Black Women for Wages for Housework campaigns against AZT malpractice and Paediatric European Network for the Treatment of AIDS (PENTA) trials in British hospitals.

September   National Network of Black Women's Organisations (NNBWO) launched, coordinated by Sia: the National Development Agency for the Black Voluntary Sector; National Black Women's Network Planning Group and Black Women in Europe Network merge.

November   Black Women's Rape Action Project campaigns for withdrawal of episodes of television series *Cracker* which portrays stereotypical African Caribbean male rapist.

Liverpool Black Sisters, Black Women for Wages for Housework and other organisations campaign against the Child Support Act.

African Women's Support Group established in Aberdeen.

EARLY 1990S

Asian women from all over Britain demonstrate in Huddersfield against gangs of Asian men organised to hunt down women who have escaped violent households.

Meridian Black and Ethnic Minority Women's Information and Resource Centre established in Glasgow.

Newham Asian Women's Project, Southall Black Sisters and other black women's refuges campaign against 'One Year Rule'.

International Network of Women of Colour (INWOC) formed in London in preparation for UN conference in Beijing.

1995

Warwickshire African, Caribbean and Asian Women's Network (WACAWN) launched.

Mental Health and the Muslim Woman Conference held by Muslim Women's Helpline in northwest London.

Collection of writing by black lesbians, *Talking Black: Lesbians of African and Asian Descent Speak Out* launched in Brixton.

June/July   National Network of Black Women's Organisations' (NNBWO) conferences in Nottingham and Leeds attract over 100 women of African and Asian descent.

September   Fourth United Nations World Conference on Women held in Beijing, attended by several British black women's organisations; UK government adopts 'platform for action' which recognises women's unpaid work; Professional African and Asian Women's Association National Conference, Breaking Through Barriers, held in London.

October   National Lottery Charities Board announces first grants; press backlash against funding of 'exotic' black charities; in second round of grants, Panahghar Asian Women's Group in Coventry receives £250,000 to build new premises.

November   Wai Yin Chinese Women's Society launches new European Community funded centre in Manchester; A Step Forward Conference for black and ethnic minority women in Grampian held in Aberdeen, over seventy women attend.

December   Refugee Women's Network, an umbrella organisation of refugee women's groups, joins Campaign Against the Immigration and Asylum Bill in lobby of parliament.

1996

INWOC, NNBWO, Cambridge Black Women's Support Group and others publicise outcomes of Beijing conference and campaign for involvement in post-Beijing implementation meetings.

Bibliography

Ackah, W. (1993) 'In Our Own Image: Understanding Afrocentricity', *Charles Wootton News* (June), Liverpool: Charles Wootton College.

Afshar, H. and Maynard, M. (eds) (1994) *The Dynamics of Race and Gender*, London and Bristol, PA: Taylor & Francis.

Agnihotri, R. K. (1987) *Crisis of Identity: The Sikhs in England*, New Delhi: Bahri Publications.

Akina Mama wa Afrika (1995) *African Women Prisoners Project*, London: Akina Mama wa Afrika.

Albrecht, L. and Brewer, R. (eds) (1990) *Bridges of Power: Women's Multicultural Alliances*, Philadelphia, PA and Gabriola Island: New Society Publishers.

Alexander, C. (1996) *The Art of Being Black*, Oxford: Clarendon Press.

Alexander, V. (1995) 'Black Women Organising', in Sia: the National Development Agency for the Black Voluntary Sector (ed.) *Developing Black Women's Organisations*, London: Sia.

—— (1996) ' "A Mouse in the Jungle": the Black Christian Woman's Experience in the Church and Society in Britain', in D. Jarrett-Macauley (ed.) *Reconstructing Womanhood, Reconstructing Feminism*, London and New York: Routledge.

Ali, M. M. (1996) *The Muslim Community in Britain: an Historical Account*, Malaysia: Pelanduk Publications.

Alkalimat, A. (1973) 'The Ideology of Black Social Science', in J. Ladner (ed.) *The Death of White Sociology*, New York: Vintage Books.

Allen, S. (1982) 'Gender, Race and Class in the 1980s', in C. Husband (ed.) *'Race' in Britain: Continuity and Change*, London and Melbourne: Hutchinson University Library, 1987.

Amamoo, N. A. (1993) 'Skin-bleaching: the Politics of Black Beauty', *African Woman* 8, London: Akina Mama wa Afrika.

Amos, V. and Parmar, P. (1984) 'Challenging Imperial Feminism', *Feminist Review* 17: 3–20.

Amos, V., Lewis, G., Mama, A. and Parmar, P. (eds) (1984) 'Many Voices, One Chant: Black Feminist Perspectives', *Feminist Review* 17.

Ani, M (1994) *Yurugu: An African-Centered Critique of European Cultural Thought and Behaviour*, Trenton, NJ: Africa World Press.

Anthias, F. (1990) 'Race and Class Revisited: Conceptualising Race and Racisms', *Sociological Review* 38 (1): 19–42.

Anthias, F., Yuval-Davies, N. and Cain, H. (1992) *Racialized Boundaries*, London and New York: Routledge.

Anwar, M. (1986) *Race and Politics: Ethnic Minorities and the British Political System*, London and New York: Tavistock Publications.

—— (1991) 'The Content of Leadership: Migration, Settlement and Racial Discrimination' , in P. Werbner and M. Anwar (eds) *Black and Ethnic Leaderships in Britain: The Cultural Dimensions of Political Action*, London and New York: Routledge.

Anzaldua, G. (1990) 'Bridge, Drawbridge, Sandbar or Island: Lesbians of Color Hacienda Alianzas', in L. Albrecht and R. Brewer (eds) *Bridges of Power: Women's Multicultural Alliances*, Philadelphia, PA and Gabriola Island: New Society Publishers.

Asante, M. K. (1990) *Kemet, Afrocentricity and Knowledge*, New Jersey: Africa World Press.

—— (1993) *Malcolm X as Cultural Hero and other Afrocentric Essays*, New Jersey: Africa World Press.

Aziz, R. (1992) 'Feminism and the Challenge of Racism: Deviance or Difference', in H. Crowley and S. Himmelwelt (eds) *Knowing Women: Feminism and Knowledge*, Cambridge: Polity Press.

Back, L. and Nayak, A. (1993) *Invisible Europeans? Black People in the 'New Europe'*, Birmingham: All Faiths for One Race.

Bains, H. (1988) 'Southall Youth: An Old-Fashioned Story' , in P. Cohen and H. Bains (eds) *Multi-racist Britain*, Basingstoke and London: Macmillan Press.

Bannerji, H. (1995) *Thinking Through: Essays on Feminism, Marxism and Anti-Racism*, Toronto: Women's Press.

Bar On, B. (1993) 'Marginality and Epistemic Privilege', in L. Alcoff and E. Potter (eds) *Feminist Epistemologies*, London and New York: Routledge.

Barrett, M. and McIntosh, M. (1985) 'Ethnocentrism and Socialist Feminist Theory', *Feminist Review* 20: 23–49.

Bellos, L. (1995) 'A Vision Back and Forth', in V. Mason-John (ed.) *Talking Black: Lesbians of African and Asian Descent Speak Out*, London and New York: Cassell.

Ben-Tovim, G., Gabriel, J., Law, I. and Stredder, K. (1986a) 'A Political Analysis of Local Struggles for Racial Equality', in J. Rex and D. Mason, *Theories of Race and Ethnic Relations*, Cambridge: Cambridge University Press.

—— (1986b) *The Local Politics of Race*, London: Macmillan.

Bhavnani, K. (1988) ' "Is Violence Masculine?": a Black Feminist Perspective', in S. Grewal, J. Kay, L. Landor, G. Lewis and P. Parmar, *Charting the Journey: Writings by Black and Third World Women*, London: Sheba Feminist Press.

Bhavnani, K. and Coulson, M. (1985) 'Transforming Socialist-Feminism: the Challenge of Racism', *Feminist Review* 23: 81–92.

Bhavnani, K. and Phoenix, A. (eds) (1994) *Shifting Identities Shifting Racisms*, London: Sage.

Bhavnani, R. (1994) *Black Women and the Labour Market: A Research Review*, Manchester: Equal Opportunities Commission.

Black Women for Wages for Housework (1994) 'Open Letter to all Anti-Racists', London, 16 June.

—— (1995) 'Beijing Report', London, 17 November.

Bondi, L. (1993) 'Locating Identity Politics', in M. Keith and S. Pile (eds) *Place and the Politics of Identity*, London and New York: Routledge.

Bourne, J. (1983) 'Towards an anti-racist feminism', *Race and Class* 25 (1): 1–21.

—— (1987) 'Homelands of the Mind: Jewish Feminism and Identity Politics', *Race and Class* 29: 1–24.

Brah, A. (1992a) 'Difference, Diversity and Differentiation', in J. Donald and A. Rattansi (eds) *'Race', Culture and Difference*, London and Milton Keynes: Sage and Open University Press.

—— (1992b) 'Women of South Asian Origin in Britain: Issues and Concerns', in P. Braham, A. Rattansi and R. Skellington (eds) *Racism and Antiracism: Inequalities, Opportunities and Policies*, London and Milton Keynes: Sage and Open University Press.

—— (1993) 'Re-framing Europe: En-gendered Racisms, Ethnicities and Nationalisms in Contemporary Western Europe', *Feminist Review* 45: 9–29.

—— (1996) *Cartographies of Diaspora: Contesting Identities*, London and New York: Routledge.

Brah, A. and Shaw, S. (1992) *Working Choices: South Asian Young Muslim Women and the Labour Market*, London: Department of Employment.

Brent, L. (1973) *Incidents in the Life of a Slave Girl*, New York: Harcourt Brace Jovanovich.

Brixton Black Women's Group (1980) *Speak Out*, London.

—— (1984a) 'Black Women Organising', *Feminist Review* 17: 85–7.

—— (1984b) 'Black Feminism', in H. Kanter, S. Lefanu, S. Shah and C. Shedding (eds) *Sweeping Statements: Writings from the Women's Liberation Movement 1981–83*, London: The Women's Press.

Brown, C. (1984) *Black and White Britain: The Third PSI Survey*, London: Heinemann.

Brown, W. (1984) *Black Women and the Peace Movement*, Bristol: Falling Wall Press.

Bryan, B., Dadzie, S. and Scafe, S. (1985) *The Heart of the Race*, London: Virago.

Bulmer, M. (1982) *Social Research Ethics*, London and Basingstoke: Macmillan Press.

Bunch, C. (1990) 'Making Common Cause: Diversity and Coalitions', in L. Albrecht and R. Brewer (eds) *Bridges of Power: Women's Multicultural Alliances*, Philadelphia, PA and Gabriola Island: New Society Publishers.

Bush, B. (1995) 'Defiance or Submission? The Role of the Slave Woman in Slave Resistance in the British Caribbean', in D. C. Hine, W. King and

L. Reed (eds) *'We Specialize in the Wholly Impossible': A Reader in Black Women's History*, New York: Carlton Publishing.

Campbell, H. (1985) *Rasta and Resistance: From Marcus Garvey to Walter Rodney*, London: Hansib Publications.

Carby, H. (1982) 'White Woman Listen!: Black Feminism and the Boundaries of Sisterhood', in Centre for Contemporary Cultural Studies, *The Empire Strikes Back: Race and Racism in 70s Britain*, London: Hutchinson.

Caribbean Times (1995) 'What We Never Heard About the Beijing Women's Conference', London: Hansib Publications, 21 October.

Caribbean Times (1997) 'Steppin' Out', London: Hansib Publications, 23 January.

Carter, T. (1986) *Shattered Illusions: West Indians in British Politics*, London: Lawrence & Wishart.

Cashmore, E. (1979) *Rastaman: The Rastafarian Movement in England*, London: Allen & Unwin.

Castles, S. and Kosack, G. (1985) *Immigrant Class Structure in Western Europe*, London: Oxford University Press.

Centre for Contemporary Cultural Studies (1982) *The Empire Strikes Back: Race and Racism in 70s Britain*, London: Hutchinson.

Chapeltown Black Women Writers' Group (1992) *When Our Ship Comes In: Black Women Talk*, Castleford and Leeds: Yorkshire Art Circus and Chapeltown Black Women Writers' Group.

Chatterjee, D. (1995) 'Harnessing Shakti: the Work of the Bengali Support Group', in G. Griffin (ed.) *Feminist Activism in the 1990s*, London and Bristol: Taylor & Francis.

Cheney, D. (1996) 'Those Whom the Immigration Law has Kept Apart – Let No One Join Together: a View on Immigration Incantation', in D. Jarrett-Macauley (ed.) *Reconstructing Womanhood, Reconstructing Feminism*, London and New York: Routledge.

Coard, B. (1971) *How the West Indian Child is Made Educationally Subnormal in the British School System*, London: Beacon.

Cobham, R. and Collins, M. (eds) (1987) *Watchers and Seekers: Creative Writing by Black Women in Britain*, London: The Women's Press.

Cole, M. (1993) ' "Black and Ethnic Minority" or "Asian, Black and other Minority Ethnic": a Further Note on Nomenclature', *Sociology* 27 (4): 671–3.

Collins, P. H. (1986) 'Learning from the Outsider Within: the Sociological Significance of Black Feminist Thought', *Social Problems* 33 (6): 14–32.

—— (1990) *Black Feminist Thought: Knowledge, Consciousness and the Politics of Empowerment*, Boston, MA and London: Unwin Hyman.

Combahee River Collective (1983) 'The Combahee River Collective Statement', in B. Smith (ed.) *Home Girls: a Black Feminist Anthology*, New York: Kitchen Table Women of Color Press.

Confederation of Indian Organisations (1995) *Directory of Asian Organisations*, London: Confederation of Indian Organisations.

Connolly, C. (1991) 'Washing Our Linen: One Year of Women Against Fundamentalism', *Feminist Review* 37: 68–77.

Cross, M. (1993) 'Black Workers, Recession and Economic Restructuring in the West Midlands', in M. Cross (ed.) *Ethnic Minorities and Industrial Change in Europe and North America*, Cambridge: Cambridge University Press.

Crowley, H. and Himmelwelt, S. (eds) (1992) *Knowing Women: Feminism and Knowledge*, Cambridge: Polity Press.

Davis, A. (1981) *Women, Race and Class*, London: The Women's Press.

Daye, S. (1994) *Middle Class Blacks in Britain: A Racial Fraction of a Class Group or a Class Fraction of a Racial Group?*, London and New York: Macmillan Press and St Martins Press.

Deleuze, G. and Guattari, F. (1988) *A Thousand Plateaus*, London: Athlone Press.

Desai, R. (1963) *Indian Immigrants in Britain*, London: Oxford University Press.

Emecheta, B. (1986) *Head Above Water*, London: Fontana.

Equal Opportunities Commission (1993) *Making Voices Heard: All Wales Black and Ethnic Minority Women's Conference*, Cardiff: Equal Opportunities Commission.

—— (1994) *Equal Opportunities For Black and Minority Women in Scotland*, Glasgow: Equal Opportunities Commission.

Essed, P. (1990) *Everyday Racism: Reports from Women of Two Cultures*, Claremont, CA: Hunter House.

—— (1996) *Diversity: Gender, Color and Culture*, Amherst, MA: University of Massachusetts Press.

Evans, G. (1995) *Moyenda Project Report 1991–1994*, London: Exploring Parenthood.

Feminist Anthology Collective (1981) *No Turning Back: Writings from the Women's Liberation Movement 1975–80*, London: The Women's Press.

Feminist Review Collective (1986) 'Feminism and Class Politics: a Round Table Discussion', *Feminist Review* 23: 13–20.

—— (1992) 'Editorial', *Feminist Review* 40.

Fernando, S. (1993) 'You Can't Beat a Woman: Sonali Fernando Talks to Pragna Patel', *Shebang* 2 (February).

Ferree, M. M. and Martin, P. Y. (eds) (1995) *Feminist Organizations: Harvest of the New Women's Movement*, Philadelphia, PA: Temple University Press.

—— (1995) 'Doing the Work of the Movement: Feminist Organizations', in *Feminist Organizations: Harvest of the New Women's Movement*, Philadelphia, PA: Temple University Press.

Fitzgerald, M. (1984) *Political Parties and Black People*, London: Runnymede Trust.

Frankenberg, R. (1993a) *White Women, Race Matters: The Social Construction of Whiteness*, Minneapolis, MN: University of Minnesota Press.

—— (1993b) 'Growing up White: Feminism, Racism and the Social Geography of Childhood', *Feminist Review* 45: 51–84.

Frazier, E. F. (1965) *Black Bourgeoisie*, New York: Collier Books.

Freire, P. (1972) *Pedagogy of the Oppressed*, London and New York: Penguin.

Fryer, P. (1984) *Staying Power: The History of Black People in Britain*, London: Pluto Press.

—— (1988) *Staying Power: The History of Black People in Britain*, London: Pluto Press.

Fuss, D. (1989) *Essentially Speaking: Feminism, Nature and Difference*, New York and London: Routledge.

Gamman, L., Hall, C., Lewis, G., Phoenix, A., Whitehead, A. and Young, L. (1993) 'Thinking through Ethnicities', *Feminist Review* 45: 1–3.

Garrison, L. (1979) *Black Youth, Rastafarianism and the Identity Crisis in Britain*, London: African Caribbean Educational Resource.

Gates, H. L. (1988) *The Signifying Monkey: A Theory of African American Literary Criticism*, Oxford and New York: Oxford University Press.

Geddes, A. (1993) 'Asians and Afro-Caribbean Representation in Elected Local Government in England and Wales', *New Community* 20 (1): 43–58.

Giddings, P. (1988) *In Search of Sisterhood*, New York: Quill William Morrow.

Gilroy, P. (1987) *Ain't no Black in the Union Jack: the Cultural Politics of Race and Nation*, London: Hutchinson.

—— (1990) 'The end of Anti-Racism', *New Community* 17 (1): 71–84.

—— (1992) 'It's a Family Affair', in G. Dent (ed.) *Black Popular Culture*, Seattle, WA: Bay Press.

—— (1993) *The Black Atlantic: Modernity and Double Consciousness*, London and New York: Verso.

Glucksmann, M. (1994) 'The Work of Knowledge and the Knowledge of Women's Lives', in M. Maynard and J. Purvis (eds) *Researching Women's Lives from a Feminist Perspective*, London and Bristol, PA: Taylor & Francis.

Goldsmith, J. E. and Makris, M. L. (1993) *Staring at Invisible Women: Black and Minority Ethnic Women in Rural Areas*, London: National Association of Women's Organisations.

Goulbourne, H. (1990) *Black Politics in Britain*, Aldershot: Avebury.

Greater London Council (1984) *Rastafarianism in Greater London*, London: Greater London Council.

—— (1986) *The GLC Women's Committee 1982–86: A Record of Change and Achievements for Women in London*, London: Greater London Council.

Grewal, S., Kay, J., Landor, L., Lewis, G. and Parmar, P (eds) (1988) *Charting the Journey: Writings by Black and Third World Women*, London: Sheba Feminist Press.

Griffin, G. (ed.) (1995a) *Feminist Activism in the 1990s*, London and Bristol, PA: Taylor & Francis.

—— (1995b) 'The Struggle Continues: an Interview with Hannana Siddiqui of Southall Black Sisters', in G. Griffin (ed.) *Feminist Activism in the 1990s*, London and Bristol, PA: Taylor & Francis.

Gunew, S. (ed.) (1991) *A Reader in Feminist Knowledge*, London and New York: Routledge.

Hall, N. (1990) 'African-American Women Leaders and the Politics of Alliance Work', in L. Albrecht and R. Brewer (eds) *Bridges of Power: Women's Multicultural Alliances*, Philadelphia, PA and Gabriola Island: New Society Publishers.

Hall, S. (1980) 'Race, Articulation and Societies Structured in Dominance', in UNESCO *Sociological Theories: Race and Colonialism*, Paris: UNESCO.

—— (1988) *The Hard Road to Renewal: Thatcherism and the Crisis of the Left*, London: Verso.

—— (1992) 'What is this "Black" , in Black Popular Culture?', in G. Dent (ed.) *Black Popular Culture*, Seattle, WA: Bay Press.

—— (1996) 'New Ethnicities', in D. Morley and K. Chen (eds) *Stuart Hall: Critical Dialogues in Cultural Studies*, London and New York: Routledge.

Hall, S., Held, D. and McGrew, T. (1992) *Modernity and its Futures*, Cambridge: Polity Press.

Hansib Directory (1994) *Third Sector*, London: Hansib Publishing.

Haraway, D. J. (1991a) *Simians, Cyborgs, and Women: The Reinvention of Nature*, New York: Routledge.

—— (1991b) 'Situated Knowledges: the Science Question in Feminism and the Privilege of Partial Perspective', in *Simians, Cyborgs, and Women: The Reinvention of Nature*, New York: Routledge.

—— (1991c) 'Reading Buchi Emecheta: Contests for "Women's Experience", in Women's Studies', in *Simians, Cyborgs, and Women: The Reinvention of Nature* , New York: Routledge.

Harding, S. (1991) *Whose Science, Whose Knowledge?: Thinking from Women's Lives*, Ithaca, NY: Cornell University Press.

—— (1993) 'Rethinking Standpoint Epistemology: What is "Strong Epistemology?"', in L. Alcoff and E. Potter (eds) *Feminist Epistemologies*, London and New York: Routledge.

Hare, N. and Hare, J. (1984) *The Endangered Black Family: Coping with the Unisexualization and Coming Extinction of the Black Race*, San Francisco, CA: Black Think Tank.

Hart, G. (1984) 'Black Women in Britain: From Agonizing to Organizing', in A. Johnson (ed.) *Critical Perspectives of Third World America: Women, Race and Class in a Cultural Context*, Berkeley, CA: University of California.

Hayfield, A. (1995) 'Several Faces of Discrimination', in V. Mason-John (ed.) *Talking Black: Lesbians of African and Asian Descent Speak Out*, London and New York: Cassell.

Hazareesingh, S. (1986) 'Racism and Cultural Identity: An Indian Perspective', *Dragon's Teeth* 24.

Heineman, B. W. (1972) *The Politics of the Powerless: A Study of CARD*, London: Institute of Race Relations and Oxford University Press.

Hensman, S. (1995) 'A Retrospective: Black Together Under One Banner', in V. Mason-John (ed.) *Talking Black: Lesbians of African and Asian Descent Speak Out*, London and New York: Cassell.

Hine, D. C., King, W. and Reed, L. (eds) (1995) *'We Specialize in the Wholly Impossible': A Reader in Black Women's History*, New York: Carlton Publishing.

Hiro, D. (1971) *Black British, White British*, London: Eyre & Spottiswoode.

hooks, b. (1981) *Ain't I a Woman: Black Women and Feminism*, Boston, MA: South End Press.

—— (1984) *Feminist Theory: From Margin to Centre*, Boston, MA: South End.

—— (1989) *Talking Back: Thinking Feminist, Thinking Black*, London: Sheba Feminist Press.

—— (1990) *Yearning: Race, Gender and Cultural Politics*, Boston, MA: South End Press.

—— (1991) 'Sisterhood: Political Solidarity between Women', in b. hooks and C. West, *Breaking Bread*, Boston, MA: South End Press.

—— (1993) *Sisters of the Yam: Black Women and Self Recovery*, London: Turnaround.

—— (1994a) *Teaching to Transgress: Education as the Practice of Freedom*, London and New York: Routledge.

—— (1994b) *Outlaw Culture: Resisting Representation*, London and New York: Routledge.

—— (1995) *Killing Race, Ending Racism*, New York: Henry Holt.

Hull, G. T., Bell Scott, P. and Smith, B. (eds) (1982) *All the Women are White, All the Black are Men, But Some of Us are Brave*, New York: The Feminist Press.

Jaggar, A. M. and Bordo, S. R. (eds) (1989) *Gender/Body/Knowledge: Feminist Reconstructions of Being and Knowing*, New Brunswick, NJ and London: Rutgers University Press.

James, J. and Farmer, R. (eds) (1993) *Spirit, Space and Survival: African American Women in (White) Academe*, New York: Routledge.

James, S. (1985) *Sex, Race and Class*, London: Housewives in Dialogue.

—— (ed.) (1995) *The Global Kitchen: The Case for Governments Measuring and Valuing Unwaged Work*, London: Crossroads Books.

Jantjes, G. (1993) 'The Artist as Cultural Salmon: A View from the Frying Pan', *Third Text* 23: 103–6.

Jarrett-Macauley, D. (ed.) (1996) *Reconstructing Womanhood, Reconstructing Feminism*, London and New York: Routledge.

Jawanza (1996) 'The Black Economy: How Can We Begin to Make It Work?', *The Alarm* 17: 9.

Jayaweera, H. (1993) 'Racial Disadvantage and Ethnic Identity: the Experiences of Afro-Caribbean Women in a British City', *New Community* 19 (3): 383–406.

Jeffers, S. (1991) 'Black Sections in the Labour Party: the End of Ethnicity and "Godfather" Politics?', in P. Werbner and M. Anwar (eds) *Black and Ethnic Leaderships in Britain: The Cultural Dimensions of Political Action*, London: Routledge.

Jewell, S. K. (1993) *From Mammy to Miss America and Beyond: Cultural*

Images and the Shaping of US Social Policy, London and New York: Routledge.

Joly, D. (1995) *Britannia's Crescent: Making a Place for Muslims in British Society*, Aldershot: Avebury.

Jones, T. (1993) *Britain's Ethnic Minorities*, London: Policy Studies Institute.

Josephides, S. (1991) 'Organisational Splits and Political Ideology in the Indian Workers Association', in P. Werbner and A. Muhammad (eds) *Black and Ethnic Leaderships in Britain: The Cultural Dimensions of Political Action*, London and New York: Routledge.

Julien, I. (1992) ' "Black Is, Black Ain't": Notes on De-Essentializing Black Identities', in G. Dent (ed.) *Black Popular Culture*, Seattle, WA: Bay Press.

Julien, I. and Mercer, K. (1991) 'True Confessions: A Discourse on Images of Black Male Sexuality', in E. Hemphill and J. Beam (eds) *Brother to Brother: New Writings by Black Gay Men*, Boston, MA: Alyson Publications.

Kazi, H. (1986) 'The Beginnings of a Debate Long Due: Some Observations on "Ethnocentrism and Socialist-Feminist Theory"', *Feminist Review* 22: 87–91.

Kunjufu, J. (1991) *Black Economics: Solutions for Economic and Community Empowerment*, Chicago, IL: African American Images.

—— (1993) *Hip-Hop vs. MAAT: A Psycho/Social Analysis of Values*, Chicago, IL: African American Images.

Ladner, J. (ed.) (1973) *The Death of White Sociology*: New York: Vintage Books.

Lawrence, E. (1982) 'Just Plain Common Sense: the "Roots of Racism"', in Centre for Contemporary Cultural Studies, *The Empire Strikes Back: Race and Racism in 70s Britain*, London: Hutchinson.

Layton-Henry, Z. (1984) *The Politics of Race in Britain*, London: Allen & Unwin.

—— (1992) *The Politics of Immigration: Immigration, 'Race' and 'Race' Relations in Post-War Britain*, Oxford and Cambridge, MA: Blackwell Publishers.

Layton-Henry, Z. and Rich, P. (1986) *Race, Government and Politics in Britain*, London: Macmillan.

Lees, S. (1986) 'Sex, Race and Culture: Feminism and the Limits of Cultural Pluralism', *Feminist Review* 22: 92–102.

Lewis, G. (1996) 'Situated Voices: "Black women's experience" and social work', *Feminist Review* 53: 24–54.

Lewis, G. and Parmar, P. (1983) 'Book Review: hooks, Moraga and Anzaldua, Hull *et al.*, Davis', *Race and Class* 25 (2): 85–91.

Liverpool Black Caucus (1986) *The Racial Politics of Militant in Liverpool*, Liverpool and London: Merseyside Area Group Profile and Runnymede Trust.

London Women's Liberation Newsletter (1984a January/February, 1984b July, 1984c August) 349–52, 372, 376.

Longino, H. E. (1993) 'Subjects, Power and Knowledge: Description and

Prescription in Feminist Philosophies of Science', in L. Alcoff and E. Potter (eds) *Feminist Epistemologies*, London and New York: Routledge.

Lorde, A. (1982) *Zami: A New Spelling of My Name*, New York: The Crossing Press.

—— (1984) *Sister Outsider*, New York: The Crossing Press.

—— (1988) *A Burst of Light*, New York: Firebrand Books.

—— (1990) 'African American Women and the Black Diaspora', in L. Albrecht and R. Brewer (eds) *Bridges of Power: Women's Multicultural Alliances*, Philadelphia, PA and Gabriola Island: New Society Publishers.

Lyotard, J. F. (1984) *The Postmodern Condition: A Report of Knowledge*, Manchester: Manchester University Press.

McLeod, M. (1991) *Trading with the Innercity: Ethnic Minorities and the Development of Caribbean Trade*, Coventry: Centre for Research in Ethnic Relations.

Mama, A. (1989a) *The Hidden Struggle*, London: London Race and Housing Research Unit.

—— (1989b) 'Violence Against Black Women: Gender, Race and State Responses', *Feminist Review* 32: 30–48.

—— (1995) *Beyond the Masks: Race, Gender and Subjectivity*, London and New York: Routledge.

Marable, M. (1995a) *Beyond Black and White*, London and New York: Verso.

—— (1995b) 'Beyond Racial Identity Politics: Towards a Liberation Theory for Multicultural Democracy', in *Beyond Black and White*, London and New York: Verso.

Marshall, A. (1994) 'Sensuous Sapphires: a Study of the Social Construction of Black Female Sexuality', in M. Maynard and J. Purvis (eds) *Researching Women's Lives from a Feminist Perspective*, London and Bristol, WA: Taylor & Francis.

—— (1996) 'From Sexual Denigration to Self-Respect: Resisting Images of Black Female Sexuality', in D. Jarrett-Macauley (ed.) *Reconstructing Womanhood, Reconstructing Feminism*, London and New York: Routledge.

Marx, K. and Engels, F. (1965) *Manifesto of the Communist Party*, Beijing: Foreign Languages Press.

Mason, D. (1990) 'A Rose By any Other Name? Categorisation, identity and social science', *New Community* 17 (1): 123–33.

Mason-John, V. (1995a) 'Herstoric Moments', in V. Mason-John (ed.) *Talking Black: Lesbians of African and Asian Descent Speak Out*, London and New York: Cassell.

—— (ed.) (1995b) *Talking Black: Lesbians of African and Asian Descent Speak Out*, London and New York: Cassell.

Mason-John, V. and Khambatta, A. (1993) *Making Black Waves: Lesbians Talk*, London: Scarlet Press.

Maxine and Arati (1984) 'Two Black Women's Perspectives of the Spare Rib Collective', *London Women's Liberation Newsletter* 349 (January).

Maynard, M. and Purvis, J. (eds) (1994) *Researching Women's Lives from a Feminist Perspective*, London and Bristol, WA: Taylor & Francis.

Medas, M. (1994) *From City Challenge to The Single Regeneration Budget: A Black Perspective*, London: Sia.

Mercer, J. (1994) *Welcome to the Jungle: New Positions in Black Cultural Studies*, London: Routledge.

Miles, R. (1988) 'Racism, Marxism and British Politics', *Economy and Society* 17 (3): 428–60.

—— (1993) *Racism after 'Race Relations'*, London and New York: Routledge.

Mirza, H. S. (1986) 'The Dilemma of Socialist-Feminism: A Case for Black Feminism', *Feminist Review* 22: 103–5.

—— (1992) *Young, Female and Black*, London and New York: Routledge.

Modood, T. (1988) ' "Black", Racial Equality and Asian Identity', *New Community* 14 (3): 397–404.

—— (1990) 'Political Blackness and British Asians', *Sociology* 28 (3): 859–76.

—— (1994) *Racial Equality: Colour, Culture and Justice*, London: Institute for Public Policy Research.

Mohanty, C. T. (1992) 'Feminist Encounters: Locating the Politics of Experience', in M. Barrett and A. Phillips, *Destabilising Theory*, Cambridge: Polity Press.

Moraga, C. and Anzaldua, G. (eds) (1983) *This Bridge Called My Back: Writings by Radical Women of Color*, New York: Kitchen Table Women of Color Press.

Ms (1996) January/February issue.

Mukherjee, T. (1988) 'The Journey Back', in P. Cohen and H. Bains (eds) *Multi-Racist Britain*, Basingstoke and London: Macmillan Press.

Myers, N. (1996) *Reconstructing the Black Past: Blacks in Britain 1780–1830*, London and Portland, OR: Frank Cass.

Ngcobo, L. (ed.) (1988) *Let it Be Told: Black Women Writers in Britain*, London: Virago.

Oakley, A. (1981) 'Interviewing Women: A Contradiction in Terms', in H. Roberts (ed.) *Doing Feminist Research*, London: Routledge & Kegan Paul.

Ocloo, J. (1995) 'A Strategic Black Unity', unpublished conference paper, London: Campaign Against Police Harassment and Abuse.

Ogunyemi, C. O. (1985) 'Womanism: the Dynamics of the Contemporary Black Female Novel in English', *Signs: Journal of Women in Culture and Society* 11 (1): 63–80.

Olusegun, V. (1995) 'Joyce Sampson: Pro-Black Community Leader or Self-Seeker?', *Black Perspective* (January/February).

Omi, M. and Winant, H. (1994) *Racial Formation in the United States: the 1960s to the 1990s*, New York: Routledge.

Omolade, B. (1995) *The Rising Song of African American Women*, New York and London: Routledge.

Organisation of Women of African and Asian Descent (OWAAD) (1979)

FOWAAD!, London: Organisation of Women of African and Asian Descent.

—— (1980) *FOWAAD!*, London: Organisation of Women of African and Asian Descent.

Osaba Women's Centre (1992) *Black Women Speak Out*, Coventry: Osaba Women's Centre.

Ouseley, H. (1995) 'Political Correctness: the Dangerous Myth', *Municipal Journal* 29, 21–7 July.

Owen, D. (1993) *Ethnic Minorities in Great Britain: Economic Characteristics*, Coventry: Centre for Research in Ethnic Relations.

—— (1994) *Ethnic Minority Women and the Labour Market: Analysis of the 1991 Census*, Manchester: Equal Opportunities Commission.

Pardo, M. (1995) 'Doing it for the Kids: Mexican American Community Activists, Border Feminists?', in M. M. Ferree and P. Y. Martin (eds) *Feminist Organizations: Harvest of the New Women's Movement*, Philadelphia, PA: Temple University Press.

Parmar, P. (1982) 'Gender, Race and Class: Asian Women in Resistance', in Centre for Contemporary Cultural Studies, *The Empire Strikes Back: Race and Racism in 70s Britain*, London: Hutchinson.

—— (1989) 'Other Kinds of Dreams', *Feminist Review* 31: 55–65.

—— (1990) 'Black Feminism: the Politics of Articulation', in J. Rutherford (ed.) *Identity, Community, Culture, Difference*, London: Lawrence & Wishart.

Patel, P. (1991) 'Alert for Action', *Feminist Review* 37: 95–102.

Pheterson, G. (1990) 'Alliances Between Women: Overcoming Internalized Oppression and Internalized Domination', in L. Albrecht and R. Brewer (eds) *Bridges of Power: Women's Multicultural Alliances*, Philadelphia, PA and Gabriola Island: New Society Publishers.

Phizacklea, A. (1990) *Unpacking the Fashion Industry: Gender, Racism and Class in Production*, London and New York: Routledge.

—— (1992) 'Jobs for the Girls: the Production of Women's Outerwear in the UK', in M. Cross (ed.) *Ethnic Minorities and Industrial Change in Europe and North America*, Cambridge: Cambridge University Press.

Phizacklea, A. and Miles, R. (1980) *Labour and Racism*, London: Routledge & Kegan Paul.

Prince, M. (1987) 'The History of Mary Prince', in H. L. Gates (ed.) *The Classic Slave Narratives*, New York: Penguin.

Qaiyoom, R. (1992) *From Crisis to Consensus: A Strategic Approach for Local Government and the Black Voluntary Sector*, London: Sia.

—— (1993a) *Empty Vessels, Hollow Sounds: Local Government and Minority Ethnic Consultation*, London: Sia.

—— (1993b) *Bitter Sweet Charity: Issues of Charitable Status and the Black and Minority Ethnic Voluntary Sector*, London: Sia.

Ramazanoglu, C. (1986) 'Ethnocentrism and Socialist-Feminist Theory: a Response to Barrett and McIntosh', *Feminist Review* 22: 83–6.

—— (1989) *Feminism and the Contradictions of Oppression*, London and New York: Routledge.

Ramdin, R. (1987) *The Making of the Black Working Class*, Aldershot: Wildwood House.

Rattansi, A. (1994) '"Western" Racisms, Ethnicities and Identities in a "Postmodern" Frame', in A. Rattansi and S. Westwood (eds) *Racism, Modernity and Identity on the Western Front*, Cambridge: Polity Press.

Reagon, B. J. (1983) 'Coalition Politics: turning the Century', in B. Smith (ed.) *Home Girls: a Black Feminist Anthology*, New York: Kitchen Table Women of Color Press.

Reddock, R. (1995) 'Women and Slavery in the Caribbean: A Feminist Perspective', in D. C. Hine, W. King and L. Reed (eds) *'We Specialise in the Wholly Impossible': A Reader in Black Women's History*, New York: Carlton Publishing.

Reeves, F. and Ward, R (1984) 'West Indian Business in Britain', in R. Ward and R. Jenkins (eds) *Ethnic Communities in Business*, Cambridge and London: Cambridge University Press.

Rex, J. (1991) *Ethnic Identity and Ethnic Mobilisation in Britain*, Coventry: Centre for Research in Ethnic Relations.

Riggs, M. (1995) *Black Is, Black Ain't: a Personal Journey Through Black Identity*, London: Independent Television.

Riley, D. (1988) *'Am I That Name?': Feminism and the Category of 'Women' in History*, Hampshire and London: Macmillan Press.

Roy, A. (1995) 'Asian Women's Activism in Northamptonshire' , in G. Griffin (ed) *Feminist Activism in the 1990s*, London and Bristol, WA: Taylor & Francis.

Saggar, S. (1992) *Race and Politics in Britain*, New York and London: Harvester Wheatsheaf.

Sahgal, G. (1992) 'Secular Spaces: the Experience of Asian Women Organizing', in *Refusing Holy Orders*, London: Virago Press.

Scales-Trent, J. (1995) *Notes of a White Black Woman: Race, Color, Community*, Pennsylvania: Pennsylvania State University Press.

Scarman, Lord (1982) *The Scarman Report: The Brixton Disorders*, Harmondsworth: Pelican.

Sewell, T. (1993) *Black Tribunes: Black Political Participation in Britain*, London: Lawrence & Wishart.

Shah, S. (1988) 'We Will Not Mourn Their Deaths in Silence', in S. Grewal *et al.* (eds) *Charting the Journey: Writings by Black and Third World Women*, London: Sheba Feminist Press.

Shaila (1984) 'Angry Opinion', in H. Kanter, S. Lefanu, S. Shah and C. Shedding (eds) *Sweeping Statements: Writings from the Women's Liberation Movement 1981–83*, London: The Women's Press.

Shaw, S. (1995) 'Black Club Women and the Creation of the National Association of Colored Women', in D. C. Hine, W. King and L. Reed (eds) *'We Specialize in the Wholly Impossible': A Reader in Black Women's History*, New York: Carlton Publishing.

Sheffield Black Women's Resource Centre (1994) *Progress Report*, Sheffield: Sheffield Black Women's Resource Centre.

Shukra, K. (1990) 'Black Sections in the Labour Party', in H. Goulbourne (ed.) *Black Politics in Britain*, Aldershot: Avebury.

Shyllon, F. (1977) *Black People in Britain 1553–1833*, London: Oxford University Press.

Sia: the National Development Agency for the Black Voluntary Sector (1994) *Agenda 2000: The Black Perspective*, London: Sia.

—— (1995) *Annual Report*, London: Sia.

—— (December 1995) *Information Bulletin*, London: Sia.

—— (1996a) *Developing Black Women's Organisations*, London: Sia.

—— (1996b) *National Directory of Black Women's Organisations*, London: Sia.

—— (1996c) 'White Backlash in the Scramble for Lottery Money', *Information Bulletin* 15, London: Sia.

—— (May 1996d) *Information Bulletin*, London: Sia.

Siddiqui, H. (1991) 'Winning Freedoms', *Feminist Review* 37: 78–83.

Simonds, W. (1995) 'Feminism on the Job: Confronting Opposition in Abortion Work', in M. M. Ferree and P. Y. Martin (eds) *Feminist Organizations: Harvest of the New Women's Movement*, Philadelphia, PA: Temple University Press.

Sisters in Study (1988) 'A Reappraisal of *The Heart of the Race*', in S. Grewal, J. Kay, L. Landor, G. Lewis and P. Parmar (eds) *Charting the Journey: Writings by Black and Third World Women*, London: Sheba Feminist Press.

Sivanandan, A. (1974) *A Different Hunger: Writings on Black Resistance*, London: Pluto Press, 1982.

—— (1990) *Communities of Resistance*, London and New York: Verso.

Small, S. (1983) *Police and People in London: A Group of Young Black People*, London: Policy Studies Institute.

—— (1994) *Racialised Barriers: the Black Experience in the United States and England in the 1980s*, London and New York: Routledge.

Small, V. S. (1994) *From Arts to Welfare: A Bibliography of the Black and Minority Ethnic Voluntary Sector*, London: Sia.

Smith, B. (ed.) (1983) *Home Girls: a Black Feminist Anthology*, New York: Kitchen Table Women of Color Press.

Smith, D. E. (1990) *The Conceptual Practices of Power: A Feminist Sociology of Knowledge*, Boston, MA: Northeastern University Press.

Smith, H. (1975) *Strategies of Social Research: The Methodological Imagination*, Englewood Cliffs, NJ: Prentice Hall.

Solinger, R. (1994) *Wake up Little Susie: Single Pregnancy and Race before Roe v. Wade*, London and New York: Routledge.

Solomos, J. (1992) 'The Politics of Immigration Since 1945', in P. Braham, A. Rattansi and R. Skellington (eds) *Racism and Antiracism: Inequalities, Opportunities and Policies*, London and Milton Keynes: Sage and Open University Press.

Solomos, J. and Back, L. (1995) *Race, Politics and Social Change*, London and New York: Routledge.

South London Black Feminist (1984) 'A Revolutionary Anger', in H. Kanter, S. Lefanu, S. Shah and C. Shedding (eds) *Sweeping Statements: Writings from the Women's Liberation Movement 1981–83*, London: The Women's Press.

Southall Black Sisters (1989) *Against the Grain: A Celebration of Survival and Struggle, Southall Black Sisters, 1979–1989*, London: Southall Black Sisters.

Spare Rib (1992–3) 'Letters', London: Spare Rib Collective (July, October/November, December/January).

Spare Rib Collective (1992) 'Who's to Blame?', *Spare Rib*, London (July).

Spelman, E. (1988) *Inessential Woman*, Boston, MA: Beacon Press.

Spivak, G. (1987) *In Other Worlds: Essays in Cultural Politics*, New York and London: Methuen.

—— (1990a) *The Post-Colonial Critic: Interviews, Strategies, Dialogues*, New York and London: Routledge.

—— (1990b) 'The Post-Modern Condition: the End of Politics?', in *The Post-colonial Critic: Interviews, Strategies, Dialogues*, New York and London: Routledge.

Stanley, L. and Wise, S. (1993) *Breaking Out Again: Feminist Ontology and Epistemology*, London and New York: Routledge.

Staples, R. (1973) 'What is Black Sociology? Towards a Sociology of Black Liberation', in J. Ladner (ed.) *The Death of White Sociology*, New York: Vintage Books.

Subira, G. (1994) *Black Folks Guide to Making Big Bucks in America*, New Jersey: Very Serious Business Enterprises.

Sudbury, J. (1994) 'Self Reliance No Easy Option for Black Groups', *Third Sector*, London, 6 October.

—— (1995) 'Out of the Mainstream', *Voice*, London: Association of Chief Executives of Voluntary Organisations (December).

Sulter, M. (1988) 'Notes of a Native Daughter', in L. Ngcobo (ed.) *Let it Be Told: Black Women Writers in Britain*, London: Virago.

Takaki, R. (1989) *Strangers from a Different Shore: A History of Asian Americans*, New York and London: Penguin Books.

Tang Nain, G. (1991) 'Black Women, Sexism and Racism: Black or Antiracist Feminism?', in *Feminist Review* 37: 1–22.

The 1990 Trust (1993) 'Shades of Blackness', *Black to Black* 2 (September).

Troyna, B. and Williams, J. (1986) *Racism, Education and the State: the Racialisation of Education Policy*, Beckenham: Croom Helm.

Turner, T. E. (ed.) (1994) *Arise Ye Mighty People!: Gender, Class and Race in Popular Struggles*, New Jersey: Africa World Press.

—— (1994) 'Rastafari and the New Society: Caribbean and East African Feminist Roots of a Popular Movement to Reclaim the Earthly Commons', in T. E. Turner (ed.) *Arise Ye Mighty People!: Gender, Class and Race in Popular Struggles*, New Jersey: Africa World Press.

Visram, R. (1986) *Ayahs, Lascars and Princes*, London: Pluto Press.

Voice (12 December 1995) 'Would-be Voters Urged to Register', London: Vee Tee Ay Publishing: 2.

—— (5 March 1996) 'What it Takes to Be a Man', London: Vee Tee Ay Publishing: 37.

—— (26 March 1996a) 'Designs of the Future', London: Vee Tee Ay Publishing: 20.

—— (26 March 1996b) 'War of Words', London: Vee Tee Ay Publishing: 25.

—— (9 April 1996) 'Lessons in Education', London: Vee Tee Ay Publishing: 19.

—— (23 April 1996a) 'Book is Withdrawn after Race Row', London: Vee Tee Ay Publishing: 6.

—— (23 April 1996b) 'Should Women be on Top?', London: Vee Tee Ay Publishing: 4.

—— (23 April 1996c) 'Wilting Men put Blame on Career Girls', London: Vee Tee Ay Publishing: 4.

—— (7 May 1996) 'The Mixed Generation', London: Vee Tee Ay Publishing: 13.

—— (2 May 1997) 'Labour to Axe Law', London: Vee Tee Ay Publishing: 3.

Wadsworth, M. (1992) 'Black Politics: a Historical Perspective', *Race and Class* 34 (2): 63–74.

Walker, A. (1985) *In Search of Our Mothers Gardens,* London: The Women's Press.

Wallace, M. (1978) *Black Macho and the Myth of the Superwoman*, London and New York: Verso.

Walter, R. W. (1973) 'Towards a Definition of Black Social Science', in J. Ladner (ed.) *The Death of White Sociology*, New York: Vintage Books.

Walvin, J. (1971) *The Black Presence: A Documentary History of the Negro in England*, London: Orbach & Chambers.

Ware, V. (1992) *Beyond the Pale: White Women, Racism and History*, London: Verso.

We Are Here Collective (1988) *We Are Here: a Magazine by and for Black Women Only*, 1, London: We Are Here Collective.

Weekly Journal (1995) 'Pioneering Group Evicted', London: Vee Tee Ay Publishing, 12 October.

Welch, K. (1984) 'Racism in the Feminist Movement', in H. Kanter, S. Lefanu, S. Shah and C. Shedding (eds) *Sweeping Statements: Writings from the Women's Liberation Movement 1981–83*, London: The Women's Press.

Wenham, M. (1993) *Funded to Fail: Nuff Pain, No Gain: the Under-resourcing of the African Caribbean Voluntary Sector in London*, London: London Voluntary Service Council.

Werbner, P. (1991) 'Black and Ethnic Leaderships in Britain: a Theoretical Overview', in P. Werbner and A. Muhammad (eds) *Black and Ethnic Leaderships in Britain: The Cultural Dimensions of Political Action*, London and New York: Routledge.

West, G. (1990) 'Conflict and Cooperation among Women in the Welfare Rights Movement', in L. Albrecht and R. Brewer (eds) *Bridges of Power: Women's Multicultural Alliances*, Philadelphia, PA and Gabriola Island: New Society Publishers.

Whelehan, I. (1995) *Modern Feminist Thought: From the Second Wave to 'Post-Feminism'*, New York: New York University Press.

Williams, P. J. (1991) *The Alchemy of Race and Rights*, Cambridge, MA and London: Harvard University Press.

Wilson, A. (1978) *Finding a Voice: Asian Women in Britain*, London: Virago.
—— (1984) 'Developments in the Eighties', *Finding a Voice: Asian Women in Britain*, London: Virago.
—— (1991) 'Against the Grain: Review', *Feminist Review* 39: 193–5.
Wilson, M. (1993) *Crossing the Boundary: Black Women Survive Incest*, London: Virago.
Wolpe, H. (1986) 'Class Concepts, Class Struggle and Racism', in J. Rex and D. Mason (eds) *Theories of Race and Ethnic Relations*, Cambridge and New York: Cambridge University Press.
Women Against Fundamentalism (1994) 'Editorial', *WAF Journal* 5 (1).
Yawney, C. (1994) 'Moving with the Dawtas of Rastafari', in T. E. Turner (ed.) *Arise Ye Mighty People: Gender, Class and Race in Popular Struggles*, New Jersey: Africa World Press.
Yeebo, Z. (1995) 'Now is the Time to Save the African Man from Extinction', in *The African* 1 (29): London: African Development Communications Network (September).
York, J., Leonard, D., Liensol, C. *et al.* (1991) 'We Are the Feminists That Women Have Warned us About', includes 'Feminist Practice Notes from the Tenth Year', in S. Gunew (ed.) *A Reader in Feminist Knowledge*, London: Routledge.
Young, L. (1996) 'The Rough Side of the Mountain: Black Women and Representation in Film', in D. Jarrett-Macauley (ed.) *Reconstructing Womanhood, Reconstructing Feminism*, London and New York: Routledge.
Yuval-Davis, N. (1994) 'Women, Ethnicity and Empowerment' , in K. Bhavnani and A. Phoenix (eds) *Shifting Identities Shifting Racisms*, London: Sage.
Zamimass (1992) 'Zaminews' 2 (2), London: Zamimass.
Zimbabwe Women's Resource Centre (1995) *News Bulletin: Fourth Conference on Women*, Harare (November).

Index